Robert B. Ives
Sept 1986
Oxford
3139

A HISTORY OF OXFORD UNIVERSITY

A HISTORY OF
OXFORD
UNIVERSITY

V. H. H. GREEN

3139

B. T. Batsford Ltd, *London*

First published 1974
Reprinted 1984
© V. H. H. Green 1974

ISBN 0 7134 1132 5

Printed and bound in Great Britain by
Redwood Burn Limited, Trowbridge, Wiltshire
for the publishers
B. T. Batsford Ltd
4 Fitzhardinge Street
London W1H 0AH

Contents

List of Illustrations

Foreword

The fascination and interest of Oxford's history are perennial. Currently scholars are at work on a massive project which will ultimately result in a definitive history of the university. No such claim can be made for this brief survey, some of the findings of which may well be modified by detailed research. Its aim is simply to describe and illustrate some of the principal features of the university's life during the past 700 years.

Acknowledgments

The Author and Publishers would like to thank the following for permission to use illustrations in this book: Bodleian Library (Pls. 2 and 23); British Museum (Pl. 13); Cuddesdon Collection (Pl. 20); Fitzwilliam Museum, Cambridge (Pl. 14); Lady Margaret Hall (Pl. 24); Lincoln College (Pls. 19 and 22); Mansell Collection (Pls. 3 and 6); Merton College (Pl. 21); Oxford City Library (Pl. 25). The remainder are from the Publisher's collection.

I

The Origin and Growth of the University c. 1100-1400

Development and early organisation

Universities were among the permanent creations of medieval civilisation. Although they were tied to the cultural and social scene which gave them birth, their teachers and students were joined together in an exploration of knowledge, pushing through the frontiers which had hedged the ideas of men since the ending of the Roman Empire. The earliest universities, Bologna and Paris, became flourishing centres of study before Oxford began to attract scholars, but once a university was established there in the mid-twelfth century, its prestige mounted quickly, so that for a time at least it took second place only to Paris.

How and when the university actually came into being we do not know. Medieval publicists, proud of their own society and eager to discredit the claims to antiquity made by the university of Cambridge, supposed that Oxford owed its existence to the coming to Britain of Brutus and his Trojans who established an academy of classical studies at Cricklade (viz. Greeklade) and subsequently settled in Oxford. By such criteria the assertion which a writer made in the fourteenth century that University College had been founded by the Anglo-Saxon king, Alfred, might seem reasonable. The claim was upheld by the court of King's Bench in 1727, but it too was wholly legendary. 'If ever there was a lie in the world', William Smith wrote bluntly, 'the Devil never told a greater'.

The mists which cloak the real origins of Oxford may be less thick than the legends which early scholars perpetrated but, like the sallow fog which in winter so often engulfs the city, they are sufficiently impermeable to make it impossible to speak of Oxford's early days with any degree of precision. It was, however, plain that a revolution was taking place in twelfth-century Europe, generating everywhere a zest for intellectual enquiry which the existing cathedral and monastic schools could not meet.

Oxford was a by-product of this development and the child of an expanding, affluent society concerned for the education of its children.

That Oxford rather than London, Stamford or Exeter should have been the place where these streams coalesced to form a river was largely accidental. It had no cathedral school from which a university might have evolved. Its early scholars appear to have had no connection with the Augustinian priory of St Frideswide's, founded in 1122, though two other Oxford societies, the priory of Oseney and the college of secular canons of the church of St George in the Castle, had some association with learning. Oxford was, however, easily accessible, situated at the junction of many routes and close to one of the royal residences, at Woodstock. It is also possible that scholars were attracted to Oxford, and the growth of the university stimulated, by the comparatively low cost of property and rentals, an effect of the migration of the clothing industry from the town which was experiencing a period of some economic decline.

In practice the steady growth of the schools, which clustered around St Mary's Church, reflected the reputation of the individual teachers who attracted disciples. For the most part these early scholars are obscure figures. There was an Anglo-Norman scholar from Caen, Theobald of Etampes, who early in the twelfth century, described himself as a 'master of Oxford', instructing 'sixty or a hundred clerks more or less.' A future cardinal, Robert Pullen, was probably teaching at Oxford between 1133 and 1138, before becoming a master of theology at Paris. There too we find the Roman lawyer, Vacarius, lecturing in the reign of King Stephen. John of Cornwall, later archdeacon of Worcester, who was holding classes at Oxford in the middle of the twelfth century, was the first secular master in theology in Oxford of whose writings there is a record. A further stimulus may have been given to the youthful university by the return of the English scholars from France, probably in 1167, which Henry II had ordered in retaliation for the French king's support of Archbishop Becket.

By the end of the twelfth century the picture becomes much clearer. That vain Welshman, Gerald, spent three days in Oxford in 1184-5, reading extracts from his *Topographica Hibernica*, to the satisfaction of the assembled scholars as well of himself. Twelve years later a group of Oxford scholars was entertained by Abbot Samson of St Edmundsbury, 'and the Abbot was praised for the magnanimity of his generous expenditure'. It was evident that Oxford's prestige as a centre of scholarship was well established before the end of the twelfth century. In 1201 we learn for the first time the name of a master of the schools, John Grim. Prior Senatus of Worcester writing to Clement, the prior of Oseney, exclaimed that at Oxford there were 'many eloquent orators and men who are well able to weigh the words of the law' who 'bring forth from their treasures things new and old for everyone that asks.'

Then, in 1208–9, a crisis occurred which could have ruined the still youthful foundation. A student, accidentally (*casu*) or shamelessly (*turpiter*), slew a woman. In their anger the outraged townsmen promptly hanged two or three clerks. Many scholars, fearful of further reprisals, fled to other towns, among them Cambridge where they either founded, or reinforced, another university. In this quarrel, the first of many that split town and gown, the citizens may have enjoyed the sympathy of King John, himself then in dispute with the Church. But when five years later the king came to terms with the pope, the clerks were better placed to get compensation for the wrongs they had endured. In 1213/14 the citizens had to make a humiliating apology to the papal legate. They agreed not only to do penance but to accept a legatine ordinance which gave substantial privileges to the scholars. Nor did the scholars who had earlier come to terms with the townsfolk escape censure. They were suspended from teaching for three years. In this charter we may see an affirmation of the university's established position.

If papal authority played its part in confirming and extending its privileges, the university owed its continued strength mainly to the patronage of the crown and, to a lesser extent, of the bishop of Lincoln. Apart from the pope's confirmation in 1254 of the charter of 1214, papal intervention in the university's affairs was relatively unimportant. Oxford was, however, situated on the fringe of the great diocese of Lincoln. Its chancellor, if not a member of the cathedral chapter, was in some sense the bishop's representative. By comparison with the authority which the bishop of Paris wielded over the chancellor at Paris, the bishop of Lincoln's actual powers over the university were limited; when exercised, as in the town and gown riots of 1298 and 1355, they were used in its favour. Nor did the bishop's other official, the archdeacon of Oxford, ever exert much control over the university; in 1346 he explicitly surrendered all his rights in this connection save the proving of wills.

Archiepiscopal intervention, exercised by virtue of the archbishop of Canterbury's metropolitical powers, could be more critical. The archbishop intervened to censure some of Aquinas' propositions in 1277 and 1284, and to condemn John Wyclif in 1382. But only on one occasion, in

1411, was there an active collision between the university and the archbishop. Some 16 years earlier, in 1395, Pope Boniface IX conferred a bull
on the university exempting it from archiepiscopal and episcopal jurisdiction. Archbishop Arundel, angry at interference with his rights, persuaded Richard II to revoke the privilege. Before, however, this could be
done, Arundel was in exile and the king deposed. After Arundel's re-
instatement, he determined to restore his authority over the university,
strengthened in his intention by the university's association with the
Lollard heresy. But when the archbishop visited the university, demanding
an oath of loyalty from its members, the protectors forcibly barred his
entry to St Mary's Church. Arundel left Oxford in high dudgeon, placing
it under an interdict, while the riot degenerated into a struggle between
northerners and southerners.[1] The university, for once lacking royal
support, was obliged to give way and to entreat the pope to revoke the
bull of 1395.

In general the university enjoyed royal favour. It was the king who
promoted its privileges, protected it against the townsfolk and bestowed
his patronage in favour of its clerks. That he should have done this may
have represented his belief that it was a royal duty to patronise scholarship;
but he realised that Oxford was training the men who were most likely to
do him and his kingdom the best service. The university, moreover,
promoted the prestige of his kingdom abroad. In the series of disputes
which divided the university from the town, the king invariably intervened in favour of the university.

The uneasy relationship between the scholars and the townsfolk led not
merely to constant dispute but to acts of violence. In 1263, because the
town sympathised with the baronial cause, Henry III ordered the scholars
to move to Northampton (where, paradoxically, it appears that some at
least fought against the king). In 1290 the citizens of Oxford appealed to
parliament against the chancellor's oppressive rule; but the crown only
reaffirmed the university's rights and privileges, asserting the chancellor's
authority over all crimes involving scholars, except murder and mayhem.
In every ensuing conflict, and there were many, the townsfolk failed to get
redress from king or parliament. The town argued that criminals took
advantage of the privileged position of the scholars to masquerade as

---

[1] The students of medieval universities were grouped into so-called nations, regional or racial
in origin. At Oxford the division was between north and south (which included the Welsh
and the Irish), and the territorial line of division was, as Dr A. B. Emden has shewn, the river
Nene rather than the river Trent.

clerks; occasionally the clerks' activities gave substance to this belief. That the townsfolk used the opportunity to wring what they could from the scholars, by fair means and foul, can hardly be doubted; they extracted extortionate prices for food, gave wine in short measure, sold food and drink of poor quality. The scholars complained of the refuse piled high in the streets near the schools and the unsavoury practice of melting tallow and slaughtering beasts in the public highway.

The frustration from which town and gown both suffered led to frequent riots which sometimes developed into minor battles. In 1298 there was a skirmish between the students and the bailiffs of the town in the vicinity of Carfax. In 1334 the masters and scholars considered moving the university to the quieter atmosphere of Stamford (where the earl of Warenne promised them his patronage). But the king forbade the move and ordered the scholars to return to Oxford, simultaneously confirming their rights and strengthening the control which the university exercised over the town.

This was the background to another major explosion which took place on St Scholastica's day, 10 February 1355. Some students, led by Walter Spryngeheuse and Roger de Chesterfield, both priests who held livings in the west of England, arguing with the innkeeper of the Swyndlestock tavern at Carfax, terminated the discussion by throwing a quart pot of wine in the host's face and proceeding to beat him up. His friends rushed to ring the bell at St Martin's to call out the townsfolk. The chancellor, hastily brought on the scene, tried to pacify the rioters but was himself eventually obliged to retreat. The bells of St Mary's summoned the clerks to the fight. When the town's mayor, John de Bereford, rode the next day to Woodstock to bring the town's grievances to the notice of the king, Edward III, the townsmen made common cause with the villagers outside the city walls. Collecting in St Giles, they attacked the students in Beaumont Fields. The battle went in favour of the town: as the scholars fled to the sanctuary of their inns and halls, the triumphant townsmen followed, beating and wounding many, killing some, sacking and firing their rooms. The chancellor hurried to Woodstock as many students, defeated and humiliated, wearily fled from the town.

Oxford was, however, soon to rue its triumph. The bishop of Lincoln imposed an interdict. The mayor and some of his colleagues were sent to prison. A new charter, dated 27 June 1355, extended the wide powers which the chancellor already enjoyed. The townsmen had to pay a substantial fine and the major and bailiffs were henceforth compelled, under penalty of a fine of 100 marks, to attend the mass for the souls of the clerks slain in the riot every St Scholastica's day, a penance which in attenuated form survived the Reformation and was not abolished until 1825.

The wide measure of support which Oxford received from the crown, and the comparative independence which it enjoyed from bishop and pope, gave the university the opportunity to order its own affairs. It very early became a self-governing society in enjoyment of substantial privileges. Its chancellor wielded considerable authority. He could deprive masters of their licence to lecture and he could prevent students from taking their degrees. He summoned and presided over meetings of the Great Congregation, the assembly of the masters. He was responsible for the maintenance of law and order, and through his court could fine, imprison and excommunicate offenders. He could expel undesirable persons from the town, ten miles in the case of prostitutes. So, in 1444, the chancellor, Thomas Gascoigne, expelled one Lucy Colbrand whose activities as a prostitute had been the cause of sundry 'litigation, fornication, fights and homicides in the university.'

In spite of his considerable powers, the chancellor was not an autocrat. He came to be elected by the regent masters[1] by indirect vote, the proctors nominating a regent from each of the higher faculties, and the same number from the faculty of arts; in a real sense the chancellor shared his powers not merely with the proctors but also with the masters (though not, as in some continental universities, with the students). His authority was rather presidential than monarchical. To be really effective it had to have the assent of the resident masters whose interests the proctors represented.

The proctors were the most influential figures in the university. They were elected annually after Easter by two boards representing the northern and southern masters, the southern proctor ranking as the more senior. The division of university posts among northerners and southerners did something to assuage the *magna dissensio et discordia* to which strong regional antipathies constantly gave rise. The proctors had very wide powers. In addition to acting as a check on the chancellor, they had to protect the privileges of the regent masters. They were entitled to veto university legislation. They supervised the university's income. They saw that the statutes of the university were properly observed, kept lists of offenders and imposed punishments and fines.

[1] They were called regent masters because they ruled a school, usually no more than a room which they hired for lectures.

Collectively the masters of the university formed a body known as the Great Congregation, the *Congregatio Magna*, or Convocation. The regent or teaching masters had been originally grouped into the so-called Black Congregation which met in St Mildred's Church; proposed changes in the statutes and other university business were discussed there before these were brought forward at another assembly of masters, the Lesser Congregation or *Congregatio Minor*. Gradually the powers of the Black Congregation passed entirely to the Lesser Congregation with which it became merged. The work of the Lesser Congregation, whose membership was confined to the regent or teaching masters, overlapped with that of the Great Congregation which consisted of the non-teaching or non-regent masters as well as the teaching or regent masters. But while the Lesser Congregation could make ordinances, it had no authority to pass statutes, a right which belonged alone to the Great Congregation.

The university was then, and in this it resembled the medieval English Parliament, more of a process than an institution. Its own financial resources were trifling. For long it had few buildings which it could call its own. Most of its proceedings took place within the walls of St Mary's Church in the High Street. There the Congregation of Faculties met, degrees were awarded, university records, administrative and loan chests were stored.

Halls and colleges

Since the sixteenth century the university, apart from its few central buildings, has consisted of its colleges, housing both schools and teaching masters. But this was not the case in the Middle Ages when the majority of the undergraduates lived in private halls under the superintendence of a principal, who was a regent or teaching master, or a non-regent master, not appointed by the university but responsible to it. The halls, which usually housed some 12 to 20 students, and were 69 in number in 1444, were not self-governing communities of students, but were under the jurisdiction of their master. They had none of the elaborate regulations, embodied in statute, which became typical of a college, and they lacked the traditions sustained by a series of benefactions and religious observances, so much a part of early college life. Although the principal might have his own oratory, halls rarely had their own chapels or libraries, nor, unlike colleges, did they own corporate property. Of these ancient halls, St Edmund Hall is the sole survivor, built on the site of the house in which the future archbishop of Canterbury, Edmund Rich, taught his pupils in logic. Acquired by Oseney Abbey in 1291, it came after the suppression of the monasteries under the virtual control of Queen's College and did not achieve full independent status until 1957; its Elizabethan quadrangle is one of the most charming in Oxford.

The colleges were from the very start architecturally more impressive than the halls. They owed their existence to wealthy benefactors who hoped not merely to forward learning but for the opportunity to win credit in heaven through the promotion of good works. A college was essentially a religious foundation, largely staffed by priests who would say mass for the souls of the founder and benefactors of the society. At first they were small communities, governed by a body of statutes and administered by a head and fellows who shared in their common life and drew a modest sum from the college's revenues for their maintenance. In addition to the resident fellows, many of whom would be studying for a higher degree, the college might provide lodging for other regent masters, disqualified by their wealth from being fellows but who were able to reside in college as paying boarders; even some non-teaching masters, preferring to live for a part of the year in Oxford rather than in their parishes, might rent rooms. In general the colleges were not primarily undergraduate societies, except in so far as they might have a place for a servitor, like the bible clerk, who was not a graduate. Because, however, they often housed some of its leading scholars and officials—the first fellow to be chancellor was elected in 1297—colleges soon came to exercise an influence in the university out of proportion to their numbers.

Even in the first two centuries of the university's existence the colleges varied in their wealth and character. University College long claimed to be the earliest of the foundations, not simply because of its suppositious connexion with King Alfred but because, in 1249, William of Durham had bequeathed 310 marks to be invested in rents to sustain 10 or more needy masters studying divinity. The Oxford colleges seem to have been modelled on the colleges of the University of Paris. William of Durham, who had left Paris in 1229 after the dispersal of scholars following a riot between clerks and citizens at carnival time, may have intended his masters to form a separate society, but it was not until the 1280s that the university actually sponsored the setting up of a residential hall. In its comparative poverty and unimportance, University College contrasted with two other early foundations, Balliol College and Merton.

As an act of penance, a wealthy north-country nobleman, John Balliol, acting in collaboration with his wife, the Scottish princess, Dervorguilla of

Galloway, between 1255 and 1260, gave *summam certae sustentationis* to maintain some scholars at Oxford. After Balliol died in 1269, his widow added to the college's resources. Established outside the Northgate, near the church of St Mary Magdalen, it soon attracted other benefactors and began to accumulate property.

While the date of its foundation enabled University to claim to be the oldest, Balliol was probably the first college to exist as a more or less independent institution. But as early as 1262 Walter de Merton, chancellor of England and later bishop of Rochester, had planned a college. At the start the college, which was to be known as the House of the Scholars of Merton, was designed by the founder to administer estates, the manors of Maldon in Surrey and Farleigh in Hampshire, for his eight nephews and other kin, and a dozen older men from the diocese of Winchester studying at Oxford. Its headquarters were to be at Maldon in Surrey.

Extensions to the Oxford properties followed the transfer of the warden and his small society from Maldon to Oxford, and the scope of the foundation was widened. A hall was built before 1277, a treasury or muniment room between 1288 and 1291. The old church of St John the Baptist was dismantled and replaced by the magnificent new chapel which was fitted out in 1291. The choir of the chapel and Mob quad were constructed under the active supervision of one of the early fellows, Walter of Cuddington, *custos operum omnium collegii*, between 1289 and 1311.

Merton's outward magnificence and its endowments made it one of the noblest of the early colleges; it had some 40 fellows and 25 scholars. Its early history appears, however, somewhat chequered. There were complaints of internal strife and abuse of statute; but the college recovered its poise, supplied the English Church with many bishops and elected fellows who were to be reputed as outstanding mathematicians and scientists; among them, John Gaddesden, the author of *Rosa Medicinae*, who became the Black Prince's physician, Simon Bredon, John Ashenden, the *Calculator* Richard de Swyneshed, John Dumbleton and William of Heytesbury who was to define uniform acceleration and uniform retardation, and to prove arithmetically the rule for mean speeds.

Merton, like other colleges, was, however, principally concerned with the study of theology. This was the main object behind the foundation of the four colleges of the fourteenth century, Exeter, Oriel, Queen's and New College. Walter de Stapledon, like de Merton a bishop and royal minister, founded Exeter between 1314 and 1316. A Devonian by birth and bishop of Exeter, he was strongly imbued with local patriotism and eager to give boys from the west country an opportunity to make use of an Oxford education. His scholars had only a lean income, tenpence a week for commons, clothes or liveries (raised to a shilling in 1408) and a stipend of 10 shillings a year; their fellowships ceased on their becoming masters of arts or if they accepted a benefice or enjoyed an income of 60 shillings a year.

Oriel College owed its existence to another royal servant, Adam de Brome, almoner to Edward II and also vicar of St Mary's Church. He obtained the king's patronage for his foundation; but Edward II's fortunes failed and to protect the infant society de Brome paid court to the anti-Edwardian bishop of Lincoln, Henry Burghersh, who became the new college's Visitor.

Seventeen years later, in 1341, yet another royal chaplain, Robert of Eglesfield—he was chaplain to the queen, Philippa of Hainault, described in the statutes as 'a foundress rather than a patroness'—established a college. Eglesfield was a Cumberland man and his society, the Queen's College, bore, as it long continued to do, a distinctly north-country flavour. In some respects his statutes were even more markedly religious in character than those of other colleges, the founder's chief aim being to increase the number of scholarly clergy, especially in his native county. The college was founded, the first statutes affirmed, 'in order that this fruitful tree of theology may be carefully cultivated to the glory of God, the defence of the Church and the salvation of souls'. The fellows, who were to be in priest's orders and to hold a master's degree, were required to wear a blood-red livery in remembrance of Christ's passion; at the high table the provost was to sit in the centre with the fellows on either side as it was conventionally believed that Christ had sat with the apostles at the Last Supper.

Thirty years after the foundation of Queen's, a great churchman, William of Wykeham, issued in 1379 a charter for a society of 70 'poor and indigent' scholar clerks who were to form the 'Seinte Marie College of Wynchestre' in Oxford. The college was intended as a sequel to the grammar school which Wykeham had set up at Winchester to provide the grounding necessary for an Oxford foundation. Although the scholars were to be poor, the scale of the new foundation was more grandiose than that of any other Oxford college, its buildings more magnificent, and its warden more affluent.

No significant vestige of medieval Balliol, Exeter, Oriel or Queen's remains; but the grand quad of New College, the cloisters and the bell-tower were erected between 1380 and 1400 under the superintendence of the warden, Richard Malford, and the architect, William Wynfold, who had built Winchester College. Of the fine chapel, its size dictated by the large collegiate body it had to serve, little that is medieval, apart from the frame, survives; and the original plan has been obscured by the restorations of James Wyatt and Gilbert Scott. But New College, so massive in scale and impressive in appearance, was the first College where the quadrangle embraced all the buildings essential for the life of the society.[1]

If New College, and two of the colleges founded in the fifteenth century, All Souls and Magdalen, were well-endowed wealthy institutions, all college statutes stressed the need for sobriety of behaviour and the repudiation of luxury, expected of men who were dedicating their lives to religion and learning. Both in their personnel and manner of life these societies were essentially clerical seminaries. Their fellows were reminded continually of the eternal verities they served; they were exhorted to be constant in prayer, to be sober in their garb as in their conversation, diligent in their attendance at the mass.

In addition to the colleges for secular masters there were also houses established by the religious orders for their members in Oxford. Gloucester College was founded in 1283 for 13 monks from St Peter's monastery, Gloucester, but it was opened in 1298–9 to Benedictines from houses throughout the province of Canterbury; even this restriction was removed in 1336. The fifteenth-century *camerae* of Gloucester College, now the southern side of the quad of Worcester College, form the most important visible remains of a monastic hall. Durham College was founded in 1289 by Richard Holton, prior of the Benedictine house at Durham, for monks of his order. Canterbury Hall, founded by the monks of Christ Church, Canterbury, in the early fourteenth century, was for a short while turned into a college for both regulars and seculars (with John Wyclif as warden in 1365), reverting to its purely religious use in 1371. The Cistercians had Rewley Abbey (*c.* 1280) and, after Rewley failed as a result of the opposition from the Cistercian abbots, St Bernard's College (1437) was set up by Archbishop Chichele. In 1435, St Mary's College was founded for Austin Canons.

The friars were soon prominent in the university. They had a distinguished patron in Robert Grosseteste, who was lector to the Franciscans

---

[1] By composition with the founder, the university agreed that members of New College should be exempted from the exercises for degrees, and also from the obligation of supplicating for them, a privilege which the college voluntarily renounced on 12 November 1834.

from 1229/30 to 1235 when he became bishop of Lincoln. They had their own houses to which friars were sent for instruction from friaries in Great Britain and even from the continent. They soon won a reputation as exponents of scholastic theology. But their relations with the secular masters deteriorated. The latter insisted that no candidate could be given a licence in theology who had not first graduated in arts. The friars, forbidden to study secular subjects, resented this obligation and thought the study of theology should take priority. There were a series of bitter crises. In 1253 Thomas of York, a Franciscan, requested permission to supplicate as a master in theology without having first taken a degree in arts. His supplication was accepted, but the angry regent masters passed a decree that 'no one shall incept in theology unless he has previously incepted in arts.'

The dispute was renewed in the early fourteenth century. When, in 1303, the Franciscans were required to fulfil that part of the necessary exercise for the degree, the statutory sermon in St Mary's Church, they refused, alleging that the church was too noisy. A statute was passed in 1311 insisting that no lectures should be given on the Scriptures before the lecturer had become a bachelor in theology. This meant that the lecturer had first to lecture for a year on the *Sentences* of Peter Lombard, an obligation resented by the friars. Once more the controversy escalated when a Dominican, Hugh of Sutton, refused to take an oath to observe the statute and was consequently expelled. When the Dominicans secured a favourable ruling from the pope, the university refused to accept it. Eventually an agreement was reached in 1320, largely through the good offices of the archbishop of Canterbury, which left the honours with the secular masters.

Teaching and syllabus

Scholarship in the service of religion, reflected in Oxford's motto *Dominus, illuminatio mea*, may be said to epitomise what was taught in the medieval university. Medieval Oxford was intellectually an exciting place. All education at that time was basically theological, in that it was founded upon an accepted philosophy of existence designed to promote the ultimate salvation of man. But university education was not itself narrowly theological in its ingredients; it encompassed logic, philosophy and mathematics as well.

A medieval undergraduate lacked many of the aids to learning enjoyed by his successors. What libraries there were, were mainly confined to colleges.[1] Each book was secured by a staple to a chain, and the chain was attached to a cross bar which ran underneath the desk or lectern which housed the books, some 30 at a maximum. Fellows usually possessed a key to the room, but they were not permitted to remove the books, mainly heavy folios in manuscript,[2] from the library itself. There was, however, a system by which they could borrow books to read in their own rooms. In addition to the books kept in the library, there were others normally stored in a chest which could be distributed to the fellows. At All Souls this annual *electio*, as it was called, took place at a general court or assize of the College held within a week of All Souls Day; an early All Souls' list of *libri distribuendi* consists of 164 items. The books were given out in return for receipts delivered by the borrowers. Merton College still possesses these ancient indentures, small strips of parchment inscribed with the borrower's name and the title of the book. Such libraries could, by their very nature, be only comparatively large. An early inventory of All Souls records 466 books (of which 36 or 38 still survive). The earliest catalogue of Lincoln College, *c.* 1474, lists 135 books, the majority of which were donated to the college by the founder and other benefactors.

The student was unlikely to have possessed more than a small number of well-thumbed text books. The current value of books is demonstrated by the extent to which they were used as guarantees or *cautiones* for loans from the university chests.[3] An official called a *stationarius* or stationer, who acted primarily as a bookseller, was responsible both for lending copies of texts to students and for keeping a list of pledges, *cautiones*, in the form of books deposited by masters and scholars in return for cash.

The student had therefore to depend for the most part on lectures, sometimes lasting as much as three hours, which generally took the form of a commentary or gloss on a set text such as the *Sentences* of Peter Lombard. He would copy this down laboriously and use it as the basis of his study. The statute of 1431 decreed that masters should first read the

[1] The bibliophile bishop of Durham, Richard de Bury, intended to found a college and endow it with his valuable collection of books, but he was so much in debt at his death in 1345 that his executors sold the books, so many that they filled five large carts.

[2] The 49 books given to All Souls by its founder, Archbishop Chichele, weighed 312 lbs.

[3] The chests contained money which members of the university could borrow upon security, and were largely established by benefactions. The University Chest, the name still used to describe the university's finance department, which was known as the Chest of the Four Keys, contained the university's own valuables. The proctors kept two of the keys; the other two were in the custody of the regent masters selected from the two nations. The chest became overcrowded, and in 1412 (and again in 1427) chests with five keys were purchased; the keys were kept by the chancellor and four representatives, two regent masters and two non-regent masters from the colleges.

text, then explain and comment on it; lecturers were urged to be relevant and to keep closely to the text.

The lectures were given by the regent or teaching masters in a room or school which the master had hired or in a hall of residence. As soon as a student had graduated, he had to give lectures for the next two years as a part of his master's degree; hence the description of graduation as inception, that is, the beginning of lectures. The period was known as a necessary regency. Until the middle of the sixteenth century university teaching was thus based upon the lectures delivered by the regent masters.

The system had much to commend it. It was cheap, for the student paid his fees and so it cost the university nothing. It meant that the teaching was mainly in the hands of young men, newly-fledged masters, in some respects inexperienced, but still enthusiastic about their subject and likely to be in touch with their audience. It stimulated competition, so that lecturers tried to make their material interesting. 'There could not be better teaching here', a scholar noted, 'for students of civil law, than is to be found this year; because there are two doctors here continually lecturing, whereas there used to be only one; and each of the two tries, in emulation of the other, to make better progress and to offer more useful teaching.'

The course in arts was concerned to develop the students' capacity for reasoned argument, for the oral disputation, so long the focal point of university education, represented far less the accumulation of knowledge than its active employment in debate. A man's progress towards his first degree was thus punctuated by a series of exercises. After he had studied for two years, he became a 'general sophister' and engaged in logical discussions, acting either as a respondent or opposer in a debate on a set theme. In his fourth year, he became a questionist, engaging in disputations in grammar and logic with a master in what was known as Responsions. Eventually he was brought before a board of masters or university teachers. He had to convince them that he had mastered the appropriate texts and had fulfilled the necessary exercises. They had to assure themselves of his character and other attainments, testified by witnesses. If their verdict was favourable, he was given permission to 'determine' that is, to uphold or determine a thesis against an opponent. For many this may have been the end of the scholastic road, but there were others who studied for another three years, so that they might proceed to inception (at a ceremony called the Act) and so join the rank of the masters. They undertook a further series of exercises the best-known of which was Austins, so called because it took place at the convent of the Austin Friars, though under the supervision of the masters. At length the candidate was able to supplicate for his degree. Some 15 regent masters, including his own master who was to present him, testified to his suitability in the presence of the chancellor and proctors. Then the chancellor licensed the inceptor who subsequently went the round of the schools, inviting the masters to attend his inception and possibly to the banquet (on which he had promised that he would not spend more than 3,000 *livres tournois*) with which he celebrated the occasion. If a master wished to qualify for a higher degree, in theology, law or medicine, he had to enter on a further lengthy period of study, amounting in all to 16 years of labour before he acquired the cherished doctorate.

Scholasticism, and Lollardy

By the close of the fourteenth century Oxford's prestige in the world of scholarship stood high. The university had come into being at a time when the character of medieval learning was itself being shaped anew. The narrower theological concepts, so strongly influenced by the ideas of the fifth-century African, St Augustine of Hippo, were giving way to a broader synthesis in which the re-discovered philosophy of Aristotle had a major part to play. In the future development of scholastic thought Oxford was to be deeply involved, though its role was to be subordinate to that of the university of Paris. Oxford had become a centre of Aristotelian scholarship in the thirteenth century, though the majority of its teachers remained long loyal to more traditional types of thinking. Before the first decade of the century John Blund, a regent master, was lecturing on Aristotle's *Sophistici Elenchi*, and in its middle years Oxford produced a number of capable exponents of Aristotelianism, among them a group of friars, Robert Bacon, Richard Fishacre (whose work was said to have won praise from Thomas Aquinas), Simon of Hinton, Richard Rufus, Thomas of York and Robert Kilwardby.

Oxford theologians at first looked somewhat askance at the synthesis which Aquinas compounded of Christian doctrine and Aristotelian philosophy. To the Oxford Dominicans, more especially to Kilwardby who had become archbishop of Canterbury in 1272, Aquinas' ideas seemed of too radical a character, and in an effort to stem their spread he called a special Congregation at Oxford on 18 March 1277 which censured some 30 Thomist propositions. It was, however, a vain effort, for Aquinas soon had followers in the university: Richard Knapwell, William Hothum and Thomas Sutton, a fellow of Merton. Moreover, no sooner was Thomism respectable than Oxford produced in Duns Scotus and William of Ockham two of its most formidable critics.

Both men, members of the Franciscan order, spent the greater part of their academic careers in Paris; but their ideas had been first formulated at Oxford. Scotus was probably at Oxford between 1297 and 1304 and was lecturing there on the *Sentences*, a function that William of Ockham who entered the Franciscan house at Oxford, was performing between 1317 and 1319. In their different ways both men challenged the validity of the synthesis which Aquinas had conceived in so masterly a fashion, drawing a distinction between the disciples of theology and philosophy which he had sought to resolve. But it was left to Ockham to establish the basic form of scholasticism, known as nominalism, which conditioned the academic life of Oxford, as of so many other European universities, in the late fourteenth and fifteenth centuries.

Naturally enough there were those who regarded the new development with distaste, and looked back to the realist philosophy of Aquinas and the more traditional thinking of Augustine. Such a scholar was Thomas Bradwardine of Merton, a future archbishop of Canterbury, who in his *De Causa Dei*, tried to demonstrate God's omnicausality by a series of mathematically ordered proofs and corollaries.

But the most distinguished representative of this reaction was John Wyclif, possibly a fellow of Merton, certainly for a short time master of Balliol and latterly a resident of Queen's. He belonged to the more conservative group of thinkers in the university, owing much to Grosseteste, Augustine and the fathers of the Church, critical of the all-prevailing nominalism which, as he made plain in his *Summa de Ente*, seemed to suggest that it was beyond man's capacity to attain any knowledge of absolute truth. This seemed to him to contravene the teaching of Scripture where in all its literalness the divine word was revealed. He made the Scriptures not so much the sole as the basic criterion by which the Christian faith was to be interpreted and judged. He was drawn by his studies to a belief in determinism and to a repudiation of the contemporary notion of transubstantiation.

The lectures which Wyclif delivered at Oxford, the learned, ponderous commentaries he wrote there, demonstrated his relative conservatism, but he soon aroused controversy within the university. He had a following among the younger dons, Nicholas Hereford of Queen's (associated with Wyclif and Purvey in the translation of the Bible into English), John Aston of Merton, Thomas Hutman of Merton, Laurence Stephen or Bedeman of Exeter, and an able Austin Canon, Philip Repingdon, who in later years became bishop of Lincoln. An Oxford Carmelite, John Kenningham, trounced Wyclif for the heterodox propositions which he deduced from his writings. When the archbishop himself intervened in the dispute, many Oxford dons saw the move less as an attack on Wyclif than on their own cherished privileges. Repingdon declared in a university sermon that Wyclif was only saying what the church had long taught.

Such a view was unacceptable to the archbishop, long alarmed by fear of spreading heresy and made anxious by the influence which the Oxford schoolman was wielding in court circles. Wyclif, like some dons in more recent times, was a poor politician, happier in the sophisticated argument of the schools than in the realities of political manipulation. Momentarily he had won the favour of John of Gaunt and the anti-clerical lay barons, only to be discarded when it was evident that his notions were unorthodox as well as doctrinaire. A council of bishops, theologians and canon lawyers met at Blackfriars on 17 May 1382, and condemned his views as heretical. The archbishop decided that the university must itself be brought low. He summoned the chancellor and proctors to London, snubbed them when they arrived by keeping them waiting, and then overawed them with bland threats and powerful arguments. Of the delegation only one, Thomas Brightwell, a fellow of Merton, for a time withstood the primate's measured words.

Oxford was, however, not yet ready to kowtow to the archbishop. When the chancellor, Robert Rygge, read out the decrees passed by the Blackfriars Council at St Mary's, there was a murmur of dissent. Hereford and Repingdon made a vain attempt to win the support of Gaunt; riding to London from Gaunt's house, they distributed Lollard literature. It was a gesture both imprudent and dangerous. Brought before Archbishop Courtenay, Hereford and Repingdon reluctantly agreed that the 24 extracts drawn from Wyclif's writings, which the Council had condemned, had been rightly so treated. Aston, who was rash enough to seek to conduct his own case in English, was sent to cool his heels in the archbishop's prison. To all intents and purposes the Lollard movement at Oxford had been brought to a prompt and humiliating closure.

It was, however, to linger on long after Wyclif's death in 1384. A Benedictine student of Gloucester College, who incepted in 1396-7, owned a copy of Wyclif's books, thus indicating that his writings were still circulating among the scholars. There seems little doubt that a small group of Merton dons continued to regard Wyclif's views with sympathy.

Among the Lollards, held on royal orders at Beaumaris Castle in May 1395, were three fellows of the college, Richard Whelpyngton, junior proctor in 1393–4, Thomas Lucas and John Gamlingay. Another fellow, William James, charged with defending Wyclif's teaching on the Eucharist before a meeting of Congregation, was arrested at Bristol. The authorities sent a letter to the chancellor ordering him to expel all Lollard sympathisers from the university, naming in particular Robert Lychlade who 'a long while published and taught nefarious opinions and conclusions and detestable allegations repugnant to the catholic faith in the university.'

The sequel was something of an anti-climax. Lychlade, who had criticised the religious orders in a university sermon, was banished from the university on 1 October 1395, but was reinstated by the king's order on 8 November 1399 and, by 1401, was rector of Kemerton, Gloucester. Gamlingay, who was brought with James before the king's Council in Chancery, was deprived of his fellowship. Thomas Lucas reappeared as junior proctor in 1403–4 and was still a fellow in 1408 when he borrowed 12 books from the college library. Whelpyngton, the author of a scholastic work, *Questiones Posteriorum*, was still a fellow in 1401–2.

William James was apparently the doyen of the group. He had been a fellow of Merton as far back as 1387 and was a friend of the chancellor, Rygge. He was put in prison but on his release was welcomed warmly by the subwarden on his return to college. Whether he retracted his opinions seems doubtful, for while his name disappears from the college accounts after 1411, he abjured Lollardy in the presence of the archbishop some nine years later. Archbishop Chichele absolved him and gave him permission to practice medicine within the limits of his college and manor of Maidstone. There were still pockets of Lollards at Oxford, but they no longer constituted a danger to orthodoxy.

In some sense the phenomenon of Lollardy demonstrated Oxford's intellectual vitality. It showed how reluctant the university was to prostitute its independence to archiepiscopal control. Yet, equally, as a training ground for the future priests of the Church, it could not, without detriment to its foundation, harbour heterodoxy. For a while, indeed, its flirtation with Wyclif and his ideas damaged its reputation, but no one could doubt that, by the end of the fourteenth century, it had become one of the established institutions of English society.

II

Medieval don and undergraduate

The population of the medieval university is not known precisely. At its height it may have exceeded 1,500; in the fifteenth century, a period of declining numbers, it has been estimated to have been 1,000. While lists of those taking degrees exist from the fifteenth century onwards (a register of Congregation runs from 4 December 1458 to 19 November 1463, and begins again in 1505), there was no record of matriculations before 1565 (though a list of 1552 provides the first record of all members of colleges and halls). Even after that date, the figures are not wholly reliable since there were men on the college books who had never attended the ceremony of matriculation.

No such ceremony existed in the early years of the university. Masters and scholars simply lived as lodgers and tenants in town houses. But they resented the exorbitant rents charged by the townsfolk; 'We have heard', Henry III wrote to the major and bailiffs on 3 May 1231, 'that you are so onerous and exorbitant in the letting of your lodgings to the scholars residing among you that, unless you deal more moderately and reasonably with them in this respect, they will be obliged, on account of your exactions, to give up their studies and to go abroad.' In an attempt to secure fair rentals, a board of taxors, consisting of two representatives of the university and of two townsfolk had been set up to assess the rents according to the custom of the university; but contention continued.

There was, however, another problem which led the university to exert a more rigid control over the students. They were involved constantly in brawls with the townsfolk, and were often at strife with each other. While the university invariably blamed the townsmen, it was anxious at the disorder perpetrated by the students. In 1231 the king, Henry III, complaining of the 'rebellious and incorrigible clerks' who would not submit to the discipline of the chancellor and masters, and of 'ruffians who took advantage of clerical privilege to masquerade as clerks', ordered that no clerk should remain at Oxford who was not 'under the discipline or tuition of one of the masters of the schools.' Henceforth every scholar was required to put his name on the roll (*matricula*) of a master, and the master was ordered to keep a list of those attending his lectures. While such a method may have helped to diminish idleness, it did not eliminate the indiscipline latent in the student population. Because, as the statute of 1410 worded it, 'the peace of this university is known frequently to be disturbed by divers persons who in the guise of scholars abide in divers places within the university and the precincts of the same, not residing in halls nor having principals, who are called by the name of chamber dekenys and who sleep all day and at night lurk about taverns and brothels, bent on robbing and homicide', students were in future to be obliged to reside in 'a hall or college of the university, where commons are kept, or in halls annexed to the same', and townspeople were forbidden to take in undergraduates as lodgers.

The population of the halls had been growing gradually—that of the colleges remained only a tiny, privileged minority—before this statute, reiterated in 1421, was promulgated. Until that date it had been possible for a rich student to rent a house, and for poorer students to live in lodgings. Chaucer's poor scholar, the 'hende Nicholas' had 'a chambre ... in that hostelrye' which was kept by John the carpenter. Although the *Miller's Tale* can be regarded, as Dr Pantin has suggested, as the first of the many novels written about Oxford, the portrait of Nicholas may well have been representative of the less responsible scholars. 'Al his fantasye was formed for to learne astrologye', so Chaucer informs us; but he seemed even more intent on seducing his landlord's wife, Alisoun, and in playing crude jokes on the carpenter and the parish clerk.

The halls brought the medieval student within the framework of an organised community. They were of varied size, but in addition to the large open hall used for lectures, meals and other communal assemblies (two of which survive in Tackley's Hall on the south side of the High Street and Beam Hall in Merton Street), they had a kitchen and buttery, a principal's room or rooms and chambers in which the students lived. The hall of both halls and colleges would be strewn with straw and rushes, renewed on the great religious feast days, and heated by a central hearth (the medieval louvre survives in the hall of Lincoln College). As in the colleges, two or more scholars shared the chambers in which they lived; the ends or corners of the rooms would be partitioned off to form small studies which afforded privacy and could be locked up. The central space was used as a common room and bedroom. By the end of the fifteenth century the windows would have been glazed, and the room heated by a fireplace. Surviving inventories show that the furniture was adequate if sparse. There would be a truckle bed, with a mattress or straw palliasse, sheets and blankets, possibly adorned with a set of hangings; chests and coffers in which the student could keep his goods; forms, stools and chairs.

The undergraduate's daily routine followed a familiar pattern. He probably rose between 5.00 and 6.00am, and attended lectures in the early morning; either in his hall or in the schools. He might at some stage attend an early mass, though this would only be a matter of obligation on Sundays and festivals. The ordinances of 1483–90 decree that on other days scholars are required to attend high mass, matins and vespers *secundum exigenciam sui ordinis vel condicionis*. The demands made on fellows of colleges, the majority of whom were in priests' orders, would naturally be more exacting. At New College, where the fellows were not obliged to attend every statutory service, they had to be present at High Mass and say the Hours on Sundays, on 46 major feasts and on all non-legible (i.e. days on which there were no lectures or disputations) saints days. It is probable that at some stage in the morning the student would break his fast with a piece of bread and a pot of ale.

Between 10.00 and 11.00am he was summoned to dinner by a bell or a horn. Grace was said before and after the meal, usually by the man with the first seat at the table. For failure to say grace, or laughter or noise during its recital, students were liable to a fine of ¼d, a sum also exacted from late arrivals who might forego the meal altogether unless they had an adequate excuse; their portions of meat or fish would, however, be kept for the next meal. The scholar provided his own knives, and trencher; though there were cups, dishes, salt-cellars and table-cloths for common use. As in colleges and monasteries the meal was accompanied by a reading. The food was probably adequate rather than luxurious. At New College there were two meals a day except on Fridays, Saturdays and in Lent when there was only one. Besides bread and beer, (New College baked its bread but did not brew its own beer), the food comprised beef and mutton, and fish on fast days. When, in Lent, butter was not served, spices and mustard were provided for the fish. On Fridays in Lent figs, raisins, almonds, honey and rice were substituted for fish. Much to the ire of the local shopkeepers, the college bought its spices, salt meat and fish wholesale. Most colleges and halls had gardens in which they grew their own vegetables: cabbages, onions, parsley and leeks. Students were forbidden to remove any crockery or tablecloths from the halls nor were they to carve their names or otherwise deface the furniture, or to spill liquor on the rush floor. They were urged not to stay too long over their meals, and were prohibited from taking meals in the buttery or kitchen.

The domestic side of the hall was presided over by a manciple (who might combine his office with that of cook). The undergraduate paid his fees for his lodging and instruction to the principal, but settled his account for his board with the manciple. The regular allowance for food and drink, forming a part of the stipend of the fellows of colleges, was known as commons; hence the expression still used of 'commoner' to describe undergraduates of Oxford and Cambridge who do not hold scholarships. If a student wanted more food and drink than was provided by the commons, he could buy it at his own charge; this constituted his battels. By statute any food left over was to be given to the servants or to the poor. It appears that there were some halls, evidently because of their smallness, which did not provide meals; their students had to make arrangements to take these at another hall.

After dinner the undergraduate would be free to take some exercise, walking in company with another (to walk alone was regarded with great disapproval) or possibly to indulge in one or other of the more active amusements condemned by his elders as unbecoming to the life of the scholar and future cleric. Inventories reveal the possession of musical instruments, mainly lutes, with which scholars beguiled their time. Chaucer's poor student had a 'presse i-covered with a faldying reed, and al above ther lay a gay sawtrye, on which he made a nightes melodye, so swetely, that al the chambre rang'.

The founder of New College thought it necessary to forbid dancing or wrestling in the hall and games of ball in chapel. It will be recalled that Chaucer's clerk, Absalon, had learned dancing 'after the scole of Oxenforde.' Halls and colleges must soon have developed their own customs, often unrecorded but passed down from one generation to another. Contemporary continental universities had embarrassing initiation ceremonies of which no trace can be found at medieval Oxford; though at Merton in the early seventeenth century, according to Anthony Wood, freshmen had to 'speake some pretty apothegime, or make jest or bull, or speake some eloquent nonsense' on penalty of 'tucking' (i.e. splitting the chin with the thumb-nail) on certain days before Christmas. It seems likely that there were similar functions at some of the medieval halls.

Sooner or later, however, the student would settle down to work. Lectures and disputations took place at 12.30 or 1.00. In the halls 'cursory' or 'extraordinary' lectures (by contrast with the 'ordinary' lectures of the morning) occurred where the content of the morning's lecture might be discussed. He would be expected to work also in his study. Supper would be served at 5pm. After the evening exercises or recreation, possibly spent in the local tavern or in roaming the streets, he would reassemble in hall for a *collatium* or *biberium*. On Saturday evenings the *Salve Regina* or an antiphon to Our Lady would be sung, followed by a recitation of faults (by a scholar known as the *impositor* specially nominated to do this task) and the imposition of penalties by the principal. Bed followed about 9.00pm.

Although the halls were subject to rules—the only surviving set dates from 1483–90—the student had a considerable degree of liberty. He was liable to be fined for breaches of regulations which were necessary, as they still are, for civilised living within a community. He was properly fined 1d for washing his dirty hands in a bucket from the well which gave the college or hall its supply of fresh water. He was made responsible for breakages in the dining hall or in his rooms, and for walking on the grass or destroying the plants. He was forbidden to keep sporting dogs, ferrets or hawks. He was required not to 'prevent his fellows from studying, by noisiness, by shouting, by playing a musical intrument, or by any sort of clamour or roudiness, under penalty of ¼d fine.' Disobedience or insubordination made him liable to expulsion.

University towns were among the very few places in the medieval world where a large number of young men, often high-spirited and impulsive, were brought together. Once a man's studies were complete—and he could hardly be expected to work all the day—there were few legitimate outlets for a student's energy. 'Many scholars are of this disposition', a writer commented in the fifteenth century, 'that they will keep themselves in their chamber from morning till night to be seen as virtuous fellows, but nevertheless when it is night they will rush out in arms into the streets, as foxes do out of their holes, to rob men of their money if they meet any . . .'

In general the authorities frowned on most forms of exercise; hunting and hawking were thought to be unsuitable for future clerks. Ball games were sometimes indulged in, occasionally with dire results, but generally they were prohibited. Bull and bear baiting afforded occasional entertainment. No doubt the local taverns provided the greatest consolation; they gave an opportunity for gambling and horse-play, rough practical jokes and bawdy conversation. Excessive drinking often led to violence among the students, between northerners and southerners, between town and gown. Although they were expected to be celibate (though not all students were yet in holy orders), the young men sometimes availed themselves of the services of the town girls. As early as 1234 the king ordered the scholars' concubines to be released from gaol. At the start of the fourteenth century, as a result of agitation by the university's chancellor, a special room in the Oxford gaol was reserved for women, in the main prostitutes. Others found the exercise and the excitement they needed by poaching on the game outside Oxford. Some even banded together to lie in wait for innocent travellers. In 1421 some undergraduates broke into the bishop's prison, releasing the prisoners with whom they joined company, roaming the countryside in dangerous bands.

The university records are frequently punctuated by episodes in which clerks were guilty of theft, poaching, disorder, wounding and even murder. Henry Kinnieton, caught trespassing in 1231 with bows and arrows in Shotover Wood, was handed over by the king's officers to the chancellor for condign punishment. In December 1301, Nicholas de la Marche attacked a fellow clerk, Thomas de Horncastel, in his lodgings by the 'great schools' in Schools Street. An unfortunate colleague, John de Hampslape, who tried to stop the fight was stabbed to death by de la Marche in Catte Street. A similar fate came to William de Roule, who was killed by Welsh clerks when he went to the aid of friends by whom they had been attacked in Schools Street on 22 February 1303. A north countryman, Richard de Langeleghe, was charged with stabbing another clerk in the neck with a bodkin in Schools Street on the night of 16 March 1343. On 29 June 1389, Richard Gille knifed John Martyn in a room in Queen's College with fatal effects. John Kirkeby, accused of housebreaking and robbery in October 1374, may have been the same Oxford clerk who led a riot against the Welshmen in 1389. In 1442 William Bysshop of St John Hall was hauled before the chancellor for assault arising out of a game of sword and buckler. A decade later Robert Wrixham, a priest and B.A. of St George's Hall, was convicted with a schoolmaster of entering the house of a fishmonger and beating him up. A member of Beam Hall was convicted in 1469 of stealing necklaces and precious stones from the shrine of St Frideswide's and debarred from proceeding to a higher degree.

Graduates seem to have been as much involved in such breaches of the peace as undergraduates. Richard Lytham, a young fellow of Merton, was expelled from the university by the chancellor for going to brothels in 1387, but was eight years later reinstated by the king's order. Another fellow of Merton, a century later, in 1492, was charged with frequenting suspect places, and with playing tennis and dice in public. William Harbord, who rented a school from University College in 1461-2, was released from prison in the Oxford Castle in March 1465, on promising that he would not poach again in Woodstock and Beckley parks; he ended his life as rector of Market Harborough. John Crosby, later a resident and benefactor of Lincoln College, stabbed a glover because he had failed to make his gloves by an agreed time.

The Welsh[1] and Irish students, possibly stimulated by the Celtic temperament, were among the prime offenders. In 1430 Hugh Thomas, later principal of Grove Hall, was accused with others of waylaying an Oxford ironmonger at the Bullstake, Binsey. Thirty years later, two Welsh students, sons of Roger Vawghane, assisted by their tutor, stole a horse from Robert Knolles, guest of John Vincent, mine host of the Cardinal's Hat, for their journey to Wales. The Welsh and Irish were well to the front in more tumultuous affrays. In 1238 the papal legate, Cardinal Otho, was residing at Oseney Abbey. When some students called to pay their respects, an officious janitor repulsed them rudely from the door. To add to the confusion the abbey's cook threw a pot of boiling water over a begging Irish clerk, whereupon one of his Welsh colleagues shot the cook dead with an arrow. The Celtic temperament momentarily triumphant, the cardinal hastily crossed the river and withdrew to Abingdon, threatening excommunication, interdict and other reprisals until the university's protector, Bishop Grosseteste, managed to still the legatine wrath.

The University's population represented a cross-section of all classes. There was no examination for admission; but no student who did not possess the rudiments of Latin grammar and some skill in spoken Latin could have made a profitable use of his time. Ordinarily he would have attended some grammar school before coming into residence. There were a number of grammar schools in Oxford itself; among them Inge Hall, Lyon Hall, Tackley Hall, Cuthbert Hall and White Hall, controlled by the university which appointed two masters of arts to superintend them. William of Waynflete, bishop of Winchester, founded a special grammar school attached to the college which he had established, Magdalen, to enable the demies[2] of his college to get a grounding in grammar before

[1] Of the 400 Welshmen who came to medieval Oxford, the majority naturally came after the Edwardian conquest—only 24 before 1284, and the majority, 260, in the fifteenth century.
[2] So-called because they had half the commons which a fellow enjoyed.

they started their arts course. More aristocratic members of the university would have had schooling from a private tutor before they came into residence.

There were always a number of *generosi*, men of wealth and birth, in residence at Oxford and these increased in the later Middle Ages. The future cardinal, Henry Beaufort, rented an *alta camera* at Queen's between 1390 and 1393. John Rous asserted that Beaufort's nephew, the future Henry V, attended the college under his tutelage; though his statement lacks confirmatory evidence. Alexander Neville, a younger son of the lord of Raby, and a future archbishop of York, resided at Oxford, as did his brother, Thomas, in 1348. Two other members of this affluent and aristocratic family who studied at Oxford were Robert, the bishop of Salisbury, and George, who supplicated for his B.A. in 1450, and subsequently became chancellor of the university and archbishop of York. The majority of the students must, however, have come from a more modest background. Some had their expenses paid by their parents, while others won the patronage of a churchman, a religious house or a wealthy layman. In 1419 Bishop Langley of Durham provided 100 marks for the support of an Oxford student, William Ingleby. In 1483 Lady Margaret Chocke bequeathed John Langley '6 marks yerely during 4 yeres for to goo to Oxford to scole'. Admissions were made in a haphazard fashion. While entry to a hall may sometimes have been arranged beforehand as a result of negotiation between a parent or patron and the principal, it is probable that the majority simply signed on at a hall when they arrived at Oxford. There were also a fair number of beneficed clerks who had been given leave of absence from their livings to further their studies. A number of foreigners were attracted to Oxford by the growing reputation of its scholars, among them Peter de Candia, the future Pope Alexander V, who was sent to attend the Oxford house of the Franciscans to study for the bachelorship of divinity.

Then, as now, a student's expenses varied in accordance with his tastes. On the one hand there are ample complaints of penury by the undergraduate; on the other hand, of extravagant spending by the parent. Both were doubtless assisted by the actual dearth of cash and ready money, a feature of late medieval society. As early as the second decade of the thirteenth century, Elias, a canon of St Frideswide's, wrote to Richard Neville, bishop of Chichester, informing him that Thomas de Bosco, a scholar, whom the bishop supported with an exhibition, was placed in great difficulties when the payment of his exhibition was in his arrears by his inability to buy books and other necessities. A fifteenth-century scholar was so short of money that he had to pawn his bedclothes. The letter-book drawn up by Thomas Sampson, the Oxford writing master *c.* 1380, contains examples of letters written by undergraduates and parents. 'I know not', runs one, 'what to offer you, my sweet father, since I am your son and after God, entirely your own creature, and so completely yours that I can give you nothing. But if I can remember what the child's instinct prompts it to say, I might sing, as does the cuckoo unceasingly 'Da, da, da, da': which little song I am at this moment compelled to sing, for the money, which you so liberally gave me last time for my study is now completely disbursed, and I am in debt to the tune of five shillings and more.' 'To recover your honour and put slander under foot', an angry parent wrote to his son, 'you will now cease from such ribald behaviour, knowing that on no account will I give you any aid or financial help, if you require it, while you behave thus madly and outrageously, and that you will possess my curse as you had my blessing before.' The son sought to reassure his father: 'As you have been given to understand that I have no desire to learn and that I am doing no work, pray believe me, sir, that my hope on the contrary, is that you will understand matters aright, for, when I next come, I will tell you clearly how it is with me. . . . Wherefore I pray to God the Father on high that you will not have cause to forget my master, but will aid me to pay my expenses to him.'

The normal expenses of the medieval university seem to have been reasonable enough. A student had to pay the rent of his study, his commons, a contribution to the wages of the manciple and cook, lecture fees, 2d a term to the bedel of his faculty and small sums for special feasts or gaudies. His personal expenses varied, but would probably include payments to the laundress and the barber, for clothes, books and charity. 'Since I cannot get through without heavy costs', a budding lawyer told his father, 'I have scarcely enough money for my expenses till the bearer of this letter returns; for in commons I cannot manage with less than 8d a week, but in other necessaries also I have spent the money allowed me, and have to go on spending: to wit, in my journey to Oxford, for myself and my horse, 3s 4d; in the purchase of two books at Oxford, namely the *Codex* and the *Digestum Vetus* after I got here, 6s 8d *item* to the teacher from whom I hear my "ordinary" lectures, 2s; and when you reckon in the wages of our manciple and cook, the hire of my study and many other necessities with which I need not trouble you, because of their number, it will be obvious that my expenses are not unreasonable.' 'When I was a scholar at Oxforde', the grammarian Robert Whittington wrote, recalling his days there *c.* 1494, 'I lyved competently with vii pens commens wekely.'

John Arundell, later bishop of Chichester, chaplain and physician to Henry VI, kept a notebook when he was principal of St Mildred Hall in 1424 in which he noted the expenditure of the sums of money which he had received on behalf of his pupils. He estimated the expenses of an undergraduate in the first term of his third year as 16s 14½d (the sum included 6s 4¾d for commons for 12 weeks, 5¼d for battels, 12d for gaudy, 20d for lecture, 12d for manciple and cook, 1d for the barber, 1d for the laundress, 7d for shoes, 8d for a shirt, 1d for a belt, 1d for candles, 4d for clogs, 6d for a book and 1s 8d for the journey home), amounting to £3 13s 4d for a whole year, a comparatively modest sum. The son of a wealthy merchant in the mid-fourteenth century spent 2s a week on his board, 20s 8d a year on tuition, 40s on clothes (a hefty sum denoting some measure of sartorial extravagance), and 20s on sundries, in all £9 10s 8d; but it has been reckoned that an undergraduate's inclusive annual expenses in the late Middle Ages need not have amounted to more than 50s.

The university course was, however, a long one, more especially if the bachelor aspired to the doctor's degree, which could amount to as much as 18 years. It was unreasonable to expect a patron or parent to support a scholar much beyond his graduation as a bachelor. The young graduate must therefore have often watched the future with some anxiety. Hence the continuous search for benefices, which could give the graduate the income which would enable him to complete his courses, and the university's concern to preserve the process of papal provision which gave the graduate a possible alternative to private or episcopal patronage.

It was in this respect that the colleges performed so useful a function. Of the 1,500 members or so of the university, monks and friars accounted for some 150 and the colleges for a similar number, a very small fraction of the total. But a fellow of a college was placed financially in an enviable position. A don's income varied according to the society of which he was a member. The early scholars of Merton had an allowance of 40s a year. At Oriel, in addition to board and lodging, the fellows had 5d a week, with 5s at Christmas and Easter and 40d at Whitsuntide. At Lincoln the rector and fellows enjoyed commons, the amount varying according to the incidence of holy days and special benefactions; an additional allowance or pittance, was made yearly on the anniversary day of some benefactor. The weekly allowance normally came to 16d but was as much as 2s at Christmas and Easter. The subrector and bursar received 13s 4d each annually; of college servants the manciple was paid £2 6s 8d, the cook 10s , the barber 8s and the laundress 13s 4d. Various other payments were made to the fellows as allowances—for clothing, for hairdressing and so forth. Although no fellow could be described as rich—and wealth was ordinarily a disqualification for election to a fellowship—he could live reasonably well. Few men held fellowships for long, accepting preferment in the Church, but they frequently remembered the society to which they had belonged by bequeathing their books, vestments and cups to it.

Left, Arthur Cole, President of Magdalen (d.1558) Right, Robert Langton, Queen's College (d.1524)

III

The Passing of Medieval Oxford
1400-1558

Trends in fifteenth-century Oxford

The century and a half that elapsed between the fading at Oxford of the Lollard heresy and the accession of Elizabeth I, were of crucial importance in the university's history. These years saw the slow but steady injection of a humanistic style and of humanistic ideas into the syllabus; though the scholastic method was not abandoned, it was to be substantially modified. Latterly they saw too the gradual, if reluctant, acceptance of the Protestant faith and the steady intrusion of Protestant theology into the teaching of divinity and of Protestant ceremonial into college chapels.

The political and social developments which accompanied these changes were even more significant. The control which the crown had exercised over the university was deepened and magnified, though it used its powers wisely and with discretion. But the crown could no more afford to tolerate political and religious heterodoxy than could the medieval Church; it expected obedience, if not subservience, from its academic élite.

Moreover it was then that the structure of the university began to experience a socially significant transformation. As the halls of residence disappeared, they were replaced by the colleges which emerged more and more as the determinant influence in the university's life. The colleges ceased to be small societies of what we should today call research graduates and became largish communities of young men studying for a first degree. In the sixteenth century the training of the future clergy continued to be a principal object of university education; but the would-be clerics were reinforced by men, drawn from the gentry and aristocracy, who were to follow a career in law and politics.

In the early fifteenth century the university still suffered from its association with Lollardy, however evanescent this had become, for only a few scholars continued to sympathise with Wyclif's teaching. Some were involved in Oldcastle's rebellion, among them John Mybbys, the principal of Cuthbert Hall, who for a time was placed under arrest. William Taylor, principal of St Edmund Hall, who was summoned before the archbishop for preaching a heterodox sermon at Paul's Cross, was in later life to be burned at the stake. His successor as principal, Peter Payne, was an even more convinced adherent of Wycliffism and ultimately fled to Bohemia where he was to be prominent in the Hussite movement for nearly half a century.

The tarnish of heresy seems to have stimulated the university into a display of orthodoxy. In 1427 Richard Fleming, bishop of Lincoln, who had earlier aroused Archbishop Arundel's disfavour unjustifiably by his supposed support of Lollard opinion, founded a college, Lincoln, to train theologians to combat heresy. A former fellow of Oriel, Reynold Pecock, devoted much time to writing a great thesis, *The Repressor*, to combat the Lollards whom he had met at Oxford and later when he was master of Whittington College in London. Unfortunately, when he was bishop of Chichester Pecock himself was charged with heterodoxy, with placing too much trust in the power of dialectic, perhaps the fruit of his Oxford training, and, as a result, was deprived of his bishopric and placed in detention. But his books were read by some Oxford scholars, among them Thomas Leemster, a fellow of All Souls and principal of Salisbury Hall. Scholars had therefore to be careful, more so than in the past, about the nature of the theses which they wished to propound, even in disputations. In 1416, John Holand, a doctor of civil law, provoked criticism as a result of the scholastic act he intended to make, his proposition being thought to be in some degree critical of papal authority.

In the fifteenth century the university entered into what was in some respects a period of contraction. Its numbers apparently fell from 1,500 to 1,000; only 27 men took the master's degree in 1456–7. Contemporary letters complained of the shortage of students, teachers and endowments, attributing this to the impoverishment of the country and the effects of war. 'Once', the university exclaimed somewhat rhetorically in 1430, 'she was famous in the world: students flooded to her from every nation: then she abounded with men learned in every art and science; her schools were not dilapidated nor her halls and inns empty.' The university, it was urged, in 1435, in a letter to the duke of Gloucester, pleading for his patronage, 'is reduced to the greatest misery. Lectures have ceased and a complete ruin of education is imminent.' Such statements must not be taken at their face value, but, cumulatively, economic conditions, the infection of heresy and the growing pull of Cambridge contributed to promote a period of mild depression.

Only three new colleges were founded: Lincoln, All Souls and Magdalen. The first was small and poorly endowed; but its front quadrangle and its hall, built *c.* 1436/7, provide an excellent illustration of the lay-out of a late medieval college. The other foundation which Archbishop Chichele made in 1438, *Collegium Animarum Omnium Fidelium*, reflects its founder's objects. The warden and scholars, in addition to training clerks and encouraging study, were to offer prayers for the king, the archbishop, for Henry V and his brother, Thomas, duke of Clarence, and for others who had died in the French wars. The college was exempt from the jurisdiction of the bishop of Lincoln and subject only to its visitor, the archbishop of Canterbury. Building was started on the High Street frontage on 10 February 1438, and the first mass was said in the chapel on 2 April 1443. The plan of the chapel, notable for its fine hammer-beam roof, covered up in the eighteenth century and brought to light again in 1872–6, was based on that of New College. Altogether £4,156 5s 3½d had been expended on building before the end of 1442.

Ten years after the foundation of All Souls, in 1448, William of Waynflete, bishop of Winchester, a former headmaster of Winchester and Eton, and a confidant of Henry VI, was given a royal license to establish a hall for a president and 50 graduate scholars. In 1456 he was granted the moribund hospital of St John Baptist and decided to enlarge its foundation. This was to consist of a president, 40 scholars engaged in the study of theology and philosophy. Its building took some years to complete. Sited outside the city walls, Magdalen was able to purchase the wooded meadows which bestow upon the college an enduring charm.

Although Oxford's academic life was conservative in character, there were signs of a changing attitude. The more extensive study of the canon law, which was a feature of the period—nearly half the resident halls were halls of legists—was a corollary to the university's academic conservatism. Significant was the attention which the university gave to the organisation of teaching, possibly because of a shortage of teachers, partly because the lectures of the regent masters no longer effectively covered the syllabus. In 1431 the university formed the regent masters into ten groups (representing the seven liberal arts and the three philosophies, moral, natural and metaphysical), to make sure that their lectures met the scholars' requirements. They endeavoured to persuade Humphrey of Gloucester and his brother, the duke of Bedford, to endow lecturerships. In 1453 Congregation turned its attention to the appointment of masters to lecture on topics not dealt with by other regent masters. Thirteen years earlier, the Schools had been built opposite Duke Humphrey's library (and on the site of the present Bodleian quadrangle). It was not, however, until 1497 that a permanent endowment was provided for a university teaching post, with the provision of a lectureship in theology through the munificence of Lady Margaret Beaufort, and not until 1561 that the university appointed official lecturers paid by the other regent masters, who were no longer obliged to lecture.

The slow but steady intrusion of humanistic studies was probably the most significant feature of Oxford life in the fifteenth century. In its early stages it represented less a movement than a scattered stream of learned foreigners, academic savants and rich patrons; foremost among the latter Humphrey, duke of Gloucester, showy braggart as he was, was sincerely interested in promoting scholarship. Even if there was any truth in the legend that he studied at Balliol (and it seems doubtful), it was his patronage of Italians resident in England which really caused humanistic notions to circulate. In 1433 he made known that he intended to endow lectureships at Oxford. Two years later he gave the university money and books. In 1437 the university requested further favours from their patron. In response Gloucester sent 129 manuscripts, including both ancient and modern authors and translations from the Greek. Many further tokens of his goodwill followed, 17 manuscripts in 1442, 134 in 1444. As an expression of its gratitude, the university added the duke's name to the list of the benefactors for whom prayers were to be said and, in transmitting the suggestion that his books should be placed in the new Divinity School, then being built, suggested that the new library should bear his name. When he died in 1447, he left £100 towards the construction of the Divinity School and bequeathed all his Latin books to the university. But as Duke Humphrey died in the odour of political disgrace, not indeed without suspicion of poisoning, his bequest was not fully carried out; his library was, ironically, designated for the king's infant foundation at Cambridge.

Even so, the duke's gifts acted as a stimulus to humanistic studies at Oxford. His books covered a wide range of classical as well as patristic and scholastic learning. They served to open a window into a world of which few Oxford men had as yet any experience. Scholars were able to compare the different styles of classical writing, modelling their own letters on the elegent latinity of the ancient world, even when they failed to grasp the significance of the new ideas. So Thomas Chandler, chancellor and warden of New College, whose writings are fundamentally medieval in character, copied the Ciceronean style to purvey his knowledge, and patronised a young scholar, John Farley of New College, who became scribe or register of the university.

An increasing number of Oxford scholars made their way to Bologna, Padua and other Italian cities, to imbibe the new learning at its source; they brought back manuscripts and shared in the enthusiasm which these Italian schools seemed to impart. Walter Grey, future bishop of Ely, who studied under Guarino da Verona at Ferrara, bequeathed a collection of books to his college, Balliol; though these were predominantly scholastic, and specifically Scotist, in character, they included some classical and modern treatises. Robert Fleming, a nephew of the founder of Lincoln College and dean of Lincoln, likewise studied in Italy, bought manuscripts from the shop of the famous Florentine bookseller, Vespasiano da Bisticci and made a transcription of Cicero's *de Officiis* with his own hand at Padua. He was adept in the composition of Latin prose and poetry and had a working knowledge of Greek, making notes in that language on the margins of his manuscripts. In 1465 he gave a collection of classical and modern texts to Lincoln College, perhaps with the notion of widening the range of reading of the theologians studying there. Another Oxford don, John Free of Balliol, who studied under Guarino at Bishop Grey's expense, was one of the very few Greek scholars of his time at Oxford as well as an elegant stylist.

Even if Oxford scholars were unacquainted with Greek, they began to have some insight into Hellenic civilisation. An increasing acquaintance with Greek led some to examine the original Greek text of the Gospels. Above all, they acquired an appreciation of values which were in many ways alien to the scholastic atmosphere of the medieval university.

By the closing years of the fifteenth century the university housed a number of scholars dedicated to the new learning. First among them was William Grocin, so precocious as a boy at Winchester that he had composed an impromptu Latin verse for the delectation of a French envoy. Elected a fellow of New College, and subsequently reader in divinity at Magdalen, he stayed in Italy in 1488 and returned enthusiastic for the new ideas. He was less a creative scholar than a guide to younger men, 'the patron and protector of all' in Erasmus's words. Erasmus himself had such pleasant memories of his residence at Oxford in 1499 that he always held the university in higher esteem than the draughty academy where he was professor in the fens.

The circle in which he moved was brilliant by any standards. Thomas More, probably a resident at Canterbury Hall, for a time drank of its waters. Thomas Linacre, Grocin's executor and a fellow of All Souls, 'as deep and acute a thinker' as any that Erasmus met, learned Greek and Medicine in Italy, the study of which he promoted in Oxford. Another fellow of All Souls, William Latimer, was so esteemed for his knowledge of Greek that he was invited to teach the language to the chancellor of Cambridge. William Lily of Magdalen travelled to the Holy Land as well as to Italy, became the first master of St Paul's School and wrote a Latin grammar that survived the centuries. His friend and patron was John Colet, who, after studying in Italy, under Platonist scholars, sought to reconcile classical learning with Christian teaching. Although fundamentally neither a great nor an original scholar, for his knowledge of Greek remained somewhat superficial, Colet aroused the enthusiasm of his Oxford audiences by the lectures he delivered on St Paul's Epistles, so refreshing was their interpretation, so able was he to break through the crust of the scholastic gloss.

By the closing decades of the fifteenth century there were ample signs of growing humanist influence. Even the ultra-conservative Thomas Gascoigne, whose famous *Liber de Veritatibus* showed no awareness of the new trends, owned at least one humanist work, Ambrogio Traversari's translation of the Greek fathers. Correspondence sent out under the university's seal became more felicitous in style. Better instruction was provided in grammar, as the publication of the *Compendium Totius Grammaticae* of John Anwykyll, the grammar master of Magdalen College School, published in 1483, exemplifies. Nor were scholars simply content to use the valuable collections which had been bequeathed to the university and colleges. They had additional copies transcribed and, as soon as the printing press was set up, published.

The first book to be printed at Oxford was the *Exposicio Sancti Jeronomi in simbolum apostolorum*, printed by Thomas Rood, a German from Cologne, in 1478, in partnership with the University stationer, Thomas Hunt. Between 1478 and 1487 some 17 other books were published at Oxford. Printing was resumed there in 1517 by John Scoler but, after 1519, no book was printed at Oxford until 1585. Nonetheless the appearance of the printed book was to have a decisive effect on university studies. The invention of the printing press made books available at a comparatively cheaper rate—a manuscript could cost as much as a farm. The printed book was likely to be more legible than the manuscript, the text would probably be more correct and there would be a usable index. Although the traditional scholastic works were printed first, the printing press undoubtedly acted as a spur to the circulation of humanistic literature. The list which the Oxford bookseller, John Dorne, itemised in 1520 shows that of some 2,383 works sold, no less than 20 were by Erasmus. College libraries were at first reluctant to buy books, but, by the middle of the sixteenth century, as manuscripts were discarded and replaced by books, there was a flood of new accessions.

Thus Oxford had experienced a mild intellectual revolution. Scholastic learning, Scotist and Occamist in type, continued to dominate its curricula; but scholastic conservatism had been modified by classical humanism. Even run-of-the-mill scholars showed an interest in humanist writings. The Benedictine monk of Evesham, Robert Joseph, who was at Oxford between 1523 and 1529, studied many modern writers, Erasmus, Budaeus, More, Lefèvre, as well as the fathers of the Church. 'Drop Scotus and unfruitful disputes', he told his friend, Neot. Nor was Joseph alone. Surviving inventories of books owned by Oxford scholars tell a similar tale. Master Bryan, who died in 1508, left 20 books which included some five works by humanist writers, treatises by Lorenzo Valla, Augustinus Datus, Francesco Negro and the letters of Gasperini Barzizza and Pius II. Edmund Burton of Balliol, who died in 1529, left 41 books, among them many books of humane letters, including eight works by Erasmus. By the middle of the sixteenth century many dons had extensive private libraries, some of them, as for instance, the collection of books made by Sir John Mason, a fellow of All Souls in the 1520s and later chancellor, very catholic in their range. Another fellow, David Pole, bequeathed the college some 250 volumes when he died.

Critical as the older Oxford scholars might be of the Grecists, the new learning had come to stay. Of the three Oxford colleges founded in the early sixteenth century, two at least, Corpus and Wolsey's new foundation, Cardinal College, had been set up with the definite intention of promoting it. The third of the colleges, Brasenose, based on the ancient Brasenose Hall, enriched in 1512 by the curialist bishop of Lincoln, William Smyth, and his co-founder, Sir Richard Sutton, was more conservative in its objects, its design being to train men in 'sophistry, logic and philosophy' as a training for 'holy theology'. The new foundation which owed so much to the generous benefactions of Richard Fox, the bishop of Winchester, and his friend, Hugh Oldham, bishop of Exeter, was of a different order. The government and life of Corpus Christi were to be shaped by statutes, drawn up in 1517, conventional in character, but which had distinctive features designed to promote liberal studies. Its teaching on theology was to be founded more on scripture and the patristic writings than on scholastic glosses and commentaries. The Greek lecturer was required to lecture daily on grammar and rhetoric. The professor of humanity, 'sower and planter of the Latin tongue', was to lecture at eight in the morning throughout the year. All fellows and scholars, except for bachelors of divinity, were obliged to attend the lectures which were to be open to the whole university. Corpus, which Erasmus regarded as potentially 'one of the chief glories of Britain', was the first college to openly recognise humanistic studies, though its founder's main intention was to promote an educated clergy. The college was, to use one of the many metaphors which so profusely decorated its statutes, to be a bee-hive, towards which scholars from all over the university and beyond it might fly—*ut apes ingeniosae e toto Gymnasio Oxoniensi convolantes ex eo exugere atque excerpere poterunt.*

What Fox intended for Corpus, Wolsey, if less explicitly, designed for his new college. Wolsey, Smyth's successor as bishop of Durham and Fox's as bishop of Winchester, had made his mark as an Oxford scholar, as a fellow of Magdalen and master of the college school. His plans for his new college were very elaborate. There were to be a dean, 60 senior canons, 40 junior ones, 6 public professors, of theology, canon law, and philosophy, civil law, medicine and *literae humaniores*, 16 choristers, a teacher of music as well as servants, in all some 180 persons, enjoying an annual endowment of £2000 a year. The land had been acquired in a typically high-handed way, adding to Wolsey's unpopularity. For he had obtained the pope's permission to suppress the ancient monastery of St Frideswide's as well as some less important religious houses, incorporating their revenues and estates and, in the case of St Frideswide's, its buildings, into the scheme. What he did not need was demolished, as were several tenements and inns and the church of St Michael at the Southgate. Given the fact that the royal licence was only granted in July 1525, much progress had been made before the cardinal fell from power. Between 16 January 1525 and 19 December 1527, the dean, John Higdon, received £9,828 11s 4½d, much of which was spent on building operations. The superb hall, its hammer-beam roof constructed under the supervision of the king's carpenter, Humphry Coke, was complete by 1529. 'The work has all been well done', the warden of New College told the cardinal, 'as my Lord's gracious purpose is to have his meritorious act perpetually to endure.' Meanwhile

Wolsey had appointed some 30 or so canons, among them some young scholars of radical views of which he would surely have disapproved, as well as a dean, before he was disgraced.

What was to happen to this foundation? The building work was stopped. Henry VIII, momentarily contemplating the demolition of what had already been built, was too avaricious and vindictive, too surrounded by courtiers greedy for loot, to allow his minister's great scheme to survive. Fears for its future may well have been the bitterest of all the pains that Wolsey had to suffer before his death. In 1532 the king transformed Wolsey's foundation into a collegiate church, headed by a dean and a chapter of 12 prebends or canons. But although two of Wolsey's canons, Dr Cottisford of Lincoln and Robert Wakefield, were appointed canons of the new foundation, it was not a school of learning and, after the destruction of St Frideswide's shrine in 1538, its endowments again reverted to the crown. Henry was, however, tempted to perpetuate his memory by a grand gesture. After the setting up of the bishopric of Oxford in 1542 he established Christ Church, uniting the cathedral, formerly at Oseney, with the college, appointing the dean and canons by royal charter issued on 4 November 1546, allocating for their maintenance Wolsey's buildings and Oxford properties. Although the plan was a little less magnificent than that which the cardinal had envisaged, the new society was so splendid that it must outrival all other colleges.

From its start too it admitted commoners, though they were at first few in number, four in 1547, 27 in 1553, a modest fact which reflects a major revolution. By the middle of the sixteenth century Oxford was well on the way to becoming a purely collegiate university. The halls had reached their zenith by the middle of the fifteenth century when they were about 70 in number. By 1530 they seem to have sunk to less than half, and even so were not always full; within a decade (1510-20) they declined from 25 to 12. In 1526 the warden of New College said that 16 halls had 'decayed in these few years' and that only 140 students lived in them; though it is fair to add that even in 1552 some 215 were living in halls by comparison with the 444 in colleges. There were many reasons for the decline of the halls. Some fell into a natural decline and became garden plots. Others were joined together. Some were swallowed by the colleges. The foundation of a new college almost inevitably brought about the elimination or absorption of one or more halls: Hampton Hall and Sekyll Hall came into the possession of Lincoln College in the middle of the fifteenth century and were soon used for college purposes. Some 19 or 20 halls disappeared as a result of new foundations in the early sixteenth century. Colleges were so much richer that they were better placed than the halls to withstand the economic pressures of the time, especially when Oxford experienced something of a slump (which may well have stimulated the colleges themselves to take fee-paying students), following the disturbed period of the Henrician reformation.

Social and intellectual developments also helped to make the colleges more prominent. The proctors and the chancellor's commissary or vice-chancellor had for some time been selected from their members. Now they widened their sphere of activity by taking in commoners and providing tuition for them. Many parents obviously preferred their sons to reside in colleges rather than in private halls, for they realised that they were better placed to control and discipline students—the statutes of Brasenose were the first to provide for corporal punishment[1] (at Corpus and Cardinal College provision was also made for the corporal punishment of scholars or fellows up to the age of 20). They could instil in the young men the moral and social values which their parents expected.

Oxford and the Reformation

In establishing Cardinal College, Wolsey told Queen Catherine that it was his intention to set up professorships to meet the new requirements of the age. At the cardinal's college the professor of theology was required to lecture on the text of the Old and New Testaments as well as to comment on the *Questiones* of Duns Scotus; his colleague in humanity taught, in addition to Cicero and Quintilian, Lucian, Homer, Hesiod, Aristophanes, Euripides, Sophocles and Pindar. Wolsey asked Pole to help him secure a professor of oratory from Italy. Such was his concern to attract talent that he sought migrants from Cambridge. The authorities were, however, soon made uneasy by the radical views of some of these young scholars. Bishop Longland of Lincoln remonstrated with Wolsey, but the cardinal appeared outwardly indifferent. Perhaps he did not relish being told what to do by one of his subordinates. Yet the avowed object of his foundation was 'to extirpate the many heresies and schisms which had spread themselves on the Christian world.'

In fact Oxford had walked very delicately since its unfortunate flirtation with Lollardy. The influence which humanism exerted was indirect. There

[1] The statutes of Queen's had provided for corporal punishment of the 'poor boys'. At Brasenose such punishment could be meted out for unprepared work, for laughing or talking in lectures, for speaking English (instead of Latin), for non-attendance at chape and various other offences.

were, indeed, scholars who criticised the 'new learning' and found in it an explanation for the unquietness of their times; but More, with the approval of king and cardinal, had strongly refuted these so-called 'Trojans' who 'raged', as Tyndale recalled, 'in every pulpit against Greek, Latin and Hebrew.' The infection of Lutheranism was carried from Cambridge to Oxford, not least by those migrants whom Wolsey had bidden (among those invited Cranmer) to join his new college. Six members of Wolsey's college, among them John Clarke, who had been used to expound St Paul's Epistles, were placed in detention and excommunicated. Most of them recanted, processing in penitent fashion from St Mary's to St Frideswide's, carrying faggots, a fitting symbol, and some heretical literature which they flung into a bonfire at Carfax. 'Wold good my lord', Warden London of New College commented plaintively, with reference to Clarke, 'is grace hadd never be motyonyd to call hym nor any other Cambridge man unto hys most towardly college.'

Protestantism's early appearance at Oxford was unimpressive; but the events which followed Wolsey's disgrace and death, the divorce and the legislation of the Reformation parliament, inevitably created tensions within the university. It was inconceivable that in a learned community there should not be some who were attracted by the new ideas, who were critical of the established order in the Church and who were in secret correspondence with fellow-sympathisers in Cambridge and on the Continent. The fall of Wolsey, whom Oxford regarded rightly as a princely benefactor and a protector of its privileges, must have been a great shock. The university's response to the king's enquiry on the validity of his marriage to Queen Catherine had been uneasy. 'And iff the youth of that university,' Henry wrote angrily, 'will playe maistres as they beginne to doo, we doubte not that they shall wele perceyve that "*Non est bonum irritare crabrones*" ' (it is not good to stir up hornets.) Oxford women threw stones at the royal visitors, one of whom was unfortunately relieving himself at the town wall. The regent masters, most especially the younger ones, havered. The king expressed surprise at their unwillingness to commit themselves, and their chancellor, the pliant Archbishop Warham, some dismay. Reluctantly the faculty of arts agreed to accept the ruling of a committee headed by the bishop of Lincoln, which accorded with royal wishes. Whatever murmurs of dissent there were to be, as an institution the university was obliged to obey the royal will.

For many dons the future of the university in the 1530s and subsequent years must have seemed ominous. For the majority were probably of a conservative disposition, whatever impression the young radical hot-heads might give to the outside world. Most dons were in priests' orders; they owed more to the scholastic learning of the past than to the fashionable humanism of the present. They may have looked to the pope as the ultimate defender of their rights, though as far as the university was concerned he had always been a distant prelate. The king, upon whom they depended for favours and charity, was surrounded by courtiers avid for riches, rejoicing, whether Catholic or Protestant in their religious inclinations, in the spoils of the religious houses. They could not hope for very much from the chancellors of the university, who were no longer resident academics but great men, virtually nominees of the crown, like Archbishop Warham, Bishop Longland of Lincoln. Doubtless they put some trust, as universities always do, in the goodwill of their former graduates occupying high posts in Church and state. But they must have realised that fundamentally they depended upon the caprice of the king himself. Fortunately, Henry VIII, like Oliver Cromwell at a later date, had a genuine regard for learning as well as a conviction that the universities were serviceable to the state and the maintenance of the established order. Much as he may have been tempted by their wealth (which was, however, small by comparison with the riches of the monasteries which fell into royal hands in 1536 and 1539), he wished for nurseries of learning where bishops, diplomats and statesmen could be trained. 'I tell you, sirs, that I judge no land in England better bestowed than that which is given to our Universities, for by their maintenance our Realm shall be governed when we be dead and rotten'. Such comments afforded balm to Oxford dons, even if the price they had to pay was that of acquiescence in the religious policy of the crown.

The outlook for the religious houses which had played so prominent a part in university life was black. According to some contemporary accounts some may already have been in decline—that of St George in the Castle had apparently no more than three residents. In the then climate of opinion the survival either of the monastic houses, Gloucester, Durham and Canterbury, or of the friaries was more than doubtful. A Cambridge lawyer, Richard Layton, assisted by John London, the warden of New College, that 'stout and filthy prebendary', who had been earlier forward in ridding Oxford of its Protestants, was empowered to visit the university. The visitors made some pretence, possibly genuine, of fostering learning, establishing Greek lectures at Merton and Queen's, Greek and Latin lectures at New College and All Souls and lectures in civil law. They condemned the old scholastic studies. The study of canon law was brought abruptly to an end. Scholastic treatises were discarded and turned, literally it would seem, to baser uses. The leaves of Duns Scotus served in houses of easement, and a Buckinghamshire squire, seeing the leaves blowing about in New College quad, gathered them 'to make hym sewelles or blawn-sherres to keep the dere within the woode.' The visitors also imposed regulations to strengthen discipline, more especially for the students who remained in the monastic houses; they were strictly forbidden to enter taverns or other houses in the town.

The fate of the monastic colleges was in practice sealed by the dissolution of the great abbeys from which they were stocked. Gloucester College was to pass eventually as Gloucester Hall into the hands of St John's College, much later to evolve into Worcester College. Durham College lost its estates to the chapter of Durham cathedral and its buildings passed to the crown, falling eventually into the possession of Sir Thomas Pope, the founder of Trinity College. Canterbury College was soon to be absorbed into Christ Church. St Bernard's, a comparatively recent founda-tion, was granted by the king to Christ Church which subsequently sold it to Sir Thomas White, the founder of St John's. St Mary's, after continuing for a while as a private hall, was sold to Brasenose by Lord Huntingdon in 1580. The friars' houses met a similar fate; closed were the Carmelite house in Beaumont, and the house of the Austin Friars which, after many vicissi-tudes, was to be absorbed into Wadham. The Franciscans and the Dominicans houses were also dissolved.

The accession of Edward VI aroused anew fears of confiscation and spoliation. Legitimately the colleges feared expropriation. The act for dis-solving the chantries could easily have been applied to colleges which were statutorily obliged to say masses regularly for their founders and bene-factors. They escaped outright depredation, but the government instituted a Visitation to ensure that the universities were tied to the new order. Somerset's own attitude was not unlike that of the previous king. 'If learning decay', he said, 'which of wild men make civil, of blockish and rash persons wise and godly counsellors, of obstinate rebels obedient subjects, and of evil men good and godly Christians; what shall we look for else but barbarism and tumult?' The universities were to be centres of order as well as of scholarship.

The Visitors' powers were very wide. They could deprive heads and fellows. They could eliminate, alter or amend out-moded statutes. They were entitled to make a revision of university and college finances, to provide new syllabuses and even, if they thought it desirable, to amalgamate colleges or to insist that a college should concentrate its studies on a single subject; it was mooted that All Souls might be confined to the study of the law, New College to the study of divinity and the arts. Many dons must have awaited their findings with apprehension, more especially as they brought with them new statutes, drawn up with the approval of the council.

In addition to the new statutes the Visitors issued orders or injunctions for the colleges. By and large these seem to have been no more than a repetition of earlier regulations, encouraging plainness of living, prohibiting flamboyant clothes and frivolous games except at Christmastime. They forbade English as a medium of conversation, reminded colleges that the funds they administered were held on trust and deplored too great an expenditure on food and drink. The colleges had been founded, they stressed, for the education of poor children. The Visitors' religious injunctions were naturally much more radical. Symbols of Roman idolatry, altars, superstitious pictures, images, bells, vestments, were prohibited. The catechism was to be taught; the Holy Communion to be celebrated in College Chapels every Sunday.

The triumph of Protestantism was the most obvious result of the Visitors' work. This was necessary if the university was to fulfil satisfactorily its task of training young men for the ministry of the reformed church. The Visitors tried to see whether there was any way in which the pro-Romanist, Henry Cole, warden of New College (who was a few years later, in March, 1556, to urge the burning of Cranmer in a sermon at St Mary's) could be ousted from office. But even so they were not generally immoderate in their attitude. They allowed the fellows of Oriel to elect a conservative as provost in spite of an expressed wish on the part of the government to procure a contrary appointment. Nonetheless encouragement was given to men of outright Protestant views such as Richard Cox the dean of Christ Church, Bentham and Bickley at Magdalen, Jewel and William Cole at Corpus.

The situation remained, however, a very confused one. Lincoln, under Rector Weston, and Exeter were strongholds of reaction; Nicholas Harpsfield, professor of Greek, James Brooks, master of Balliol (whom Mary Tudor was to make a bishop), and Morgan Phillips of Oriel were all protagonists of the old cause. John Calvin, writing to Somerset on 25 July 1551, deplored the continued hold which popery had in the English universities. Peter Martyr's windows were once broken by local rowdies; he commented gloomily that of 20 recent B.D.s he found that their views were for the most part papistical. Even so, papists were undoubtedly placed on the defensive. They were unable to resist the Visitors' injunctions, especially as these had been in part drafted by an Oxford resident, Dean Cox. Cox was accused of favouring the more malevolent critics of the old faith, allowing them to disseminate their invective in sermons designed to discredit the old ceremonies. He permitted the reformer and theologian, Peter Martyr, to keep his wife within the precincts of Christ Church and took no action when the younger scholars 'nose(d) and impudentize(d)' their seniors. There were many other acts of vandalism aimed at the Romanists, more especially at Magdalen and All Souls where the reredos was taken down. The libraries were purged of popish manuscripts and books; even the collection which Bishop Grey gave Balliol was pillaged. So many manuscripts, some from Duke Humphrey's donation, appeared on the market that the second-hand bargain hunter was rarely favoured.

The design of the reforming party had been well demonstrated by the appointment of the Italian Protestant, Peter Martyr, as professor of divinity in 1549. He used his lectures on St Paul's Epistles to the Corinthians as a means by which to criticise Romanist doctrine and ceremonial. The Romanists, headed by Richard Smith, the former holder of the chair, challenged Martyr to a public disputation which he was at first reluctant to accept. By the time the vice-chancellor had agreed, Smith had himself fled to the Continent, but some of his fellow sympathisers, Dr Tresham of Christ Church, Cheadsey of Corpus and Morgan Phillips, took up the gage. The debate which was held in the presence of Cox, the vice-chancellor, was naturally indecisive, though Cox was accused by his critics of favouring Martyr. It is a tribute to the underlying vitality of the university that, in spite of the 'hurrying and noise' about Oxford, there should have been no apparent lack of scholars, some 761 in the colleges and 260 in the halls according to an estimate of 1552.

The death of Edward VI and the accession of the Catholic Mary Tudor had great repercussions, though less so at Oxford than at Cambridge where Protestant sentiment had always been stronger. The vessels and vestments were brought out from their hiding places; old statues were re-erected, old services revived. Most of those who had accepted Edward VI (and would equally well have accepted Lady Jane Grey) proved ready to take the oath to Mary, among them the university's chancellor, Sir John Mason. Ultra-conservatives like Richard Smith and Hugh Weston, who had found it expedient to absent themselves from Oxford, reappeared. Contrariwise there was a flow of Protestant dons to the Continent. Protestant fellows who did not conform suffered ejection. At Corpus a scholar was lashed with a whip for every verse he had written against the mass and consequently lapsed into orthodoxy and a fellowship at All Souls.

The university became the scene of the historic collision with the leading protagonists of the Protestant cause, ironically all of them graduates of Cambridge, and ultimately of their bitter humiliation and death. Cranmer, Ridley and Latimer were brought to Oxford to debate on the Eucharist in St Mary's Church. Their opponents included Tresham, Oglethorpe, Richard Smith, Cheadsey, John Harpsfield and Henry Cole; the Romanist rector of Lincoln presided as moderator but revealed his bias by his intemperance. It was a sorrowful spectacle. Latimer, afflicted by a failing memory and unable to debate without lack of books, faltered. After the disputation was over the reformers were placed in detention. In September 1555, Cranmer was brought to trial in St Mary's under Brooks, now Bishop of Gloucester, but he refused to acknowledge the court's jurisdiction. Ridley and Latimer were tried, sentenced and burned at the stake 'in the Towne Ditch, over against Balliol College.' Richard Smith preached the sermon before the committal on the text 'Though I give my body to be burned, and have not charity, it profiteth me nothing'. Yet how far was charity prevalent among the dons and students who watched the grim scene? Cranmer had longer to wait, was judged in Christ Church under bishops Bonner and Thirlby, and put to death on 21 March 1556; six shillings were paid for the wood and three shillings and fourpence for the faggots for the fire by which he died.

Oxford's reputation as the favoured home of orthodoxy seemed assured. The pious, shrivelled queen bequeathed money for the university's poor scholars in her will, and by her gift in 1554 of the rectories of South Petherwyn in Cornwall, of Syston in Leicester and Hulme Cultram in Cumberland, she proved herself to be one of the most generous of Oxford's royal benefactors. The university's privileges were confirmed and extended. Cardinal Pole became chancellor of Oxford (as well as of Cambridge). A former resident of Palmer's Hall, he issued a commission to undertake a new revision of the statutes, since the Edwardian statutes were declared null and void. In his preliminary instructions he stressed the need for eliminating heresy. He also favoured the colleges against the halls, emphasising the authority of their heads, perhaps because they were more likely to be the homes of discipline and order. When Jewel returned from exile, he deplored to Peter Martyr the poverty of Oxford's scholarship and the scandalous lives of some of its dons. But, in fact, the university survived the change of regime without apparent harm to its daily life. Yet surely, given the strife which had dogged its history for so many decades, what it needed above all was a time for consolidation.

Left, Henry Sever, Warden of Merton (d.1459) Right, Richard Wyard, fellow of New College (d.1478)

IV

Elizabethan and Stuart Oxford
1558-1660

The Elizabethan settlement

Oxford, so disturbed when Elizabeth became queen, was in the next half-century to experience a period of consolidation and steady growth. In 1558 religious conservatism was still deeply entrenched in its colleges, but there soon appeared a group of radical Protestants, whose faith had been confirmed by their exile on the Continent and who, on their return, looked forward to imposing their beliefs on their less godly colleagues. Such a situation had explosive possibilities. Yet extremism has rarely been a feature of Oxford's life. Even the university's widely-publicised attachment to lost causes has usually signified its unwillingness to commit itself to a new order rather than any deep-set loyalty to the old. Dependent as the university was for so long to be on the will of the crown and its ministers, tied to the interests of the established Church and the ruling social order, its dons never ceased to yearn for their independence and in the last resort they might criticise or even defy their masters. But, in general, they were politically compliant. The majority wished to keep their fellowships and to enjoy the fruits of patronage, and they had no wish to taste the dubious charms either of exile or martyrdom.

Elizabeth and her advisers took a continuous interest in the university. When Sir John Mason gave up the chancellorship in 1564, he was succeeded by the queen's favourite, Leicester; on Leicester's death in 1588, Sir Christopher Hatton became chancellor and, in 1591, at the queen's express wish, Lord Buckhurst. That such an office was held by distinguished lay-men who were in the sovereign's confidence led to the bestowal of patronage; deaneries, bishoprics, canonries and livings became the expected perquisites of the loyal academic. Naturally, something was expected in return for this cornucopia. Through the chancellor the crown exerted pressure to secure offices and degrees for its nominees. Leicester sought to influence elections to headships of colleges, interfered in proctorial elections and urged the university to give dispensations for degrees. The university did not always assent to such requests and was even able occasionally to parry the demands, but it could not ignore the rewards which friendships with the great brought in its train.

Yet it is doubtful whether such activities did much harm to the university. In general the Elizabethan government was to treat the universities discreetly, carrying out a tidying-up operation rather than seeking to impose what its more extreme Protestant supporters would have wished, a doctrinaire reorganisation of the dons' lives and studies. The commission which visited Oxford shortly after the queen's accession acted circumspectly. The outward symbols of Romanism were either destroyed or pushed into chests and cupboards. Pole's injunctions were disallowed. Some of the Protestant exiles were restored to fellowships, and the abler were soon recruited for higher dignities. Contrariwise the Romanists were deprived of their positions. Even so, one estimate suggests that less than a dozen suffered this fate in 1559, an illustration of the moderate policy which the government was following. The process of purification was to be a slow one. It was only gradually that colleges wedded to the old order, notably New College, Exeter, Trinity and Lincoln, were, through deprivations and new elections, reconciled to the establishment.

The steady rather than the abrupt erosion of the old faith thus prevented too radical a break with the past and enabled the university to come gently to terms with the new regime. Elizabeth and her ministers realised that the universities, as the nurseries of churchmen and politicians, had to be preserved from impurity of doctrine: but the iron hand was somehow concealed in a near velvet glove. Oxford was to be wooed, flattered and patronised rather than coerced into obedience. Elizabeth herself visited the university twice, in 1566 and 1592. Although she appears on the first visit only to have gone to Christ Church, she submitted to an array of speeches, feasts, academic disputations, plays and spectacles. If once she seemed to be bored by an over-long declamation, she declared that the visit pleased her. 'Since first I came to Oxford', she told the dons, 'I have seen and heard many things, I have been delighted with them all. For myself I have had many teachers, who tried to make me learned, but they worked upon barren soil. I know that I am not worthy of your praises. But if my speech be full of barbarisms, I will end it with a prayer—that you may prosper greatly in my lifetime and be happy for generations after I am dead.' Flattered as the university was by the queen's visit, the dons, and Christ

Church in particular which had to bear the brunt of the cost, must have been much relieved that such expensive junketings were comparatively infrequent.

The changing character of the university

An even more intimate connection came to exist between the university and the established order in the sixteenth century than had been the case in the late middle ages. Such a development had been promoted by the major changes that were taking place in the structure of Oxford, the beginnings of which we have already noted.

The colleges steadily consolidated their control over the university. After 1569 when the chancellor, Leicester, effectively made the vice-chancellor a cancellarial nominee, removing the appointment from Congregation, he was invariably the head of a college or hall or a canon of Christ Church. In the medieval university the proctors had often been fellows of colleges, but not necessarily so; from 1628, when the so-called proctorial cycle was drawn up, arranging for the election of proctors by the colleges in rotation, they were always fellows. The colleges' identification with the university was confirmed by the Laudian statutes of 1636 which made their heads, meeting every Monday in the Hebdomadal Board, the real governing body of the university instead of Congregation and Convocation. The matriculation statute of 1565 gave the colleges control over admissions to the university.

What was happening represented no conscious or sinister attempts on the colleges' part to seize power, but was the effect of the congeries of circumstances which had ended the useful existence of most of the residential halls. But the rising influence and growing wealth of the colleges was largely promoted by the increased desires of aristocrats, gentry and affluent merchants to send their sons to college. From 1550 onwards there was a spectacular, if irregular, rise in the number of entries.[1] Professor Lawrence Stone has suggested that a greater proportion of the male population experienced higher education either through the universities or Inns of Court in the early seventeenth century than at any period before 1914. The interest shewn by nobles and gentry in sending their children to the university was the most novel feature of this movement. Between 1575

[1] The correct figures are difficult to obtain since the matriculation register does not include all those in residence at college, but, allowing for this, Professor Stone has estimated the number of Oxford entrants as follows: 1560–69, c. 300; '70–79, c. 372; '80–89, 366; '90–99, 295; 1600–09, 383; '10–19, 411; '20–29, 406; '30–39, 575; '40–49, 192. There was a rise in graduations: between 1571/80, it averaged 123 taking an Arts degree between 1611/20, 226.

and 1639 sons of the gentry made up 50% of the Oxford entry (of plebeians, 41%, of sons of the clergy, 9%). It is not wholly clear why there should have been this change of attitude. Some parents may well have become convinced that an Oxford education gave a young man the credentials which would provide him with good employment in Church and state. A university education was becoming a necessary pre-requisite for a civil or political career, and, as such, a gateway to preferment and success. Of members of the Elizabethan House of Commons who are known to have been at Oxford or Cambridge, 67 sat in the parliament of 1563, 145 in that of 1584, 161 in that of 1559; over half the 825 members between 1604 and 1629 had attended a university. Others were persuaded that a university education conferred the social status necessary to a gentle-man's place in society; the training in classical literature educated a man in the values which would enable him to occupy his proper place in the social hierarchy. 'As for gentlemen', Sir Thomas Smith observed in 1564, 'they be made good cheap in England. For whosoever studieth the laws of the realm, who studieth in the Universities, who professeth liberal sciences, and, to be short, who can live idly and without manual labour . . . shall be taken for a gentleman.' A university education became then, as a public school education was to become in the early twentieth century, the hall-mark of gentility.

But the professional classes, merchants, lawyers and the like, were equally interested in securing a university education for their children, partly because they were following the fashion of their betters, partly because they believed that it provided a good and godly education in itself. More especially in founding scholarships and exhibitions to enable poor boys to study at Oxford, their motive was still basically religious. The boys who went to Oxford would learn through scholarship to discern truth more completely and so serve as faithful ministers in the Church. Yet their benefactors realised that a university education was advantageous from a secular point of view. The successful graduate had a better chance of winning preferment in the state as in the Church. While the proportion of the wealth which they gave to education was still relatively small, Professor Jordan has estimated that London merchants gave some £135,000 to Oxford and Cambridge colleges between 1480 and 1640.

It is hardly surprising that of the five colleges founded between 1550 and 1630 four were set up by wealthy laymen. Sir Thomas Pope, an efficient civil servant and treasurer of the Court of Augmentations, had amassed an immense fortune, and, though a loyal Catholic and of faithful servant

Mary Tudor, had also accumulated monastic land. In 1555 he decided to found a college in honour of the Holy and Undivided Trinity. The same year saw, through the purchase of the hall of the Old Bernardines from Christ Church by Sir Thomas White, the establishment of the college of St John Baptist. The founder, the son of a clothier, made a fortune as master of the Merchant Taylors' Company and through opening up trade with Russia and eastern Europe.[1] The only post-Reformation college that could be called a clerical, albeit a distinctly Protestant foundation, was Jesus which owed its existence to the enterprise of Dr Hugh ap Price, the Treasurer of St David's, the son of a wealthy butcher, who persuaded Queen Elizabeth, described as the college's foundress, to confer the site of the former White Hall on the small and as yet impoverished foundation.

The two early seventeenth-century colleges had founders of rather a different sort. The founder of Wadham College, Nicholas Wadham, belonged to the Elizabethan governing class. A property-owner in the west country, his grandfather had been knight of the shire for Somerset and Vice-admiral to the earl of Surrey, and his wife, Dorothy, was the daughter of Sir William Petre, the Tudor statesman who acquired vast property as a result of the dissolution of the monasteries; a former fellow of All Souls, he gave substantial benefactions to Exeter College. Having no children, Wadham designed to spend his wealth on founding a college at Oxford. He died (in 1609) before a site was acquired, and his plans were carried to a successful conclusion by his widow. Wadham, as its early associations might suggest, catered especially for the sons of country gentry.

Pembroke's foundation was more complex. Thomas Tesdale, a wealthy maltster of Abingdon who had bought an estate at Glympton near Woodstock, had originally intended his benefaction for Balliol, but difficulties arising out of that society's unwillingness to fulfil the conditions of the will, with the consent of James I and the collaboration and money of Richard Wightwick, a Balliol man who was rector of East Ilsley, Broadgates Hall was refounded in 1624 as Pembroke College and endowed with Tesdale's benefaction. The last head of Broadgates Hall, Dr Clayton, became the first master of Pembroke which owed its title to the university's

---

[1] The number of benefactors from the mercantile classes forms a striking feature of the early history of St. John's: Walter Fish, merchant taylor, also Hugh Henlie, George Palin, citizen and girdler of London, Thomas Paradyne, citizen and haberdasher of London, Sir William Craven, alderman of London, Jeffrey Elwes, alderman of London, Sir William Paddie, president of the College of Physicians, Sir Robert Ducie, alderman of London, George Benson citizen of London—all before 1636.

chancellor, William Herbert, third earl of Pembroke (whose fine statue by Le Sueur has dominated the Schools Quadrangle since 1723).

The medieval university had been a socially diversified community, drawing its pupils from many different social levels. So, in many ways, Oxford continued to be. The sons of the clergy, many of them with a very modest income, formed a new and significant ingredient in its social composition. There was an actual increase in the number of poor boys, sizars, servitors. Yet the rising number of undergraduates who were the sons of the comparatively affluent gentry sometimes helped to promote social divisions within the colleges themselves. For, though colleges continued to educate men of humble origin, some of whom were to earn distinction in Church and state, they lived in the poorer rooms and were overshadowed by their wealthier contemporaries. 'There be none now', Latimer declared with some exaggeration, 'but great men's sons in colleges.' In 1577 Harrison commented similarly. Colleges, he said, had been originally founded 'only for poor men's sons . . . but now they have the least benefit of them, by reason the rich do so encroach upon them.'

It would, however, be incorrect to stress unduly the secular aspect of sixteenth- and seventeenth-century Oxford. It remained a clerical seminary designed, as Thomas Starkey put it, to educate youth destined for the 'spirituality and the exercise therein.' Not only were the vast majority of the dons in holy orders, but a high proportion of the junior members were intended for the ministry of the Church of England. Because contemporaries held that a well-instructed clergy was not merely more likely to promote true 'godliness', but was essential to the defeat of the twin dangers of sectarianism and papistry, the number of graduates holding benefices showed a sharp upward increase: in the diocese of Ely at the end of Elizabeth's reign, 67%, in that of Worcester in 1640, 80%. The government too was interested in fostering a learned clergy, in the realisation that it was one of the best ways of maintaining public order and legitimate authority.

The curriculum of an Oxford education had not been changed in its fundamentals, though it had been substantially modified. The course still took four years, except for sons of peers, and (after 1591) sons of knights and esquires who were allowed to complete it in three, unless the university agreed to give a dispensation from the required terms of residence. The university records demonstrate that this device was freely employed: students are dispensed from their statutory obligations on grounds of poverty, illness, an opportunity for election to a college fellowship (not open to an undergraduate), ordination, the promise of a benefice, foreign travel, plague, study at an Inn of Court or at Cambridge. The undergraduate still moved towards his degree through a series of disputations and exercises in the schools.

But although the scholastic method was still the basis of his intruction, canon law and scholastic theology had been largely relegated to unused chests. Their disappearance constituted an intellectual (and by implication a political) revolution, removing an important stratum, that of canon lawyers, who had previously been very prominent. The syllabus for the arts degree became a blend of classical literature and of scholastic philosophy, the latter no longer, however, diffused through the works of the great commentators like Peter Lombard and Duns Scotus, but communicated through the text of Aristotle's own writings, notably the *Rhetoric*, the *Dialectics* and the *Nicomachean Ethics*. Classical humanism retained a scholastic foundation.

The themes of the declamations and disputations, offered at Oxford in the late sixteenth-and early seventeenth-centuries, illustrate this feature. Those in the faculty of arts were abstract and philosophical in content, the subject matter often derived from Aristotle's own works. Candidates only infrequently showed any awareness of contemporary events. In 1589 a candidate disputed on the theme, *An Angli sint validiores Hispanis ex influentia coelesti?;* a reference to the Gunpowder plot was permitted in 1606, *An inventio pulveris tormentarii faciat magis ad perniciem quam ad salutem rerumpublicarum?* Once, with a negative conclusion, it is argued as to whether there should be a third university. In 1614 the question was put, *An Jesuitae corruperint omnes scientias?* But more often candidates were engaged in asking whether mental illness is worse than bodily, whether the earth is quiescent *in medio mundi*, whether there is *materia in coelo*, whether a mother loves her children more than a father. There are questions on natural justice, the influence of comets (*noxia vel salutaris?*), the relationship of the moon to the tides, the plurality of worlds, is knowledge more productive of error than ignorance, beauty more a matter of symmetry than of skill? In 1620 whether 'sexuum transmutatio' was possible was debated. Some themes were clearly designed to entertain the audience: can a penurious wife, it was asked, be tamed more by humanity or severity? Clearly a premium was placed rather on logical argument and verbal dexterity than on abundance of knowledge.

In any case the Elizabethan and early Stuart undergraduate did not confine his interest to the list of prescribed books (such as were specified in the statutes of 1564). In this protestant theology makes no appearance unless the candidate is studying for a degree in divinity. But can one doubt that among contemporary intellectual pressures this was one of the most significant? Surviving library inventories show the purchase of books by Calvin, Beza and their fellow theologians. Contemporary diaries and reading lists, such as those of the two Cornish brothers, Matthew and William Carnsew who were at Broadgates Hall in the 1570s, demonstrate the extent to which religious discussion engaged the attention of the more serious-minded students.

Oxford's interests in the late sixteenth century were not, however, wholly centred on religion. From the Ramist movement, anti-Aristotelian in character, which so affected Cambridge, Oxford was comparatively free. centred on religion. From the Ramist movement, anti-Aristotelian in character, which so affected Cambridge, Oxford was comparatively free. Ramist views were diffused by John Rainolds, the president of Corpus; Rector Tatham of Lincoln possessed a copy of Ramus' *Dialectica*; but contemporary Oxford opinion was critical of the purport of Ramus' ideas, as Professor Kearney has shown.

Nonetheless there is much evidence, cumulative in character, to shew that Oxford men were stirred by extra-curricular literature, and were interested in some of the more adventurous and far-ranging ideas of the period. There were occasions on which tutors deemed it necessary to devise wider courses of reading for their pupils than those laid down by the syllabus. So George Abbot, a fellow of University College who later became archbishop of Canterbury, published in 1599 a book on geography which he had composed for his pupils. Brian Twyne, a fellow of Corpus, gave his men instruction in mathematics and astronomy. Young men who aspired to culture made some attempt to acquire foreign languages. Florio, who had published an Italian grammar, was teaching Italian at Oxford between 1576 and 1583.

Professor Curtis would claim more. There were, he suggests, scholars at sixteenth-century Oxford who 'championed and introduced studies which kept them abreast of the current practical and theoretical interests of English and European thought', so contributing to 'the assault on intellectual dogma and authority' which was so important a part of the European scene. In particular he cites current interest in scientific and associated studies. Even if there is an element of over-statement in his thesis, the evidence he provides suggests how vital was the intellectual life of at least a minority of dons in late sixteenth-century Oxford. We find the young Richard Hakluyt lecturing on geography and navigation: he 'produced and showed both the old imperfectly composed, and the new lately reformed maps, globes, spheres and other instruments of his art for demonstration in the common schools.' It was to Sir Henry Savile who lectured on astronomy that Henry Gellibrand, the author of *Trigonometria Britannica*, who went up to Trinity in 1615, owed his decision to devote his life to mathematical studies. The Lady Margaret professor of divinity, Dr Cradock, a friend of John Dee, also enjoyed a reputation as an alchemist. The Elizabethan Puritan, Thomas Allen resigned his fellowship at Trinity in 1570 to retire to Gloucester Hall where he studied mathematics and antiquities and natural philosophy until he died at the advanced age of 90 in 1632. Among his pupils Thomas Harriott, who graduated at St Mary Hall in 1580, was to be the scholar most responsible for the formulation of modern algebraic principles. A catalogue of individual instances is not enough to prove that Oxford was in the vanguard of scientific advance. In spite of Curtis' claims, Oxford had only a small part in forwarding mathematical and scientific studies. It would in any case have been surprising if, in a place of outstanding intellectual curiosity, there were not men who showed an interest in all branches of knowledge. Yet at least it does suggest that Oxford was no intellectual backwater.

The foundation of chairs and lectureships points in a similar direction. In 1619 Sir Henry Savile set up and endowed two professorships, one of astronomy and one of geometry, the latter of which was held until 1631 by the distinguished mathematician, Henry Briggs. In 1618 Sir William Sedley bequeathed money for a chair of natural philosophy, which was set up in 1621. The same year Thomas White founded a professorship of moral philosophy, while the Camden professorship of ancient history, to be held for a quarter of a century by Digory Wheare, was established in 1622. In 1624 Richard Tomline founded a lectureship in anatomy, which was to be held with the professorship of medicine. William Heather gave money for a professorship of music, and for a *choragus* or master of musical praxis in 1626. Archbishop Laud made provision for a chair of Arabic in 1636. In 1621 Henry Danvers, earl of Danby, gave five acres of land opposite Magdalen College, formerly used as a Jewish burial ground, for the encouragement of the study of physics and botany, so creating the Botanic Gardens, the gateway of which was built by Nicholas Stone. It was indicative of the ethos of Oxford that the frieze in what is now the upper reading room of the Bodleian library, seventeenth century in date, should include among its divines and scholars portraits of men of more adventurous intellect, such as Copernicus, Tycho Brahe, Galileo, Paracelsus, Vesalius, Mercator and Ortelius.

Oxford and religious increments

However catholic the character of the university's interests, religion remained not merely its chief business but the issue which most affected its life. Oxford and Cambridge were the two great bastions of Protestantism, into which Romanism infiltrated occasionally and of which sectarians were continuously critical. From 1581 all those who matriculated over the age of 16 had to subscribe to the Thirty-nine Articles. All intellectual discussions, whatever their political undertones, took place within a framework of spiritual ultimates. Throughout the sixteenth century, there were dons and undergraduates who still adhered to Rome; they reappeared on the Continent as priests at Douai and Rome and made their way back as members of the Roman mission, sometimes paying for their mistaken loyalty with their lives. It was a matter of some concern to the government, especally in the 'seventies and 'eighties, that so many traitors had been educated at Oxford. After the arrest of Edmund Campion and his associates the Council remonstrated with the university 'forasmuch as their Lordships finde by experience that most of the Seminarie Priests which at this present disturbe this Chirche have been heretofore schollars of that Universite.' But if the pestilence of Romanism was but slowly eliminated, extreme Puritanism, especially in its more extreme manifestation, was in some respects as great a danger, since it could involve, if its exponents achieved power, a revolution in the university's studies, and probably in its organisation.

From early in Elizabeth's reign the authorities had kept a watchful eye on any manifestation of left-wing Protestantism. It had two main advocates among the heads of colleges, Thomas Sampson, the dean of Christ Church, and Laurence Humphrey, president of Magdalen. Sampson, like Humphrey originally an alumnus of Cambridge, had lain low in London in the early years of Mary's reign, though observed, according to Henry Machyn, to have been seen doing 'penance' at St Paul's Cross 'for he had ii wiffes', a curious charge for which we have no other evidence; later, accompanied by only one wife, he took refuge on the Continent whence he returned, querulous and restless as even his hosts at Zurich had found him, to become dean of Christ Church, there to mark his governance by making a bonfire of 'superstitious utensils'. Humphrey, more moderate in his views though known to his contemporaries as *Papistomastix*, was, on his return in 1560, appointed regius professor of divinity, and in spite of strong opposition among the fellows, was, largely at the behest of Archbishop Parker, elected president of Magdalen. He did, as Wood commented, 'not only stock his College with a generation of Nonconformists, which could not be rooted out in many years after his decease' but 'sowed also in the Divinity Schools . . . seeds of Calvinism, and laboured to create in the younger sort . . . a strong hatred against the Papists.'

When the confrontation with authority came, it was over the wearing of vestments to which extreme Protestants greatly objected, in spite of the rubric in the prayer book and the royal injunction which authorised them. Sampson and Humphrey were summoned to Lambeth but both men refused to comply. Parker found it easy to rid himself of the stiff-necked Sampson who vacated the deanery, but it was more difficult to displace Humphrey since the Visitor of Magdalen, Robert Horn, the bishop of Winchester, was himself known to be sympathetic towards extreme Protestanism. The president discreetly withdrew from college to lodge with a Mrs Warcup in the country; but he retained his office and in due course, habited in doctor's scarlet, was to receive the queen when she visited Oxford in 1566. 'Methinks', Elizabeth commented a little wryly, 'this gown and habit become you very well, and I marvel that you are so straight-laced on this point—but I come not now to chide.'

The more moderate Humphrey rather than the extreme Sampson seemed to epitomise the spirit of Oxford puritanism, for Oxford housed far fewer radicals than its sister university. Even its avowed Puritans were men of temperance, loyal, reasonable and conciliatory, very different from their extremist brethren who would have so readily changed the character of English life. A Puritan manifesto of 1580, urging the deprivation of 'unworthy ministers', claimed that to supply the vacant places Cambridge could provide 140 and Oxford 194 worthy men. That Oxford puritanism was a continuously vigorous force, especially at the halls, perhaps by their very character likely to be more sympathetic towards Puritan notions, is shown clearly by the number of future parliamentary leaders educated at the university, among them Hampden, Pym, Strode, Oliver St John, and the younger Sir Henry Vane.

Jacobean Oxford

If Elizabethan Oxford was a flourishing place, compliant to the government but never wholly subservient, intellectually alive, hitched to the wagon of the governing class but perhaps no worse for that, it was to become more subject to strain with the accession of the Stuarts. The university was no less vigorous, the colleges even fuller, more so indeed than they were to be for some centuries. Below the surface, however, there were many problems, which were bound sooner or later to create trouble and tension. The early seventeenth century was a period of economic contraction. Some graduates actually found it difficult to obtain the preferment in the Church they wanted. There was a general air of unease, nor was the university free of its critics. It was its realisation of the need to find a defence for its interests and to provide a bulwark against a growing band of sectaries, that Oxford, like Cambridge, sought representation in parliament, a petition granted in 1604. In effect, with a few notable exceptions, Oxford's early burgesses were royal yes-men, whose political activities were little concerned with the 'necessary defence of the liberties of the university' and more with the support of the royal cause. Their activities seemed only further to align the university with Church and crown, and so to evoke further criticism from their opponents.

This too was true of the religious scene. The university was affected inevitably by the increasing bitterness of religious strife, even if in the early years of James I's reign moderate Puritanism was still holding its own against resurgent high anglicanism. Yet as the established order in Church and state realised its subversive properties, Puritanism became more and more on the defensive. As early as 1573 Matthew Hutton, then dean of York, warned Burghley that he should 'have an eye to the universities, that young wits there be not inured to contentious factions; for he has noted that those, when they have been called to serve in the commonwealth, have been greater stirrers and dealers than hath been convenient.' The comparative flexibility of Elizabethan government gave way to a more intractable attitude. The government of James I used its powers to install well-known Arminians in positions of influence. At St John's the president John Buckeridge knew, as Heylin put it, 'how to employ the two-edged sword of holy scripture; brandishing it on the one side against the papists and on the other against the puritanical nonconformists.' Buckeridge had been Laud's tutor and when he resigned, Laud succeeded to his office in spite of an attempt made by Archbishop Abbot to persuade the king, James I, to prevent his appointment. The Arminianism which Laud had so strongly championed percolated more and more into the colleges: Brian Duppa became dean of Christ Church in 1629, Juxon was succeeded at St John's by Richard Baylie, once a critic but now an admirer of the archbishop, Sheldon became warden of All Souls. The old fashioned Puritans regarded such moves with perturbation.

The movement towards Arminianism was further accelerated as a result of Laud's own appointment as chancellor of Oxford in 1630. He had a genuine love of the university, to which he proved a generous benefactor, and he had a sincere appreciation of scholarship. Above all else, he wished to bring back the university within the orbit of the Church, to ensure that it was the home of orthodoxy and that it fulfilled its duty of training future ministers for its service. Suspicious of the influence exerted in the state by both gentry and aristocracy, he wished to free the university from too close a dependence upon these two classes, seeking to counter their influence by reinforcing the power of the court and the clergy, ideally in alliance with each other. He was stimulated by a genuine desire to make the university a more efficient institution and he looked back, for he had little love for the frolics of long-haired gallants,[1] to the time when the university had been a nursery of true religion as well as the home of scholarship. As always, concerned with meticulous detail, he issued regulations banning high boots and spurs, regulating the licences of taverns and ordering undergraduates to refrain from poaching for royal game in Stow Woods or Shotover. He clamped down with typical weight on any sermons or behaviour which gave a hint of sedition or heterodoxy. When the king, Charles I, and the archbishop were at Woodstock in August, 1631, he ordered three senior members of the university, Thomas Ford of Magdalen Hall, Giles Thorne and William Hodges of Balliol, to be deprived of their places and to be banished from the university for seditious preaching. The proctors had to resign because they had not carried out their duties properly, while the rector of Exeter, then vice-chancellor, and the principal of Magdalen Hall, were both reproved for condoning the offences. The principal memorial of his chancellorship was the body of statutes, the Laudian code, which brought order out of a mass of confused rules, drawn up at his instigation by special delegates and accepted as the code of laws, by which the university was to be governed by Convocation in 1636. 'This work', he wrote, 'I hope God will soe blesse as that it may much improve the honour and good government of that place, a thing very necessary in this life both for Church and Commonwealth.' The code was to endure until 1854 as the basis of the university's laws. When Laud became archbishop of Canterbury in 1633, he revived the claim to make a metropolitical visitation of the university, a seeming infringement of the university's liberty which cannot have been welcomed even by the loyal

---

[1] 'The chiefest thing they will amend', Edmund Verney of Magdalen Hall informed his father, 'is the wearing of long hair'. The principal protested that after this day [he was referring to the royal visit to Oxford in 1636] he would 'turn out of his house' whomsoever he found with hair longer than the tips of his ears.'

dons. Before he could bring his policy to an effective conclusion the country was engulfed in civil strife.

Did these developments affect contemporary studies? Throughout Europe there were signs of a neo-scholastic revival, both anti-Ramist and anti-Calvinist in direction. Its adherents paid a renewed attention to Aristotelianism and scholastic philosophy in general, more especially to the works of the sixteenth- and early seventeenth-century writers, Suarez and Bellarmine. Oxford, as Professor Kearney has well demonstrated, was not immune from this scholastic reaction. College libraries purchased scholastic texts. Oxford dons composed them. In 1619 Richard Crackanthorpe, a fellow of Queen's, published his *Introduction to Metaphysics*. Nearly 20 years later Thomas Barlow, another fellow of the college and later bishop of Lincoln, published an edition of Scheibler's *Metaphysics*. Surviving note-books testified to current fashions in reading. Scholastic metaphysics formed a significant part of the labours of John Gaudy of Oriel. At Balliol a notebook of Francis Boughey showed that teaching of a scholastic character was taking place there in the late 1630s. At Exeter John Prideaux wrote a handbook for disputations in scholastic metaphysics. It is not very easy to deduce from all this anything more than a certain conservatism of attitude which would evidently lend support to the maintenance of the *status quo* in Church and state.

Civil war and Commonwealth

Although the townsfolk of Oxford were moderately sympathetic towards the parliamentarians, the majority of university men, dons as well as under-graduates, watched the course of events in the early 1640s with apprehension. Parliament had already revealed its temper by appointing a committee to deal with the university and by abolishing the regulations which required its members to bow towards the altar; it also ordered altars to be removed from the east ends of chapels. There was talk among some Puritan extremists of confiscation of endowments and even of the foundation of new universities. The university's statutes and registers were brought to London for investigation, while the vice-chancellor was himself summoned to Westminster. The chancellor, Laud, had been arrested and impeached and, as a consequence, proffered his resignation, seeing, as he wrote in a letter of 25 June 1641, that he could be 'no farther usefull' though his affection, 'ferventnesse and zeale to the publique good and happiness' of that place remained as deep as ever.

On 11 July 1642, the vice-chancellor, Dr Prideaux, the rector of Exeter read a letter from the king in which he disclaimed his intention to use arms against the Parliament, but suggested that financial help from the university would not be amiss. Thereupon the masters presented the contents of the university's chests, in all £864, to the king's representative, and the colleges followed suit. Parliament, resentful of an 'action so full of Loyalty and Allegiance', ordered the summary arrest of the king's aiders and abettors at Oxford. Consequently the royal declaration of 9 August 1642, which shattered the uneasy peace cannot have come as any surprise to its residents who at once looked to the defence of the city. The pro-vice-chancellor, Dr Pink, summoned the privileged men for a view of arms. Reinforced by volunteers, 330 men foregathered on Thursday, 18 August, to drill in Christ Church quadrangle until rain forced their retreat to the Schools. Two days later they were 'put into battle array and skirmished together in a very decent manner.' The mood caught on. Doctors and masters worked with students. It was 'a delightsome prospect to behold the forwardness of so many proper young gentlemen; so intent, docile and pliable in their business,' though many of the townsfolk thought otherwise and urged parliament to intervene.

It looked very much as if this was likely to be the outcome. The small squadron of royalist horse under Sir John Biron were not strong enough to hold the town. In a last minute effort to avert calamity, to prevent 'our libraries fired, our Colleges pillaged and our throats cut', Dr Pink rode over to Aylesbury to bargain with the parliament's representatives, only to find himself arrested and forthwith removed to the Gatehouse in London. The parliamentary horse under Colonel Goodwin were quartered in Christ Church meadow. The troopers inspected Christ Church 'to view the church and painted windows, much idolatry thereof; and a certain Scot being amongst them, said that "he marvelled how the scholars could go to their books for those painted idolatrous windows."' But parliament's control over the university was speedily brought to an end by the royalist victory at Edgehill on 23 October 1642. Symbolically, as he left, a London trooper discharged a brace of bullets at the stone image of Our Lady over the porch of St Mary's Church and struck off her head and the head of the infant Jesus she had in her arms.

For the next four years Oxford became the royalist headquarters and the business of the university was subject to the needs of the court and army. The ordnance and guns were lodged in Magdalen, powder and muskets in the cloisters of New College and the tower of the Schools, victuals in Brasenose tower, in the guildhall and in the schools of law and logic. A powder factory was set up at Oseney, a 'mill' for grinding swords at Wolvercote. Cloth for uniforms was stored in the astronomy and music schools. The king gave immediate orders to strengthen the city's fortifications, dragooning the reluctant townsfolk and the more enthusiastic students to this end. All members of the university between the ages of 16 and 60 were liable to be called for work a day a week. The university loyally donated another £300 from its treasury; the colleges were, in January 1643, requested to contribute their plate. A royal mint was set up in New Inn Hall which, as a Puritan society, was probably denuded of most of its members.

All this could not happen without affecting radically the character of an academic society. Only a few scholars, like the learned Archbishop Ussher, felt it possible to concentrate their attention on past learning. In many colleges the entrants declined steeply; the number of graduands, some 200 in 1641, fell to 107 in 1642, to 39 in 1644 and 30 in 1645, while those proceeding to the M.A. declined from 112 in 1642 to 30 in 1644 and 20 in 1645. 'Lectures and exercises', commented Wood (who matriculated in 1647), 'had for the most part ceased.' In deference to the royal wishes the university readily showered honorary degrees on the king's supporters. The press was almost entirely concerned with printing royal proclamations and news sheets, among the latter the *Mercurius Aulicus* edited by John Birkenhead of All Souls. Disputations were indeed still held, the chancellor's court continued to sit, but 'there was scarce the face of an University left, all things being out of order and disturbed', 'The Colleges', Wood continues, 'were out of repair, their treasure and plate gone, the books of some libraries embezzled, the chambers in the halls rented out to laics.'

Above all there hung a cloud of doubt as to the issue of the strife. The trial and execution of the chancellor, Laud, on 10 January 1645, naturally caused depression and anger. Among the many charges against him were accusations relating to his supervision of the university's affairs: the revision of the university's statutes, the placing of a statue over St Mary's porch, of a crucifix in Lincoln chapel (presumably a reference to the figure in the east window which had ironically enough been presented by Laud's great enemy, Bishop John Williams of Lincoln), the use of copes, Latin prayers, bowing to the altar. Among the witnesses were some from Oxford, among them the warden of Merton, Sir Nathaniel Brent, 'knuckle-deep in blood', while much of the evidence had been compiled by that indefatigable, cantankerous and yet loyal son of Oxford, William Prynne.

The royal cause slowly succumbed. The king left Oxford in August 1645, to lead the royalist army in the west, but Prince Rupert lost Bristol to the parliamentarians and when Charles returned to Oxford in November, his hopes were low. Special prayers were ordered to be said in College chapels, but prayer, without shot or strategy, could avail little. On 27 April 1646, his hair closely cropped, disguised as a servant, accompanied by his groom of the bedchamber, John Ashburnham, and his chaplain, Dr Hudson, Charles left the city, never to return.

The university had now to brace itself to the change of regime. 'I very much desire the preservation of that place, so famous for learning, from ruin, which inevitably is like to fall upon it unless you concur', Fairfax informed the royal governor, Sir Thomas Glanham. And the treaty of surrender signed on 24 June 1646, did provide that churches, chapels and colleges should be protected from spoliation, though it hinted at a 'reformation there intended by the Parliament.' In line with this it ordered that college elections and the granting of new leases be suspended and in the autumn despatched seven ministers to justify the religious position of parliament by sermons. At long last Parliament issued an ordinance for the Visitation of the university (on 1 May 1647), and appointed a standing committee of both houses to receive reports from the Visitors.

The Visitation started somewhat inopportunely, for though the Visitors had summoned the proctors and heads of houses to the Convocation house between 9.0 and 11.00 am on 4 June, their arrival was delayed, giving their critics time, as was wryly noted, to consult together in 'most spiritual wickedness.' When the Visitors did not arrive, the vice-chancellor and his company left. His procession met that of the Visitors as they entered the proscholium. The bedel shouted 'Room for Mr Vice-Chancellor'. Dr Fell 'very civilly moved his cap to them, saying 'Good-morrow, gentlemen, 'tis past eleven of the clock, and so passed on, without taking any further notice of them.' But the Visitors bided their time, winning fresh powers from the London Committee to deal with the contumacious, not only to visit but 'to reform and regulate the University.' After a sermon by the puritanical Henry Wilkinson, so vitriolic that some of his hearers left the church before he had finished, hardly surprising as the service lasted three hours, the Visitors ordered all heads of houses to send in their statutes, books and accounts and summoned the vice-chancellor to appear in person before them. The heads replied that they doubted the competence of the Visitors' powers. The London Committee, though reminded by Selden that it was better to move slowly lest they 'destroy rather than reforme one of the most famous and learned companyes of men that ever was visible in ye Christian world', was losing patience. Fell was dismissed from the vice-chancellorship and deanery; so were the proctors, three canons of Christ Church, and some heads of houses.

The Visitors, stimulated by the London Committee's actions, summoned some of its more outspoken critics. Mr Tozer, the subrector of Exeter, was asked whether he had not 'checked and reviled' Mr Jo. Mathewes of his college 'for not coming to Common Prayer', 'Why you permit Mr Polewheele, a scandalous person and a man of blood, to enjoy the profitts of his place at Exeter College?', 'Why you discouraged Braine, an ingenious youth, of a tender conscience, when he expressed his zeale against supersticion?', 'Why did you not punish Bridgood and others for drinking of healths to the confusion of Reformers?', 'Why you contemned the Order of the Visitors for prorouging of the terme, and permitted ingenious youthes to be sconced for observing the order aforesayd?', Tozer gave a 'frivolous answer' and was found guilty of 'high contempt'. John Webberley, the subrector of Lincoln, characteristically 'did out of insolent contempt of the Immediate Authoritie of Parliament . . . presume to affront and abuse us at two severall sessions, and pleaded that he was to be excused for his boldness because he did conceive himself to be a leading example to all the rest of the Graduates and Fellowes of Houses in the Universitie aforesaid'; for his 'insolent and uncivill carriage', the Visitors suspended him until he gave 'some convincing testimony of his submission and reformation'. Subsequently he was sent to cool his heels in Bridewell. All attempts to gain possession of the deanery where Mrs Fell was firmly entrenched were for the moment unavailing. Nor were the other heads more conciliatory. When the Visitors summoned the Convocation on 7 April, only 'Dr Hood, Rector of Lincoln College (one that loved to serve the times purposely to serve himself and his), who had a just vote and about ten masters' appeared.'

Once Parliament had removed the major offenders, it could make sure that the other residents of the colleges were loyal and religious citizens. Many refused to recognise the legality of the Visitors' office, 'I have taken an oath not to give an Answer', said Mr Forman of Magdalen 'to any but my owne Visitor in my owne Colledge.' 'If you understand any authority of Parliament excludinge the King's personall assent', John Goade of New College stated, 'I cannot in conscience (regulated as I conceive by the undoubted lawes of the land) submitt to the authority of Parliament as conceringe this Visitation.' 'I can acknowledge the Kinge only', Samuel

Jackson affirmed, 'to be Visitor of Christ Church.' Others, perhaps the great majority, hedged. They could not properly understand the question. Nonetheless a comparatively large minority submitted, a few extremists congratulating themselves on the righteousness of their action. 'I willingly submitt, and with great joy acknowledge the power and authority of the Visitation', Nathaniel Noyse of Queen's commented a trifle unctuously, 'the vindication of which hath to noe small malignity and opposition of those of the Colledge, whereof I am a member, rendered mee lyable.' The London Committee consequently issued an order expelling all those who had so far refused to submit. It would seem that between 300 and 400 were expelled and approximately the same number made their submission. The puritan sympathies of the halls was strikingly demonstrated in that no one, either at Magdalen Hall or New Inn Hall, refused to comply.

The deprivations necessarily changed the personnel of the university. Robert Sanderson, who was deprived, if reluctantly, of the regius chair of divinity, was succeeded by Dr Hoyle of Trinity College, Dublin, no extremist himself. In spite of his professed royalism, the learned Dr Pococke for the moment retained the chair of Arabic and Hebrew, though deprived of his canonry of Christ Church. In the colleges there was almost a clean sweep of the heads. Brent was restored at Merton. The puritan Bradshaw presided over the destinies of Balliol. At Exeter John Conant was to prove an outstandingly good choice as rector. Besides the Visitors, acting in close co-operation with the London Committee, proceeded to fill, even to exceed, the vacant fellowships by a system of nomination, some 296 in 1648, 114 in 1649 and 87 more in subsequent years. Royalist opinion was highly critical of the new men, 'illiterate rabble' John Fell called them, but it is impossible to generalise. Although there were some unfortunate appointments, the nominators showed some concern for scholarship as well as godliness. Later the London Committee, satisfied that colleges were toeing the line, relaxed its hold, simply charging the Visitors to exercise a general supervision over Fellowship elections.

The parliamentary victory had represented a potential threat to the university's independence and integrity. In 1649 Oxford was still the chief seminary of the established Church, but that Church was now imperilled, its head executed, its bishops disenfranchised, its services suspended, its parochial system questioned. In attacking tithes and patronage parliamentary critics were striking at the life blood of the colleges themselves. Radicals argued for their disendowment, for the replacement of theological training by more practical skills and even the opening of the university's doors to a wider range of entrants. Others urged the confiscation of its properties and the setting up of new universities, one of which, Durham, actually got off the ground. The townsfolk saw in the university's difficulties an opportunity to free themselves from their humiliating tutelage. Many condemned its scholarship as, in Milton's words 'an attempt to 'leaven pure doctrine with sophistical trash.' What point, asked the Leveller Walwyn, in teaching Latin, Greek and Hebrew when Christ's Apostles spoke their own tongue and the Scriptures should be in English? The scholarship of the universities represented the vested interests of an élite and the very means by which its authority was perpetuated, 'the learned . . . defending their copyhold.' 'The universities', as the Diggers' leader, Gerrard Winstanley commented in his *The New Law of Righteousness* 'are the standing pond of stinking waters, that make those trees grow, the curse of ignorance, confusion and *bondage* spreads from hence all the nations over.' In December, 1653, the Venetian ambassador reported that parliament seemed bent on 'abolishing what from their antiquity gave lustre to England, viz. the universities and colleges of Oxford and Cambridge, where every sort of knowledge and literature may be said to be cultivated with success.'

That Oxford surmounted this threat was in part the result of its inherent capacity to adjust itself to new circumstances. It was fortunate to have as its burgess in the Long Parliament the scholar John Selden, for though Selden was opposed to prerogative government in Church and state, he was critical of radical measures and an indefatigable defender of the university's interests. Even more important was the patronage of Cromwell himself. As a result the association between the university and the ruling clique became even closer than it had been in happier times. On Pembroke's death, Cromwell himself became chancellor, an appointment which must have pleased those who feared the confiscation of their properties and the destruction of their privileges. But Cromwell was fundamentally a conservative, averse to social revolution or academic change. Under his direction the university was to be guided to a new orthodoxy.

Some of the presbyterians were unready to take the oath of loyalty to the Commonwealth, among them Brent, the warden of Merton and Reynolds, the dean of Christ Church. In place of the latter, Cromwell's confidant, John Owen, succeeded. Although Owen showed his contempt for academic ceremonial, presiding as vice-chancellor in top-boots, he was an able, courageous man, 'one of the most genteel and fairest writers who have appeared against the Church of England.' Owen became a prominent member of the new Board of Visitors which Parliament instituted in response to a request from the university in 1652. The new board was smaller in number, mainly consisted of residents, and wanted to promote 'the advancement of Piety, the improvement of Literature, and the good Government of that place.' Its members made every effort to ensure that pupils were rightly instructed in religion and morals; tutors were requested to see that at 'some convenient time betweene the houres of seven and tenne in the evening . . . their Pupills . . . repaire to their chambers to pray with them.' All bachelors and undergraduates were required every Sunday to give an account of the sermons they had heard, and of their religious exercises on that day. Offenders were called sharply to account.

In September 1654, a new set of Visitors was appointed. In this move some have seen a decline in the authority of Owen and the rising influence of Thomas Goodwin, with whom he appears to have disagreed. Once more the Visitors reiterated the need for attendance at religious services. They ordered 'that there be catechising weekly in Colleges'. Occasionally they intervened in college elections, endeavouring to remedy abuses at All Souls which 'hath for a long season, to the dishonour of the University, suffered under a common reputation of corruption in the buying and selling of fellowships.' By 1655 the university had sufficiently recovered its confidence to put forward proposals to limit the Visitors' powers. It ordered that the board should be strengthened by the inclusion of representatives of the university, asked for the nomination of the Visitors in Convocation, and suggested that their tenure be limited to one year. But the authorities in London reminded the university that no change could be made without the sanction of parliament. Although the university had not managed to get the changes it wanted, the register of the Visitors' work ends abruptly on 8 April 1658. Owen had already been replaced in the vice-chancellorship by Conant.

Prima facie the university appeared to have recovered rapidly from the disruption which the civil wars had caused. College finances, harmed by lack of fees and room rents, began to improve. Entries increased. Whether there was a significant shift in the type of men entering the university it is difficult to say. Some men of genteel birth and royal affiliations who would have come to Oxford in earlier days were unable to do so. Yet if there was a higher proportion of men of bourgeois stock, it can only have been a matter of degree. By and large the social pattern appears little changed. Certainly a more decisive Puritan tone informed the senior common rooms and, so far as outward observance went, made its impact on the juniors of the university. 'I thank my God from the bottom of my Heart', George Trosse, Gentleman Commoner of Pembroke, wrote later, 'that I went to Oxford where there were so many *Sermons* preach'd, and so many *Excellent* Orthodox and *practical Divines* to preach them.' Discipline was stricter. Hunting, drinking, gambling and wenching were all condemned, and offenders brought to punishment. But there had been no revolution of manners or morals, and the ease with which the university was to adjust itself to the Caroline restoration suggests that the influence of the Puritan regime was superficial.

Nor was there a decisive shift in the character of the studies. A stimulus may have been given to natural philosophy and scientific experimentation, as the existence of the group of Wadham dons, Rooke, Seth Ward, Wren and Wilkins, who between 1648 and 1659 formed at Oxford the nucleus of the incipient Royal Society, illustrates. But it would be injudicious to assume that interest in science and mathematics, itself confined to a comparatively small group of scholars, represented a genuine reaction from the pressures and prejudices of scholastic learning. Scholasticism was still dominant in the university curriculum. The old scholastic text books, Scheibler, Burgersdicius, Suarez and the rest, were still the undergraduate's principal pabulum. When Thomas Duncombe of Corpus discussed the motions of the sun he did so in pre-Copernican terms, while a future fellow of Wadham, Nicholas Floyd, relied on the writings of Aquinas, Fonseca and Suarez. Aristotelianism seemed as strongly entrenched in 1659 as it had been 20 years earlier.

What would have been the outcome had the Commonwealth continued, it is impossible to predict. It is just conceivable that there would have been some degree of social change and intellectual advance. The experience of civil strife and religious radicalism had had a traumatic effect on the seniors of Oxford and even more so on the classes from which the university drew its entrants. It could hardly be doubted that the principal effect of Puritan rule would be a royalist and anglican reaction.

V

Life in Tudor and Jacobean Oxford

The process by which a modern university evolved out of a society with persisting medieval traditions was reflected in the architectural changes of Oxford. The medieval model of a college, with its quadrangles, its mullioned windows and arched doorways, Gothic chapel and hall, was copied in all the new foundations of the period: in the Gate Tower and old quadrangle of Brasenose, in the original buildings of Corpus and St John's. Oriel's quad, newly rebuilt in the early seventeenth century, was, in spite of its Carolean porch, Gothic in style. The new quadrangle which Lincoln constructed at a cost of £251 16s 8¼d in 1609, and the splendid new chapel, with its beautiful east window, which Bishop Williams built in 1630/1, were similarly gothic. Gothic too was the magnificent vaulted roof of the great staircase at Christ Church (the staircase was itself designed by James Wyatt in 1805), built by Smith, 'an artificer of London', to the order of Dean Samuel Fell between 1638 and 1647.

Yet the basic Gothic style was often suffused by classical ornament. The new chapel of Brasenose, constructed under the supervision of John Jackson who had worked on the Canterbury Quad of St John's, had Gothic windows but Corinthian pilasters and classical swags; the wood and plaster ceiling of 1659 concealed a hammer-beam roof taken from St Mary's, a college of Austin Canons until its dissolution in 1540, in New Inn Hall on the site of Frewen Hall. The new quad which Jackson built at Brasenose, in part paid for out of a benefaction by the principal, Samuel Radcliffe, who died in 1648, was predominantly Gothic but adorned with classical decoration. This was the case with two other distinguished buildings of the period, the Fellows' Quad at Merton, its central tower built under the supervision of the mason John Ackroyd of Halifax and the carpenter Thomas Holt, the columns of which represent the different orders of architecture; and the new quadrangle at Wadham. The latter, built by craftsmen from Somerset, is a singularly satisfying example of Jacobean Gothic.

Renaissance features were more boldly displayed in the Canterbury Quad of St John's which cost Archbishop Laud £5,087, though he repined more, and justifiably, at the great expense of the entertainment which he gave to Charles I when the building was opened on 30 August 1636. 'I am now come back to Croydon', he wrote, 'from my weary, expenseful business at Oxford.' With its Italianate loggia, and the bronze busts of Charles I and Henrietta Maria by Le Sueur, the quad forms the finest expression of Oxford Renaissance style, even though its ground plan was Gothic. Renaissance too was the Roman south porch of St Mary's Church, designed by Nicholas Stone, which Laud's chaplain, Morgan Owen, commissioned in 1637 (and for which Laud was brought to account at his impeachment in 1640).

If the majority of the new buildings took place under the auspices of a college, one great private benefaction, that of Sir Thomas Bodley, was made to the university. Bodley, who had spent his youth in Geneva where his Protestant family had taken refuge during the Marian persecution, returned as an undergraduate to Magdalen and became a fellow of Merton, subsequent to his entry into the diplomatic service. On his retirement in 1598, he decided that 'in my solitude and surcease from the Commonwealth affayers I could not busie myself to better purpose than by redusing that place [he meant Duke Humphrey's Library] which then in every part laye ruined and wast, to the publick use of studients.'

In four years he restored and rearranged Duke Humphrey's room, providing it with its lovely roof. It was opened on 8 November 1602, and a librarian, Thomas James, was then appointed. Between 1610 and 1612, he extended the building by constructing the Arts End or west range of the Schools quadrangle, to house the overflow of books with which he and his friends had endowed the library. The Stationers' Company was persuaded to send a copy of each book they printed to the library. Although Bodley died in 1613, his death did not terminate his plans, for, convinced of the need to replace 'those ruinous little roomes' by 'better built schools', he had made provision for the construction of new Schools; the foundation stone was laid on 30 March 1613, and the building was finished by 1624. This 'complete quadrangular pile' was Gothic in style, but classical in its details; the Tower, Gothic in spirit, 'solid, masculine and unaffected', represented the five orders of architecture. The library's beautiful Selden End, built to house the valuable collection given by Oxford's M.P., John

Selden, was erected over the new Convocation House between 1634 and 1637.

The colleges, as we have seen, were, however, now everything, the university virtually only an examining and disciplinary body. Its principal function was to admit students to its membership and to award them their degrees. When a young man arrived at his college, the head or his deputy inscribed his name in the buttery book, the day-book in which his purchases of bread, beer and other daily necessities was recorded. Every week one of the bedels of the university inspected the buttery books of the colleges and gave new names to the vice-chancellor. He summoned the new man to appear before him to be formally admitted, generally on the second Friday after the man's arrival in Oxford. In practice the system did not work very efficiently, so that up to 20% of college residents were never entered on the matriculation list.

The university was also involved through Congregation in making sure that the student was not disqualified for his degree by religious or political heterodoxy or immoral behaviour. On 25 May 1582, it refused to grant Robert Smith of Magdalen College a grace for a B.A., not because he had not done the necessary exercises but because of his misconduct. He had, it was alleged, gathered together a 'lewd company' late at night in his college hall and there they had charged the 'fellows and honest men of the colledge' with the 'most shameful crimes . . . carnall copulacion and the like'; he had called a 'master of arts unto his face . . . "arrant knave" ', and in the divinity school had kept his hat firmly on his head. Smith appealed from Congregation to Convocation which appointed a committee; it reported that Smith had no right of appeal. In the 1570s and 1580s, when there was a seeming recrudescence of Romanism, the university showed particular care in investigating the orthodoxy of those to whom it intended to give degrees.

Through the proctors the university was responsible for the maintenance of discipline and public order, subjects to which successive vice-chancellors gave considerable attention. The paternalistic attitude of the university towards its junior members is well demonstrated in the injunctions which Warden Pink of New College issued as vice-chancellor on 13 April 1635. Heads of houses were told to make sure that all members of their colleges attended university sermons, staying in their pews until the preacher had finished. The young men were forbidden to wander abroad in the streets or in villages in the neighbourhood, 'especially late in the nights or evenings'. They were not to frequent taverns or inns or houses where tobacco or beer is sold and taken.' They were ordered not to allow their 'haire to growe to an indecent length,[1] nor at any time to weare bootes either with or without spurres . . . save only at setting forth on a journey.' Nor were they to wear 'any manner of apparel slashed, or any other exotick or uncouth fashion, or that in the lightnesses of the collour, costliness of stuffe or triminge misbesemeth [their] place state and condition.' They were forbidden to keep a horse or 'greyhound, mastiff, water spaniell, land spaniell, tumbler or any other kind of dogge, nor ferrets, hawkes, crosse bowe, stone bowe, birding piece, fowling piece or the like.' As to games they were ordered to refrain from playing for money or *pattini* 'att dice, truncks, kittlepinnes, tables, cards, shove boords.'

Apart from entrance, the university exercises and discipline, a college's relations with the university were likely to be relatively tenuous. Occasionally the university called on the colleges to help support its teachers; when in 1536, a divinity lecturer was appointed at an annual stipend of £13 10s 8d, the colleges were requested to contribute according to their wealth; the entry in the Lincoln accounts reads 'to Doctor Smythe, for hys redyng, halfe a yere, 2s 11d.' From 1603 the university required the colleges to contribute towards a Poor Relief fund administered by officers known as the marshals of the poor, and later to a fund to reduce mendicancy (colleges were continually giving small sums to beggars of very varying description). They might also be requested to assist the university with the payment for repairs to its buildings: 40s in 1550 towards the repair of the Divinity School, 16d in 1616 for the mending of the chancel of St Mary's, 13s 4d in 1672 'to the making of the University [fire] engines'. From time to time the university had to entertain members of a royal commission, or visiting royalty, and called on the colleges for their help. Collections were also made from the colleges, usually at the request of the archbishop of Canterbury, to assist refugee scholars, more especially Protestant exiles, among them Benserius in 1575, Antonio de Corro in 1580, Alberico Gentili in 1585–6 and Fabricius in 1675–7.

The medieval colleges had been small societies, maintained by endowments bestowed on them by their founders and benefactors. After the Reformation they not only filled their buildings with fee-paying undergraduates, but were enriched by further benefactions. They became *rentier* societies, much occupied with the supervision of the farms and

---

[1] That this was taken seriously is shewn by an incident recorded in Crosfield's diary. The vice-chancellor reported to the provost of Queen's that the freshmen had long locks. Provost Potter summoned them before him. The delinquents sought to avoid his displeasure by wearing caps in pretence of sickness.

The Plates

1 Magdalen College Tower, an engraving by Michael Burghers
(d. 1727)

2 Warden, fellows and scholars of New College, *c*. 1463

3 Christ Church, drawn by J. Bereblock, 1566

4 The kitchen, Christ Church

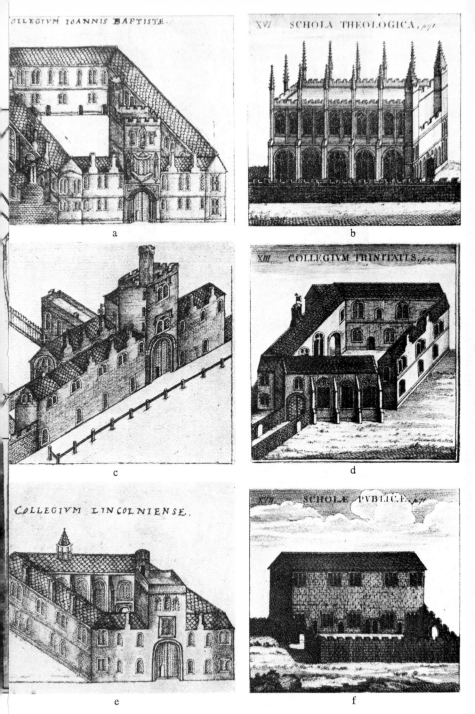

5 Oxford in 1566: (a) St. John's College (b) The Divinity School (c) Exeter College (d) Trinity College (e) Lincoln College (f) The Old School of Arts (from Thomas Neale's *Topographical Account of the University* illustrated by John Bereblock, composed for presentation to Queen Elizabeth I on her visit in 1566)

8 Christ Church by David Loggan, 1673

COLLEGIUM REGINENSE

9 Queen's College by David Loggan, 1675

10 The Bodleian Library and Old Schools by David Loggan, 1675

11 Merton College by David Loggan, 1675

12 All Souls College from the west; 18th century

13 The Sheldonian Theatre : Encaenia, 1788

14 'A Varsity Trick: Smuggling in' (T. Rowlandson)

15 Brasenose College and Radcliffe Camera, by J. M. W. Turner, 1805

16 'Bacon-faced fellows of Brasenose', c. 1811

17 Gate and Chapel, Magdalen College, by F. Mackenzie, 1826

18 The Radcliffe Camera : interior, by F. Mackenzie, c. 1835

19 John Henry Newman,
Fellow of Oriel College
and Vicar of St. Mary's

20 Mark Pattison, Rector of Lincoln College

21 A group of Merton College undergraduates, *c.* 1860

22 A group of Lincoln College servants, 1878

23 The University Museum in the course of erection, c. 1859

24 Lady Margaret Hall, 1888; the first principal, Miss Elizabeth Wordsworth, is seated in the centre

25 The procession to Encaenia by All Souls' College, 26 June, 1907. The new doctors included Mark Twain (with raised hand) and, behind him, Rudyard Kipling

26 Dons in the 1930s

27 Undergraduates outside the Examination Schools, 1934

estates from which they drew the greater part of their revenues. With land-ownership went all its varied perquisites, the holding of manorial courts and the payment of manorial dues, such as heriot (now a money payment in lieu of the best chattel or beast once the lord's right on the death of his tenant) and relief (the payment now of double quit-rent by a freeholder in every year in which there was a change in ownership). The tenant held his land by lease for a term of years at a small yearly rent on condition that at the renewal of the lease he would be liable to pay the college a substantial sum or 'fine'. These fines were treated as part of the ordinary income of the years in which they accrued and were divided among the head and fellows. Accordingly a year in which a considerable lease was granted could make a great difference to the money value of a fellowship; and the fellows were natually agog when such a lease fell for renewal.

The head and fellows' stipends varied according to the 'profitability' of the annual accounts, the college's income coming more from rentals and renewal of leases than from fees and room rents paid by undergraduates. There were besides the commons and allowances which had been for long the basis of a fellow's income in a medieval college. The money value of an Oxford fellowship, made up of so many assorted items, is not easy to estimate; but at Lincoln in 1607 it amounted to £14 16s 2½d, exclusive of the value of services, rooms and commons.

There was variation, not merely in the income of fellows but in the size and character of Oxford colleges. Yet there were certain features common to most societies. The headship of a college, partly because the heads formed the governing body of the university, was a much valued office and elections were liable to pressure from outside. Occasionally, like elections to fellowships, they were the cause of bitter internal strife. The contentious character of academic society cannot be glossed over. There were few colleges which did not from time to time experience disputes between the head and fellows. Queen's College was the scene of constant feuds between its high-church provost, Christopher Potter, and a group of Puritan fellows. When he fined the leader among the latter, John Langhorne, 10s 'for not keeping ye course of collating in ye chapell' (i.e. not taking his turn at preaching), Langhorne lost his temper and threatened to 'stiletto' the provost. Another fellow, Edward Cookes, was heard to remark of Potter in an Oxford shop that 'it mattered not much if all his sermons were burn'd for ye author of them was a dishonest man and a persecutor of all goodness.'

In Lincoln the puritanically-minded rector, the querulous Paul Hood was often at loggerheads with the fellows. A master of arts, George Ashton, had been fined 12d by the rector for wearing boots. Whereupon Ashton 'pishted' at the rector in his lodgings and in hall, and in return Hood threatened to 'pish him out of the college'. As a result Ashton was sentenced to leave the college within three days, but he had friends among the fellows who welcomed any opportunity to oppose their head. One who questioned the rector's right of punishment was accused by Hood of a 'debosht and drunken course of life'; it was alleged that 'he had broken open the cellar door of the college to fetch beer' and when as a result he had been fined by the rector, he had used such 'irreverent and unbeseeming language' that the college had ordered him to lose his commons for three months and to 'carry himself more reverently towards his governor'. The fellow in question, John Webberley, was so hot of temperament that he had struck one of his colleagues, Richard Killbye, so that the latter's head was 'sore bruised and beaten'. Later we find Webberley complaining to Archbishop Laud of the treatment he had received at the college's hands. He left the college to fight for Charles I, was elected sub-rector and, the strangest episode of all, had his room searched for Socinian literature. The puritanical Dr Cheynell rooted out 'a pestilential book very prejudiciall both to truth and peace', an odd find in the study of so convinced a royalist and Anglican. Whatever Webberley's fiery temperament, he was obviously a man of some parts.

Another of his colleagues, Gilbert Watts, deprived of his commons for 'dicing' six several nights in the town, was a constant offender. A little book which he had penned, 'being divulged redounded to the scandal and discredit of the college', was in 1629 ordered to be burned. Later he told the rector in chapel before the fellows that 'he spoke like a mouse in a cheese' and 'setting his scarlett aside, he was good a man as himself'. On Low Sunday, 1636, after administering communion in the morning to the college cook, Robert Serjeant, and his wife, he returned to their house in the evening in a drunken state and created a disturbance. But this 'incorrigible delinquent', as the rector called him, was a good linguist, an excellent wit and a 'master of so smooth a pen whether in Latin or English that no man of his time exceeded him.' It seems that he mellowed in his old age, for in 1654 the college gave him half a year's absence on the ground of his age and poverty and when he died in 1657, after having held his fellowship for 46 years, he bequeathed his books to the college library.

Colleges were long-suffering, but there were occasions when they had no alternative except to rid themselves of a discreditable member. The alcoholic Matthias Watson, 'a Fellow of our Societie', had a 'longe time both in the Colledge and elsewhere soe misbehaved himself that he hath long been a discredite and shamefull burden to the Colledge as also a notorious and unsufferable scandall in the office of his ministrie and callinge.' The college had constantly reproved him, urging him in 'all tenderness and compassion' to reform his 'notorious, lewd and deboscht course of life', but to no effect. Things came to a head in 1625. It was known that because of plague parliament was to move to Oxford. The fellows feared the discredit that their drunken colleague would bring on their society, and suggested that he might retire to the country. This he refused to do. So they ordered him, 8 August 1625, to leave the college within three days, 'yet soe charitable and compassionate did we desire to approve ourselves ... that ... we agreed to buy him a new sute of apparell[1] and to hire a messenger and horse to carrie him downe to his friends.'

Such episodes must not mislead us into supposing that there was not another side to the life of the senior common room, that if colleges were sometimes fraught by passion and dispute, they were also devoted to the pursuit of scholarship and to the cultivation of the civilised and religious life. The other side of the picture appears in the diary of Thomas Crosfield, who was elected to a fellowship at Queen's in 1627 and stayed there until he was given a college living. He sketched his daily routine in verses written on 21 June 1628:

> I'th morning pray'd & heard a Latin sermon[2]
> Wch was composed & preach'd by Mr Forman
> His text was thus: unto myselfe attend
> And to thy doctrine, constant care still bend
>
> And to my pupils read Enunciations
> Modificate, & went to disputations.
> That done we din'd, & and after did resort
> To bowle i'th garden & and to have some sport
> Then after this we heard ye disputations
> About the Vulgar & English translations.
>
> Wch done, I straight went to the lecture
> Where th'sixt of Daniel as I conjecture

[1] The suit cost the college £6 2s.
[2] Early morning chapel would have been at 6.00am, early lectures at 8.00am and dinner at 11.00am.

He did expand, & many notes did showe
Wch partly I did not & partly I did knowe
The next succeeding houre I undertooke
To write some certaine notes out of a booke
Of honour

There is ample evidence of Crosfield's scholarly interests. He read widely on a variety of subjects, including history, land-surveying (a subject, however, in which he did not persist for long, finding it of no great use to those who live by their wits . . . that have no lands, and there's the misery!) and poetry in addition to classical literature and theology. He was, besides, a conscientious tutor and a religious man. He tells us that on 7 December 1629, he had told his pupils to discourse once a week *de aliquo themate seu sententia*, and reminded them that, except on Sundays, they must converse in Latin. He takes clerical duty in Oxford and the neighbourhood, and sympathises with the provost's efforts to beautify the chapel and improve the observance of religion in the college. He fasts on the vigil of All Saints and twice a week during Lent, and tries to read over the New Testament three times a year. 'There is noe booke', he writes, on Ash Wednesday, 1627, 'that can satisfie so well as ye scripture.' When his colleague, Mr Coperthwaite, was ill and suffering from delusions, 'touching some filfynes that had been committed at Mistres Carys', Crosfield sat by his bedside, seeking to comfort him. Later in life, at Spennithorne in Yorkshire, he battled with the difficulties of keeping a parish alive during the Commonwealth.

The bleak beauty of the North Riding must have constituted a shock after the sociable life of Oxford. He loved music, vocal and instrumental, paying 16s for parts for virginals, played cards, went fishing with the 'scholars' and to bull-baiting in St Clement's. Tobacco, however, he abstained from as 'always hurtful and nocuous to ye liver.' Above all he enjoyed the entertainments staged by the wandering players, of which the university authorities (though they supported scholarly plays put on in colleges) disapproved.[1] He gives an account of a puppet show in a 100 lines

---

[1] College productions were not infrequent. The university regularly sought to entertain its royal visitors in this way but not always very successfully. When James I visited Oxford in 1606 the queen and some of the court were, strangely enough, so embarrassed by the appearance of 'five or six men almost naked' in the production of the pastoral *Alba* staged at Christ Church that the king could hardly be prevailed upon to stay. He spoke 'many words of dislike' at the second night's effort, and on the third occasion went fast asleep. In 1621 a further attempt was made to amuse the king, but it proved a tedious fiasco. In 1636, at Laud's behest, Strode's *Passions Calmed, or the Floating Island*, telling of the ill effects of rebellion, was staged at Christ Church; but in spite of its improving theme, it failed to grip the courtly audience.

of verse, and notes the variety of scenes staged on other occasions: 'the beginning of ye world besides Carfax' (10 July 1635), 'Hierusalem in its glory-destruction' invented by 'Mr Gosling, sometime scholler to Mr Camden'. He talked with Richard Kendall, the leader of the Salisbury Court Players who were lodging at the King's Arms. He had too, a lively interest in English and continental politics. A senior common room was then something more than a group of young, vigorous but quarrelsome clerics; it could be, and often was, a cultivated society, conscious of its responsibilities.

As vital to its existence as the fellows were the college servants. Their head was the manciple, a man of sufficient importance to justify his having a room in college and enjoying a fixed yearly salary though, like the bursar and the cook, he probably drew the greater part of his income from fees and perquisites. Sometimes he was allowed to transfer his office to his successor with a pension to himself (and even to his wife); often he owned a shop or rented a tavern in the town. His duty had originally been to preside over the buttery which stocked the staple articles of sustenance, but he came to have a general responsibility for the collection of battels and bad debts. Sometimes colleges were let down by incompetent manciples. In 1549–50 the manciple of New Inn Hall, Jeffrey Kyffyn, got into such a hopeless muddle that he fled from Oxford, leaving his creditors to get what they could from the assignment of his debts. The manciple often rode in company with a fellow to collect rents, to negotiate the sale of timber, to purchase provisions or to take a missive to the college's Visitor. Probably the growth in his responsibilities led to the appointment in some colleges during the early seventeenth century of another official, the butler, who took over the manciple's old routine duties as supervisor of the buttery.

The cook's function became more important as the number of undergraduates increased, and as the consumption of meat became more usual; his stipend at Lincoln rose from 13s 4d at the beginning of the sixteenth century to 20s in 1532 and 26s 8d in 1574. He had supervision over the kitchens and in larger colleges had under-cooks. These kitchens had certain conspicuous features. The vessels for salting fish and meat were prominent (salt was ordinarily bought in the form of salt loaves or stones from travelling carts) and so was the store of oatmeal. Joints were usually parboiled before being roasted. The liquor which was derived from the boiling was warmed up, thickened with oatmeal and served in pewter porringers. Another important item was the verjuice barrel. Verjuice, a liquor made from the juice of crab apples, was used partly in sauces served with meat and fish, partly to rub over meat and fish before cooking to make them tender and partly, a necessity in days of slow carriage, as a wash to remove taint. Before the middle of the seventeenth century verjuice had been replaced by vinegar, hitherto used mainly as a table relish. The cook usually had a part of the college garden for vegetables and herbs; the purchase of seeds for this is an annual item in most college accounts.

There is some reason to believe that the food in hall, if far from luxurious, had become more adequate and varied than it had been in medieval Oxford, as, with rising standards of living and the appearance of young men, many of them of good birth, among its members, we should expect. On festive days the fellows at least were given additional fare as well as more drink. Particularly relished was venison, often given by the king or the chancellor to the vice-chancellor for distribution among the colleges.

Christmas was the most festive season when the hall would be gaily decorated (1537, 'for holly and yve . . . 4d'), the floor newly strewn with rushes, illuminated more generously by candles (1559 'for candels ageynst Christenmasse 2s 8d') and warmed by extra fuel or charcoal. The linen would be clean and fragrant, the pewter newly scoured. The standing Christmas dish was brawn, the flesh of boar made into collarhead (1572, 'to a butcher for dressinge our boare against Christmas 12d; for dryncke for the brawne, 6d'); hence the abundance of boar tusks in old rubbish dumps found in Oxford. The food would be washed down by strong ale or wine, an infrequent luxury in Oxford colleges where small beer was the more normal drink.[1] Christmas saw the rules against games relaxed; so at Christmas, 1547, two quarts of wine were bought to entertain Richard Bruerne, the professor of Hebrew, and Mr Caldwell of Christ Church when they 'cam to play tyngt [tig?] her'. Since undergraduates only went home infrequently, many of them would have been in residence to share in the Christmas festivities.

By contrast Lent was observed with a measure of austerity. It was sometimes preceded by a music night (e.g. in 1513 on Quinquagesima night Lincoln spent 3s 'for the play', though what this was does not appear). The salted fish consumed in Lent seems to have brought in gross, either direct from London (1520 'for carrying of the Lent stuff, first time, from London, 3s 4d . . . second tyme, 5s 8d') or from Abingdon fair.

[1] The increasing consumption of wine in the seventeenth century, itself an indication of rising standards, is shewn by the construction of special wine cellars in colleges (as at Lincoln in 1640), the cost of which was defrayed by the sale of surplus plate.

Undergraduates' food was probably less good than that of the fellows, though they could, if they wished, supplement it by additional dishes for which they had to pay extra. They had their own gaudies or feast days, towards which in early days a proportion of the admission fees might go. Frequent breakages suggest occasional horseplay. The hall, still serving as a common room as well as dining room for the society, was sparsely furnished. The once earthen floor had been replaced by wooden boards (at Lincoln in 1507-8) which were strewn with rushes. There was often a central hearth, surrounded by a wooden pale or fender, on which the men might sit to warm themselves. The walls were gradually wainscotted, but in many colleges were still only white washed. Since forks were not in general use, handwashing facilities were provided in the hall. The furnishings consisted of tables, benches and a chair for the head of the college; the changing character of the college community is shewn at Lincoln by the addition of a third table for commoners or batlers in 1573. A bible stood on a lectern from which readings could be made during meals. Pottage was served in pewter porringers, and ale in earthenware cups, bought cheaply in large quantities. The spoons were made of pewter, the mustard pots of wood. When the company was ready for dinner, a great dish was laid on a service-table on which was the meat cut up into portions of near-equal weight. At each person's place at table a wooden trencher lay ready to be taken by a servitor to the service-table to have a commons of meat laid on it. After use the trenchers were taken to the buttery to be scraped and washed.

Undergraduate society was hierarchical in character. When, in 1641, the university repudiated certain claims made by the town it did so on the grounds that it consisted 'of the flower of the nobility and gentry of the kingdom, which will not indure to be subordinate to merchanicall persons.' The statement, which had some foundation in fact, reflects the change in the composition of Oxford which had taken place since the Reformation. Colleges now housed a certain number of gentlemen or fellow commoners who paid rents for their rooms and high fees for their instruction, and in return received some of the amenities reserved for fellows. Those of noble or genteel birth also paid fees proportionate to their rank,[1] enjoyed some privileges and wore a more ornamental gown. Scholars were boys on the foundation in receipt of an allowance from the college usually as a result of a benefaction, who sometimes had duties to

[1] In 1676 the rates of admission fees at one college were as follows: nobleman, £1 6s 8d, fellow commoners 13s 4d, commoners 4s 8d and servitors 3s 4d.

perform. They did not necessarily come from poor families, and there were complaints that scholarships were given to the sons of men who could well afford the costs of a university education. Professor Stone mentions that out of 47 scholars of Wadham between 1615 and 1639 15 were the sons of gentry, among them six sons of esquires. The largest proportion of the college consisted of fee-paying commoners. In 1572 Balliol had 46 undergraduates, including 8 scholars, 9 servitors and 29 commoners (who had increased to 70 by the early seventeenth century).

Lowliest of all were the servitors, sizars, batlers or bible clerks, originally engaged privately by fellows or graduate commoners to perform menial functions in return for instruction; so a college account book for 1527 notes the payment of 10s for Mr Sallay, a fellow, *pro camera scholasticorum suorum*. Improved standards of living, higher incomes of dons and the influx of graduates and men of quality caused an increase in the number of servitors.

The undergraduate lived his life under the supervision of his tutor, a fellow of the college. Undoubtedly the tutorial relationship did much to persuade the parent to entrust his son to college life, if it contrariwise had the effect of diminishing the amount of freedom which the student himself enjoyed. A parent might select a college because he believed that its tutors were likely to exercise the kind of control over his son of which he would approve. 'You must be ordered by your tutor in all things', Sir Daniel Fleming told his son, James, 'for your good, otherwise it will be much worse for you.' The tutor's job embraced a very wide range of functions. He received money on his pupil's behalf, and paid his bills. He might try to check his extravagant spending and seek to induce frugal habits. He tried to ensure that he was not defrauded by townsfolk or college servants. On 31 October 1549, in the vice-chancellor's court, John Edwards, a fellow of Oriel, appeared on behalf of his pupil, Richard Lymeryke, who was under age, and sued Elizabeth Griggs and Elizabeth Conwye, one for a doublet, the other for a woollen blanket which they had bought off Lymeryke and for which they had not paid. The tutor was responsible for seeing that his pupil was not unduly idle, and that he attended his lectures and disputations. He supervised his manners and morals; and sought to regulate his life so that it was free from debauchery and dissipation. He had a special care for his religious life, seeking to make sure that the young man said his prayers, read his Bible and attended college chapel; as late as the early eighteenth century Mr Steadman of Queen's used to summon his pupils to his rooms for prayers at 9.00pm. He might instruct his pupils, but his duties were basically of a more general character. He could impose penalties for breaches of college discipline, the cutting of college lectures and chapels and the like, in the form of impositions, fines or mulcts or sconces, or even corporal punishment, the more intelligible if we recall the early age at which some came to college. 'Dr Potter', Aubrey recalled, 'while Tutor of Trinity College *whipt* his pupil *with his sword by his side* when he came to take leave of him to go to the inns of court.'

What degree of success attended this relationship it is difficult to estimate. The tutor, who hoped for preferment, influence or gifts from a wealthy protégé, might readily indulge his pupil, conniving at his indolence or dissipation. Others might exercise an undue severity or neglect. In some cases pupil and tutor were bound in a lasting affection.

The puritan-minded president of Corpus, John Rainolds, agreed that students needed recreation but he felt obliged to add 'yet, in my opinion it were not fit for them to play at stoole ball among wenches; nor at Mumchance and Maw with idle loose companions, nor at Trunkes in Guild-hall nor to danse about May poles, nor to rifle in ale houses, nor to carouse in tavernes, nor to robbe orchardes.' We may be sure that some indulged in all these things. In practice undergraduate amusements cannot have been very different from what they had been in the past; though the rise in their numbers (as well as the desire of the young dons to have some means of amusing themselves) led to the construction in colleges of ball or tennis courts and bowling alleys. Although boating did not become popular until the eighteenth century, the young man might be tempted to go on the water, to hire a horse to explore the countryside or, if he were rich enough, to hunt, to visit the cock-fighting pit in Holywell or the bear-baiting in St Clements, or, as Crosfield did, to watch the strolling players. There were no coffee houses at Oxford before 1650, but the local tavern continued to afford the undergraduate solace, as a contemporary poet reflected after disaster had temporarily overwhelmed his favourite haunt:

> Lament, lament, you schollers all
> Each weare his blackest gowne,
> The Miter yt held up your wits
> Is now itselfe faln downe.
> That dysmal fyre on London Bridge
> Shall move no heart of mine,
> For yt but over ye water stood
> But this stood over ye wine

It needs must melt each Kristian heart
That this sad newes but heares
To think how the poore hogsheads wept
Good sack and claret teares.
The zealous students of the place
Change of religion feare
That this influence may chance bring on
The heresy of beer.

The Miters then ye only signe
For its the schollers crest.
Then drinke sack Sam, and cheare thy heart
Be not dismaid at all
For we will drink it up again
Though our selves do catch a fall.
We'll be thy workmen day and night
And spite of longbeare Procters
We dranke like freshmen all before
But now will drink like Doctors.[1]

Perhaps the principal disturbance to the lives of fellows and students in this period was the pestilence, recurrent summer after summer. At its onset the undergraduates were usually sent home, while the fellows sought refuge outside Oxford. The summer of 1512 found half the fellows of Lincoln residing at the Buckinghamshire village of Chilton; in 1526, and again in 1536, they rented a house at Launton, one fellow, William Hynkerfeld, being segregated from the society *quod infectabatur*. In 1571, another year of pestilence, Balliol dispersed in May and did not reassemble at Oxford until February, 1572. Lincoln sought refuge at Over Wichendon in Buckinghamshire, leaving the college in the care of the sub-rector, the cook, the maniciple (who unfortunately caught the sickness) and his wife. In 1604 the pestilence was again so bad that the bursar was granted a special allowance for the shortage in his fees.

The ceremonies which came collectively to be known as the Act formed the climax of the academic year, being fixed by the Elizabethan statute for the Saturday to Monday which included 7 July. Formerly the Act had been of little importance, and had taken place on different days in the year, but it

---

[1] The poem was recently discovered by Dr Oakeshott on a visit to the Huntingdon Library, California (Commonplace Book MS 116) and is printed by his kind permission and that of the librarian, Dr James Thorpe.

now took a pre-eminent position in the calendar, not simply as the season for the final steps in the creation of masters and doctors, but for the reception of guests and for general festivity.

The Act was much more than a purely academic occasion. Even the tedium of the disputations was occasionally lightened by the inclusion of themes which could be treated wittily. Should, one disputant asked, Aristotle have included a wife among the goods of a philosopher? At some stage a comic touch was introduced through the medium of the *Terrae Filius* who, as a jester or buffoon licensed by the proctors, could regale his audience with wit and occasional obscenities. No wonder that the Puritan vice-chancellor, John Owen, sought to abolish this part of the Act; while, in 1658, his successor, Dr Conant, obliged one such holder of the office to ask for pardon on bended knees for the *pudenda illa obscenitate* which marred his speech. The last *Terrae Filius* was appointed in 1763.

During the Act Oxford took on a festive air. Processions thronged the streets, bells rang and everyone was dressed in their best clothes. For some weeks beforehand colleges had been preparing for the great event; new rushes were purchased for hall and chapel, the linen washed, the pewter scoured, the plate cleaned, buttery and kitchen limewashed, the windows repaired, the dirt removed from the cellar, new gravel laid in the quadrangles, the streets swept and garnished, the gardens weeded and the cesspool cleaned out (e.g. 1605 'for buryinge the stinking earth that lay in the backside, before the Act, 6d.'). College tenants sent gifts of dainties (e.g. 1604, 'to Sir Henry Poole's men which brought the bucke at the Act, 7s.'), and sometimes came themselves to see the sights and partake of college hospitality (e.g. 1539, 'spent in wyn on Thomas Palmer and his wife, on the Act Day, 5d.'). The kitchens were busy preparing for feasts and gaudies. It was customary for the senior inceptors in the superior faculties to give a supper at the college of the senior among them on the Saturday evening; because of the expense the costs were after 1670 divided equally among them all. The formal proceedings were closed by a Latin sermon on the Tuesday morning, and the university reverted once more to the formal academic routine which governed its life for the greater part of the year.

This routine was most seriously disturbed by the Civil War. Strangely enough the war does not appear to have greatly diminished College revenues from estates, but in many other ways it entailed loss and inconvenience. Colleges found it difficult to collect money due for battels from members who had suddenly left the university at the start of the war; Lincoln, for instance, was still in 1660 trying to collect £7 10s from one of its members, Dr Peirce, a medical practitioner at Bath, who had left in 1642. The war emptied the colleges of undergraduates, especially just before and after the siege. By 1645 few ordinary members were in residence.[1] Many rooms were occupied by royalist officials, clerical and lay, who were expected to pay room rents, but frequently failed to do so. While the king's chaplain paid £2 13s 6d for room rent, many of his lay colleagues defaulted on their obligations. The war brought heavy requisitions from the military authorities. After the battle of Naseby Oxford was bound to face a siege by the parliamentary forces, and colleges, like houses, were required by the royalist governor to lay in additional stocks of food and fuel. Ordinary repairs were neglected, and great dilapidations were incurred by colleges, with consequent damage to their finances.

Thus at the end of the war colleges were temporarily in an impoverished state. They had to follow a policy of retrenchment, they had to make good repairs and recoup losses; the rapid rise in entries following the return of peace caused colleges to replace to some degree the plate which they had contributed to the king's mint. Effective management, however, brought a rapid improvement in their finances, and, in spite of the stricter regulations on conduct and religion, life soon returned to the norm. Thus when Charles II was restored, comparatively little had to be done at Oxford, apart from the removal of fellows intruded by the parliamentary regime, to ensure continuity with the past.

---

[1] The fluctuation is shewn in the accounts of Lincoln's College by revenues from 'incomes and gaudies of freshmen', i.e. admission charges: 1641, £8 10s; 1642, £5 18s 8d; 1643, 13s 4d; 1645, 6s 8d; 1646, 6s; 1647, £11 6s 8d; 1655, £2 17s 4d; 1656, £1 13s 4d; 1660, £5 18s.

VI

The University in Decline
1660-1800

Criticisms of post-Restoration Oxford

The university's history in the century and a half which followed the restoration of Charles II is usually described as one of steady decline. Such is the impression created by the writings of many contemporaries. The bilious antiquary, Anthony Wood, deplored what seemed to him the permissiveness of Caroline Oxford. 'A strange effeminate age', he wrote, 'when men strive to imitate women in their apparell, viz. long periwigs, patches in their faces, painting, short wide breeches like petticoats. . . . Lying and swearing much-used Atheisme-Disrespect to seniors, sauciness.'

The chorus of criticism was to continue for the next two centuries. In the late seventeenth century, an oriental scholar and former rector of St Clement's, Oxford, Humphrey Prideaux, unleashed a stream of scorn. He thought that the tenure of fellowships should be limited, fellows overtaken by senility or indolence being housed in a special institution which he named appropriately enough as Drone Hall. Many dons were no better than 'dunces and knaves', and the colleges no more homes of learning than the neighbouring alehouses.

At first sight the cumulative evidence to support these charges is considerable. Intrigue and scandal were endemic features of college life. After the Restoration, Wood recalled how Exeter had been 'much debauched by a drunken governor' who succeeded the high-minded Dr Conant until he was fortunately persuaded to exchange the rectorship for a canonry of Exeter cathedral where bouts of intoxication may have been thought less reprehensible or less inconvenient. The master of Pembroke, Henry Wightwick, 'his person ridiculous, like a monkey rather than a man', went drinking with masters and bachelors and was obliged to resign in 1664. A candidate for the bedelship of divinity drew votes because he was an 'adorer of the pitcher and pint pot'; another was killed by falling from his horse in a state of intoxication.

There were other scandals, heterosexual and homosexual, which seemed ill-becoming to those in holy orders. In 1739 Warden Thistle-thwaite of Wadham was obliged to flee the country for an indecent assault on an undergraduate, Mr French. It appeared that the warden had previously made approaches to the butler, whom he had invited to dine with him, 'endeavouring to kiss and tongue him, and to put his Hand into his Breeches.' 'He would not', said the warden 'give a Farthing for the finest Woman in the World; and that he loved a Man as he did his Soul.' The barber had also found the warden 'tickling about his Breeches'. 'How does thy Cock do, my dear Barber? Let me feel it; and then he went to kiss him: That upon this he said to the Warden, Damn you, you Son of a Bitch, what do you mean? And knocked him backwards into his Chair.' While Warden Thistlethwaite made his way to Boulogne, his colleague, the tutor, Mr Swinton, was charged with sodomising a College servant; but the offence was not proved and Mr Swinton ended his days as Arch-deacon of Swindon, whom Woodforde heard preach a university sermon. Familiarity with women, since, except for heads of houses, all dons had to be celibate, was a more natural breach of the university moral code.

More serious perhaps than the occasional College scandals were the lowered standard of instruction. All this was more a feature of Hanoverian than of late Stuart Oxford, though signs of the decline were evident before George I became king. Adam Smith commented that the Oxford professors, secure in the enjoyment of a fixed stipend, had no stimulus to lecture. Had they been supported by voluntary contributions, he argued, the situation would have been very different. In fact few professors enjoyed much of a salary, and fewer still much of an audience. 'The late noble but unfortunate Professor of Civil Law', James Hurdis commented in a reply to Gibbon's strictures, 'began his office with reading lectures and only desisted for want of an audience.' Even so, Hurdis found it difficult to provide a very adequate defence of the eighteenth century professoriate. 'The Regius Professor of Divinity reads his Lectures regularly', he noted, 'and (if the author mistakes not) no young man can take orders in the diocese of Oxford without producing to the Bishop a certificate of his having attended them.' But a contemporary's account of Dr Randolph's lectures delivered by candle-light to a soporific audience hardly suggests 'that they were either interesting or significant.' Here then was the crux of the matter. Even in the twentieth century it often requires a distinguished or fashionable scholar to draw an audience if his course is unrelated to the demands of examinations.

In the eighteenth century the examination system degenerated steadily into a farce. The exercises for the degree of bachelor of arts became near-meaningless formalities. The *Disputationes in Parviso* required a disputation on three questions either in grammar or logic; but the question and answers had become 'ready-made strings of syllogisms', as Amhurst called them, which any candidate could buy. Of the other exercises there were only vestigial remains. Knox described what happened when the young man presented himself for his final examination. 'The poor young man to be examined in the sciences often knows no more of them than his bed-maker, and the masters who are to examine are sometimes unacquainted with such mysteries. But schemes, as they are called, or little books containing forty or fifty questions on each science, are handed down, from age to age, from one to another. The candidate to be examined employs three or four days in learning these by heart, and the examiners, having done the same before him when they were examined, knows what questions to ask and all goes smoothly. . . . As neither [the university officer], nor anyone else usually enters the room, the examiners and the candidates often converse on the last drinking-bout, or on horses, or read the newspaper, or a novel, or divert themselves as well as they can in any manner, till the clock strikes eleven, when all parties descend, and the testimonium is usually signed by the masters.' Such a picture is doubtless exaggerated, but the exercises for the degrees of B.A. and M.A. had become largely indefensible by the end of the eighteenth century.

Oxford and the later Stuarts

In part what was happening was a reflection of wider trends which governed and shaped the life of Oxford after the restoration of Charles II. It emerged from the crisis of the Commonwealth with its loyalty to crown and Church reaffirmed and strengthened; the exclusion of nonconformists from its membership not merely reduced the amount of talent available from which it could draw but made it less representative of the nation as a whole. Yet even its loyalty to the crown, sycophantic as it so often appeared to be, had to be placed after its adherence to the Church and its deep-felt desire to retain its independence. Basking in the favour of Charles II, it stoutly resisted the Romanist tactics of his brother, yet found little enthusiasm for the Orange prince who became king in 1689. The high churchmanship and toryism of Anne made an instant appeal, but the accession of the Hanoverians and the long continuance in power of the Whig oligarchy cast the university into the shadows. It was not until George III became king that the university was restored to royal favour, restored at the very time that it needed government support to resist once again the critics who wished to open its doors wider and to reform its studies.

The change-over from the Commonwealth to the Restoration was accomplished smoothly and with little opposition. Lord Hertford, restored to the chancellorship in 1660, appointed a widely representative commission to regulate the reformation. Old faces reappeared: Oliver at Magdalen, Sheldon at All Souls, Baylie at St John's, Hannibal Potter at Trinity, Mansell at Jesus, Thomas Walker at University, Wightwick at Pembroke and Newlyn at Corpus. Sanderson replaced Conant as regius professor of divinity. The Act of Uniformity in 1662 brought some changes leading to the deprivation of those who could not conscientiously assent to the new prayer book, among them Conant of Exeter, but the Restoration at Oxford was achieved with moderation.

Nonetheless the spirit of Oxford had become ultra-royalist and orthodox. When the new chancellor, Lord Clarendon, visited the university, he pointedly ignored the invitation to dinner proffered to him by the puritanical Henry Wilkinson. Charles II was greeted everywhere with tumultuous applause. Fear of popery was another feature of the time. On 5 November 1678 Dr Hall of Pembroke, 'a presbyterian, covetous and a clowne' according to Wood, himself suspect of papist sympathies, 'preached sharply and bitterly against the papists' at St Mary's; and 'the pope, in the shape of an old man, was burnt at a fier at Edmund Hall. He was brought out in a chaire, set before the fier, shot at, and then (his belly being full of crackers) was burnt.' In February 1679, the heads of houses were told to make returns of any in their colleges whom they suspected to be papists.

Aware of the university's loyalty, it was to Oxford rather than to London that Charles II summoned parliament in 1681. The House of Lords sat in the Geometry School, the Commons in the Convocation House. To provide adequate accommodation for the members, many undergraduates had been sent home; but those who were left were boisterous in their welcome. 'The general cry was "Long live King Charles", and many drawing up the very coach window cryed "Let the king live, and the devill hang up all roundheads": at which his majestie smiled and seemed well pleased.' But if the university demonstrated its loyalty, many of the townsfolk were strong in support of the Whigs under Shaftesbury (who was lodged at Balliol) and clamant that Monmouth (who stayed with Alderman Wright in his house at Canditch) should be declared the heir. Charles, who had rooms in Christ Church, took the opportunity to attend the races at Burford, but decided that it would be more in his interests to bring the parliament to an end. After a week's sitting parliament was dissolved.

The university applauded the royalist victory, even if the dean of Christ Church was obliged to express his displeasure when some Christ Church aristocrats attacked the Whig, old Lady Lovelace outside the Crown tavern, 'pluck'd her out of her coach, and called her "old protesting bitch".' James, Duke of York, accompanied by his wife and daughter, the Princess Anne, made an official visit to Oxford in May 1683 which gave an opportunity for ardent expressions of loyalty. Later a full house of Convocation unanimously 'consented and hum'd' the vice-chancellor's proposal to publicly burn certain books which were held to be seditious in character.

In Convocation James Parkinson, a fellow of Lincoln College, reputed for radical views, was hissed. He had already alienated his high church colleagues, John Kettlewell and George Hickes, by his 'supercilious and un-peaceable behaviour.' He was charged with proclaiming 'unwarrantable and seditious principles' of a 'popular and republican character'; he denounced the ministers of the crown as 'fooles' and 'dunces.' 'The Commons', he declared, 'were the people's representatives and could not give away the rights of the people' since 'dominion was originally in the people.' There is, he said, 'a mutual compact (tacit or expressed) between the prince and his subjects, and that no Christian was obliged to passive obedience when the prince commands anything contrary to the laws of his country.' On learning that loyal addresses were being presented to the king, he commented acidly 'H'ant the king bum-fodder enough?' His colleagues, though the rector of Lincoln, Dr Marshall, honestly enough took no part, ganged up against him and persuaded the bishop of Lincoln, the college's Visitor, to deprive him of his fellowship. A better-known victim was John Locke, student of Christ Church, whose name the Dean erased from the college books for 'whiggisme' at the request of the government.

The king thanked the university for 'so seasonable an instance' of its 'sound judgement and loyalty' but the accession of his papist brother, James, was soon to put its loyalty severely to the test. Most colleges celebrated James' accession with bonfires, the subwarden and fellows of Merton thrusting the Exclusion Bill and the first and second parts of *The character of a popish successor* into the flames, and showed equal joy at Monmouth's defeat. Nonetheless Nathaniel Boys, who preached the thanksgiving sermon was delated to the vice-chancellor for comments 'savouring of popery' and commended by the king for an 'ingenious discourse.' Boys was a fellow of University college, whose master, Obadiah Walker, was equally suspect. Walker abstained from the sacrament and opened a chapel in a private room (15 August 1686) 'for public mass, where some scholars, and many troopers were present.' The rabble shouted 'Obadiah and Ave-Maria' and had to be driven away by the soldiery. The appointment of Samuel Parker as bishop of Oxford in succession to John Fell and of John Massey as dean of Christ Church 'to the affront of the antient canons' raised further fears. Massey opened an oratory and made a Jesuit his chaplain. It was in this atmosphere of mounting tension that the death of the president of Magdalen on 24 March 1687, opened the way to a *cause célèbre* which did much to alienate the university from the king and strengthened its alliance with the Church of England.

Although the election of the new president rested with the fellows of the college, subject to confirmation by the Visitor, the bishop of Winchester, the fellows might well have accepted a royal nominee if James had behaved more discreetly. He was ill-advised enough to order the fellows to elect a manifestly unsuitable candidate, Anthony Farmer. The only thing which suggested that Farmer had even a remote aptitude for the headship of a college was the appearance of his name in a list of members of a newly constituted university scientific society. The Visitor, the bishop of Winchester, objected strongly to the nomination. After hot discussion in the chapel where the election was to take place, the fellows, the two papists among them having left, proceeded to elect one of their number, John Hough. Lord Sunderland wrote to the college to remind them of the king's will, and the Ecclesiastical Commission declared Hough's election invalid.

On 14 August, James issued another mandate, requiring the fellows to elect the bishop of Oxford, Samuel Parker, as their new president. In other circumstances Parker would have been a reputable candidate. Brought up a presbyterian, he became a critic of puritanism, chaplain to Archbishop Sheldon and archdeacon of Canterbury. He was a voluminous, scholarly writer and a strong Erastian. He was also a very ill, indeed a dying, man. In September the king himself came down to Oxford and summoned the fellows of Magdalen to his lodgings where he administered a strong, testy reproof. James was so angry that for a time he found it difficult to speak, but the majority of the fellows remained steadfast in spite of the royal command. The vice-chancellor was equally firm. 'We must observe our statutes', he told the king, 'and no power under heaven can dispense with these Oaths.' 'I hear', said James 'that in sermons and in your own writings, you ridicule my religion, and abuse it, charging it with idolatry. In which case I cannot but esteem myself abused too.'

At Oxford the debate which involved the whole nation was now in full stream. In October the king confided the matter to the Ecclesiastical Commission, three members of which were authorised to visit the college to ensure the admission of Parker as president and to deal with the recalcitrant fellows. But Dr Hough was given a rousing welcome by a 'great rabble of followers', and the commissioners had to break the lock of the president's lodgings to install the bishop's representative, his chaplain, Mr Wickers. Within the course of the next month some 25 fellows were deprived of their places. Nor did the new president relish the installation of Romanist fellows. He 'walked up and down the room and smote his breast and said, "There is no trust in men: there is no trust in Princes. Is this the kindness the King promised me? To set me here to make me his tool and his prop! To place me with a company of men, which he knows I hate the conversation of!" So he sat down in his chair and fell into a convulsive fit, and never went downstairs more till he was carried down.' Bishop Parker had been ailing when he moved into the lodgings on 2 November 1687; he died on 21 March 1688. The new president, Bonaventura Gifford, titular bishop of Madaura, found little opposition since of the original governing body some 26 fellows had been expelled, one, Hooper, was a madman, eight were absent and three submitted.

But public opinion, reinforced by the forces of the established order, was turning against James. In the hope, a desperate one, of conciliating his critics, he dissolved the Ecclesiastical Commission and instructed the bishop of Winchester as the college's Visitor to 'settle that society regularly and statutably.' Dr Hough and other fellows were reinstated in their positions, while the Romanist fellows were mocked by the Protestant undergraduates. More bonfires than usual blazed on 5 November when Mr Drake of Lincoln preached at St Mary's 'shewing the bloodyness of the conspiracy.' When the Romanist master of University, Obadiah Walker, left for London on 9 November, he was careful to secure his books and bolt his door. At the end of the month the Dean of Christ Church 'removed all things from his chapel . . . pack'd up his goods before' and on the 30th took the Hackney coach for London. 'All blowne off' was Wood's explicit phrase.

The new king, William III, was, however, greeted with only diluted enthusiasm. Most dons were too closely attached to the principles of passive obedience and divine right to welcome their Calvinistic monarch. With dismay they watched the return of presbyterian preachers and schemes of comprehension and toleration. Parliament obliged all ecclesiastics to take an oath of allegiance to William and Mary under penalty of suspension from office. Six bishops headed by Sancroft, the archbishop of Canterbury, followed their conscience and refused the oath; some 400 clergy followed suit, among them a group of Oxford fellows (though fewer than at Cambridge), headed by George Hickes, fellow of Lincoln and dean of Worcester. Oxford's temper was well revealed by its hostility to Arthur Bury, the rector of Exeter, who had in 1690 published a book, *The Naked Gospel* 'containing a great deal of Socinianisme', in which he 'pushed to an extreme Chillingworth's principle of the harmony of Scripture with natural reason.' Exeter's Visitor, Bishop Trelawny, appealed to by the fellows, deprived Bury, and the university had his book burned in the quadrangle of the Schools on 19 August 1690.

Thereafter the university adapted itself to the new situation. If the anniversary of William's coronation on 11 April 1691 was not celebrated by bells or bonfires, 'only a few boyes had a little fier in Canditch near Kettle Hall', William was welcomed warmly enough when he made a short visit to Oxford in 1695. In the changing climate the dons looked again for favours from the crown. Oxford men once more acquired royal chaplaincies and bishoprics. The university demonstrated its loyalty by selecting William's secretary of state, Sir William Trumbull, as its representative in parliament in 1695, though he was to be placed bottom of the poll in 1698. Merton, liberated from the long rule of Sir Thomas Clayton, again became Whiggish in complexion. Wadham followed suit under Warden Dunster, 'Dunster ye lousy', 'one of ye violentest Whiggs and most rascally low-church men of ye age.' The master of Pembroke, Dr Hall, elevated to the see of Bristol, also favoured Low Church politics, as did a majority of dons at Exeter and Oriel. The new provost of Queen's, William Lancaster, a target for Hearne's acid scorn, was a friend of the establishment. But Corpus, where the president was a brother of the nonjuring bishop of Ely, and St John's, under the guidance of the ineffable Dr Delaune, were stalwartly Tory, as, by and large, was Christ Church. Its dean, Henry Aldrich, scholar, architect, lover of music, was the most

eminent as well as the most attractive of heads. But his successor, Atterbury, was more intransigent. His ill-temper led to constant conflict with
canons and students. At least Atterbury's preferment paved the way for his
resignation and so to the appointment of the more discreet but Tory
Smalridge. The division of the colleges into Tory and Whig camps, if for
the moment we allow such ill-defined terms to stand, in Williamite
Oxford laid the foundation for their eighteenth-century history.

Naturally the accession of Anne in 1702 bolstered the hopes of the Tory
high churchmen, more especially after Godolphin's fall and the decline in
the influence of the Churchills. At the start of the reign the university's
expectations were high, for the new queen was herself the grand-daughter
of the university's former chancellor, Clarendon, and the niece of the second
earl, its high steward. Oxonians gave a warm welcome to Anne when she
visited the university in August 1702, and, unlike her father, did full
justice to the viands it provided; the entertainment cost the university
£344. In 1704 they lavished praise on her for restoring the tenths and first
fruits which the crown had acquired at the Reformation to the Church, 'in
so freely parting with a branch of [her] own revenue for the most com-
fortable subsistence of the poor clergy of the Church of England.' Oxford
men were preferred to the episcopate. Sir William Whitelock, in spite of
being a son of a regicide, a high churchman reputed, according to Arthur
Charlett for his 'integrity and warm zeal for ye true interest of the nation
and the church', joined another country gentleman and high churchman,
William Bromley, as a university burgess.

Yet the university's appreciation of the royal bounty was qualified by
the influence exerted by her Whig advisers. Oxford's representative in
parliament, William Bromley, fought long but in vain against occasional
conformity. The government showed its displeasure when in July 1706,
a Mr Hart of Magdalen preached a sermon at St Mary's attacking the union
with Scotland. When Dr Jane, the regius professor of divinity, died in
1707, Marlborough used his influence to procure the appointment of the
Whig Dr Potter in preference to the Tory Dr Smalridge. 'The Oxonians',
it was said, 'do extremely resent the late affronts put upon them by ye
Court. . . . They stick not to say that you endeavour to raise the reputation
of Cambridge by sinking that of Oxon.'

In the case of Dr Sacheverell, a fellow of Magdalen, this showed plainly
enough. Sacheverell's personal reputation in the university was not high,
but his cause found enthusiastic champions there, when in November,
1709, he preached his famous sermon at St Paul's, attacking ecclesiastical

liberals, to save the Church 'in perils from false brethren'. The attempt to impeach Sacheverell united Oxford opinion against the government. 'So solemn a prosecution for such a scribble will make the Doctor and his performance,' Stratford wrote a little acidly to Harley, 'much more considerable than either of them could have been on any other account.' The vice-chancellor went bail for him. The professor of poetry, a mediocre versifier, sprang to his defence whilst Oxford lit bonfires to celebrate the relatively innocuous sentence passed on him, and huzza'ed him on his return to the city. It seemed fitting that the university should send a protest to the queen in April 1710, deploring 'that Popist Republican Doctrine of Resistance of Princes, the very mention of which at this time under the best of Queens ought to be detested and abhorred.'

The revival of Tory fortunes in the latter years of Anne's reign warmed Oxford hearts. After the great Tory victory of 1710, Bromley became Speaker. A former fellow of Oriel, Bishop Robinson, negotiated the treaty of Utrecht. Oxford's chancellor, Ormonde, 'the Head of your Majestes Troops ready to oblige the Enemies by Arms to accept such Terms as you have thought fit to offer', stood high in royal favour. Yet the alliance between the Harleyites—Robert Harley whose father had been educated at a dissenting academy became earl of Oxford in 1711—and the High Church Tories was at best uneasy. Harley himself depended too much on Christ Church, a college, influential and rich as it was, that was never very popular with other Oxford societies. His recommendation of Atterbury as dean proved disastrous, his high-handed ways leading, even before his preferment to Rochester, to dissensions among the Oxford Tories. When Anne died the situation at Oxford seemed almost as confused as that at Westminster.

Oxford under the Hanoverians

Although the duke of Ormonde, the university's chancellor, took refuge overseas, the majority of Oxford dons were in no mood to defy the new regime. The Tory president of St John's, Dr Delaune, Stratford wrote on 2 August 1714, 'ordered King George to be prayed for yesterday morning in St John's Chapel, when it was objected that it was not certain the Queen was dead. "Dead", says he, "she is as dead as Julius Caesar".' Delaune characteristically rebuked the president of Trinity for toasting the earl of Oxford. 'He is out', he declared, 'what do you toast him for?' The vice-chancellor, Dr Gardiner of All Souls, presented a loyal address; the dean of Christ Church, Dr Smalridge, penned loyal verses. Whig dons soon received favours from the government: Wynne, the principal of Jesus got the see of St Asaph, Clavering, a canonry of Christ Church and the chair of Hebrew (and later the see of Llandaff, the deanery of Hereford and the bishopric of Peterborough), and Potter added the bishopric of Oxford to the regius chair of divinity. For the rest, the university was left in the cold. 'K. George', wrote Dr Hayward of St John's, 'had suspended his favours at present from the University by some ̇representations.' The professor of poetry, Joseph Trapp, commented in an unusual burst of wit:

> King George, observing with judicious eyes
> The state of both his universities,
> To Oxford sent a troop of horse; and why
> That learned body wanted loyalty.
> To Cambridge books he sent, as well discerning,
> How much that loyal body wanted learning.

The university was thus alienated from the régime. It was a process which was to condition its history for the next half century. Government opinion, supported by hostile publicists like Amhurst, became convinced that the university was the home of a 'popish, impious, rebellious spirit.' 'If', as Archbishop Wake told the vice-chancellor, 'there be no disaffection in ye Universities to the present government . . . I may truly say you are very unfortunate in the reports wch. everywhere spread abroad.' Certainly there was grumbling, occasional disorders, harsh words, though little evidence of open treason. In September 1715, Abel Evans of St John's preached a university sermon in which he alluded to 'some of our modern tyrants and usurpers . . . meaning particularly ye present Elector of Brunswick.' In similar fashion, Thomas Warton, the professor of poetry, commemorating Restoration Day, 29 May, surmised that 'Charity beareth all things, hopeth all things and restoreth all things', and was delated to the vice-chancellor and the Lords Justice for sedition. The vice-chancellor refused at first to take action, but the Lords Justice ordered him to send for a copy of Warton's sermon which the preacher had conveniently mislaid. In December 1717, the principal of Brasenose, Robert Shippen, whose brother, William, was one of the leading Tories in the Commons, introduced a motion in Convocation to the effect that 'This is the only infelicity of His Majesty's Reign that He is unacquainted with our Language and Constitution, and it is therefore the more Incumbent on His British Ministers to inform Him, that our Government does not stand on the same foundation with his German dominions', but the motion was lost by a large majority (189 to 96 votes).

There were, indeed, uglier incidents than ambiguously-worded speeches and sermons which confirmed the government's suspicions. On 28 May 1715, a group of Whigs, mainly from New College, led by George Lavington, later bishop of Exeter, belonging to the Constitution Club met to celebrate the king's birthday at the King's Head. There they were mobbed by students and townsfolk who shouted 'Down with the Whigs' 'No G(eorge)s; Ja(me)s for ever.' They smashed windows illuminated for the day and sacked the Presbyterian meeting house. No wonder that an officer was heard to exclaim: 'I never was in such a damned, villainous hellish place.' The government, fearful of Jacobite plots, quartered a regiment in the city, which quietened the situation. The undergraduates of Merton, celebrating the king's birthday on 28 May 1716, gave the troopers 24 guineas to drink the loyal toast and 'invited all the honest gentlemen in the University to repair to the Three Tuns.' There was further trouble when the Constitution Club tried to celebrate the Prince of Wales' birthday on 30 October 1716. The Club invited the soldiers to drink the loyal toast: 'Come in, Boys, and drink and then go out and do it again', and their officers encouraged the men to break the windows of those who had not illuminated them to celebrate the occasion. Both town—for the mayor's windows had been broken—and gown complained bitterly of the soldiers conduct to Townshend and the Privy Council.

The prospects for Oxford's future seemed gloomy. The government appeared genuinely frightened of Jacobites; there were rumours, entirely without foundation, of 'several thousands lying in and about Oxford ready to rise.' It was, however, realistic to see in Oxford's high church-manship and toryism a threat to the regime. Both universities, in the view of Bishop Trelawny of Winchester, 'ought to be scourg'd into perfect duty, and better manners to ye King and His family'; he suggested that Visitors of the colleges should exert their authority to bring about this desirable end. For some time there had been vague talk of a government visitation of the universities. It had been urged by one of Oxford's critics, the deist, John Toland. Towards the end of William III's reign, Lord Somers had suggested a royal visitation, which Shrewsbury advised against as impolitic; but the bishop of Ely had renewed the suggestion under Anne.

Townshend, urged on by Humphrey Prideaux, consulted with the Lord Chancellor, Cowper, the Lord Chief Justice and Archbishop Wake as how best to draw up a bill to control the universities. They recommended that the right of nominating to all offices in the universities, and possibly the control of admissions, should be vested in a commission for a limited period. The proposed bill was so radical that it threatened the university's independence. If it were passed, Oxford would become a mere puppet of the Hanoverian government. 'The King is more determin'd than ever', Sunderland wrote to Newcastle in October 1719, 'to persist with vigour in the measures you and your friends wish. He is resolv'd to push the Peerage Bill, the University Bill, and the repeal of the Septennial Bill.' But the rejection of the Peerage Bill and divisions within the ministry led to the legislation being shelved.

In effect the government abandoned coercion and fell back on a policy of persuasion and conciliation. In 1723 Walpole's ecclesiastical adviser, Edmund Gibson, bishop of London, a former fellow of Queen's, proposed a scheme which was intended to strengthen the bonds between the Whigs and the universities. This involved the creation of 12 chaplaincies from each university known as the Whitehall preacherships; each chaplain, selected from among the dons, was to officiate in the King's Chapel at Whitehall and receive £30 a month for their services. Presumably those who were appointed might reasonably expect preferment later. Next year, Gibson and Townshend recommended a more novel and interesting scheme. 'The two universities', Gibson reminded Townshend, 'being intended for a nursery of learned and able men, not only for the service of the Church but also of the State; and the service of the State by reason of continual correspondence with foreign courts and agencies therein, requiring in a peculiar manner the knowledge of the modern or living languages, both in speaking and writing, for which no provision hath yet been made in either of the Universities', proposed that the state should subsidise the studies of 24 young men in each university in order that they might be trained in modern history and modern languages. For this object the King endowed professorships at Oxford and Cambridge at a stipend of £400 a year out of which the professor was to appoint and pay teachers of modern languages.

Neither of these schemes proved effective. It was hoped that the Whitehall preachers would use their position in the university to 'answer objections against the administration, and confute the lies and misrepresentations of the enemy upon their own knowledge and observation'; but it is doubtful whether the scheme made more than a minimal difference to the government's reputation at Oxford. The other plan started well, but as a result of the government's lack of enthusiasm dwindled to nothing. The first professor of modern history, David Gregory, made some attempt to carry out the government's intentions. Fifteen men were selected for training in 1725 and another five in January 1726. The professor sent reports on his pupils to the government. Burton of Christ Church 'has made so great a progress in the French language that he both understands and writes it very well.' Burnaby and Tottie were studying Italian as well as French. Whistler of Magdalen Hall 'fearful perhaps of venturing out of the common road, seems inclined rather to follow the ordinary method of education used in our colleges'. In Gregory's third report, to which the teachers in French, German and Italian appended their signatures, Whistler had to be written off as a failure, but otherwise the men continued to make good progress. 'Thomas Veley of Queen's College understands French and Italian very well. . . . John Meyrick of St John's College has taken a great deal of pains both in French and Italian and is able to write both tolerably well. . . . William Frank of Merton College has studied history with much care, understands French thoroughly and made great progress in High Dutch.' But, Gregory added, 'I take the liberty of informing your lordship that at present there are six vacancies, and that the fifteen, who were first nominated, can be continued no longer than February next, for the three years will then have expired'. Here was the crux of the scheme's failure. The government, which only found employment for two of the students, suspended the nomination of scholars, and the regius professor of modern history joined the ranks of the professorial *rois fainèants*.

These schemes can have done relatively little to promote expectation of patronage and preferment, for which the university's leading dons could legitimately hope. They still felt that their conscientious, if unenthusiastic, loyalty had been ill-rewarded. Certain colleges, notably Merton, Wadham and Exeter, already had strong Whig affiliations. The government decided that the best way to ensure control over the university was to strengthen its hold over the colleges.

This policy explains in part the series of unedifying college elections which took place in the first half of the eighteenth century. At Jesus, after a series of disputes, the headship passed to a Whig supporter. At Merton where there was strong minority opposition to the long Whig supremacy, the Whig party managed to manipulate a number of elections to fellowships to ensure their continued control. At Wadham the election was decided in favour of Dr Baker, supported by the duke of Marlborough, through a bribe; but the fellow whose vote determined the election and who had received the bribe went mad and his colleague, who had placed the bribe in his hand, shot himself. At Exeter the Whigs emerged victorious with the election of John Conybeare as rector in 1730. Christ Church had naturally fallen into the hands of the ruling party when the crown appointed Hugh Boulter as dean in 1719.

Many other colleges were the scenes of fierce faction fights. New College, where there was a strong Tory party, elected a Whig warden, Henry Bigg, in 1725. Lincoln under the guidance of a scion of the Northamptonshire gentry, Euseby Isham, remained faithful to the Tories. There was a singularly discreditable election at Balliol as a result of which the Visitor gave his verdict in favour of his own nephew, Dr Leigh. While there were personal as well as political ingredients in these bitterly disputed elections, they demonstrate how concerned the government was in trying to exert its control over the university.

The majority of dons refused, however, to prostitute the university to the court interest. After Ormonde's desertion, they would not accept the court's nominee, Lord Pembroke, as chancellor and elected Ormonde's brother, Lord Arran, who was to hold office until 1758. Cautious as a politician, he saw to it that no Whig head of house was nominated as vice-chancellor. Yet although many dons opposed the ministry, the university prided itself on its loyalty. John Wesley might confess in cipher in his diary that he had been speaking seditiously of King George, but Jacobitism had only a negligible following. In practice there was a slow thaw in the relations between the university and the establishment. The accession of George II was welcomed loyally with appropriate, if mediocre versification. When the Prince of Orange visited Oxford before his marriage to George's daughter, Anne, he was received, perhaps because of his Stuart ancestry, with enthusiasm. A new generation of Whig leaders, men like John Conybeare who had become dean of Christ Church in 1733, John Burton of Corpus and his cousin, Edward Bentham of Oriel and John Fanshawe, the regius professor of Greek, were men of impeccable Anglican orthodoxy, able to consolidate Whig control in their colleges but untainted by deism or republicanism. When the cry of Jacobitism was raised in 1745 by Whig preachers like Francis Potter, the vicar of Burford, and John Frere of Alban Hall, the university quickly demonstrated its loyalty.

But the thaw was a slow one. Tory dons continued to return men of politically independent views to represent them at Westminster. In the 1740s, when there was a resurgence of Tory feeling at Oxford, the university conferred honorary degrees on the opponents of the ministry. The opening of the Radcliffe Camera in April 1749 provided an occasion for a demonstration of Tory feeling—the Radcliffe Trustees were all Tories—expressed in an eloquent speech by the Tory stalwart, Dr King, in which he compared the present age unfavourably with the past when 'no Britain need blush for our national honour; when our senate was uncorrupt.'

Alarmed by the continued combination of clericalism and independent Toryism, Grub Street revived again talk of a visitation, winning an advocate in Lord Hardwicke. 'Their nonsensical principles', it was said glibly, 'are the fruit only of that shallow learning (I had almost said ignorance) which is taught in seminaries half reformed from popery, and which are ready, on the first occasion to return to the bosom of that Alma Mater. Doctrines hoarded up in the repositories of luxury, laziness, bigotry and error, whose learning consists in words, wit in quibble, religion in grimace and superstition, and the most refined policy centers in the dark interests of priestcraft.'

Yet the lines, never harshly drawn, were becoming yearly more blurred, so that the accession of George III opened the way to a reconciliation of court and university, to the cornucopia of patronage and the knowledge of government support. 'The good things of this world', so Sir Roger Newdigate was told, 'are coming amongst us.' George Horne of Magdalen, preaching at St Mary's in 1761, felt able to call for the elimination of 'those diabolical principles of *resistance to government in Church and state*.' The Peace of Paris was celebrated with due acclaim. And when the university's chancellor, Lord Lichfield, died, the understanding between Oxford and the court was cemented by the election of the king's leading minister, Lord North; the more rigid Tories found themselves divided and at a loss as to how best to put forward a strong rival candidate. The choice of Lord North, George III purred, was a personal compliment to himself. The alliance was a timely one, for the tide of criticism of the university was flowing strongly, more especially against its continued insistence on the subscription to the Thirty-nine Articles at matriculation and graduation.

This issue became important in 1772/3 and was raised in the House of Commons where Sir William Meredith moved the abolition of the obligation. Among his supporters Mr Dowdeswell argued that it was beyond the capacity of a boy of 16 to understand the scholastic subtleties of the Articles; while Mr Grey, with a fine disregard of history, described them as an 'offspring of monkish enthusiasm, a jumble of contradictions.' 'Away with such fanatical stuff', he declared, 'we live in more enlightened times!' But the majority of the members sympathised with the university's member, Sir Roger Newdigate, in believing that the object of the motion

was to 'undermine the Church by sapping the foundation of the universities.' Such too was the view of Charles Jenkinson who affirmed that it
was from the universities that 'England derived its . . . superiority of knowledge, in every department of art.' 'And whence, too', he asked, 'has
England been supplied with these reams of infidel ribaldry and cargoes of
anti-Christian argument, which have spread mischief and misery around
us? . . . they were the effusions of men who might, under the tutelary influence of academic restraint, have been saved from the disgrace of reviling
Christian truth, and seeking to poison public opinion.' Oxford's chancellor, the prime minister, Lord North, nodded his head in agreement. 'The
reforming notions of the age, Sir, are dangerous in their tendency. More
than reformation is intended—something that deserves a harsher name—
something to which if we gave way, adieu to religion, adieu to everything
dear to us as men and Christians.' The motion was lost by 67 votes to 159.
At Oxford there were some who were worried by the requirement, and a
proposal was submitted to Convocation to substitute a declaration of conformity to the worship and liturgy of the Church of England in place of
subscription to the Articles; but this failed to pass. 'Our Academical
Liberty', so William Jones of University College declared, 'may be considered as a chaste virgin, whom we have educated in these bowers with a
jealous care; we have now intrusted her to a guardian (Lord North), whose
resolution it will be, not only to view her himself with a modest eye, but to
preserve her with incessant vigilance from every presumptuous suitor.'

Study and Scholarship
The fluctuations in the political attachments of the university in the late
seventeenth and early eighteenth century go far to explain Oxford's
low reputation in this period; but they screen its achievements.

Tutorial instruction naturally varied in quality. We are only too familiar
with Gibbon's indictment of the fellows of Magdalen and are perhaps too
easily persuaded of its general truth. Of his second tutor he remarked
pungently that he 'well remembered that he had a salary to receive, and
only forgot that he had a duty to perform.' But his first tutor, Waldegrave,
cursorily described as the 'best of the tribe', read Terence with his pupil
between ten and eleven every morning. The hour, which Gibbon criticised
as a 'slight and superficial discharge of an important task', would seem to
have been passed in no less worthy a fashion than most modern tutorials.
Closer examination reveals other instances of the conscientious performance of tutorial duty. The relationships between the Fleming brothers and

their tutors at Queen's and St Edmund Hall in the late seventeenth century were cordial. George Fleming wrote in 1696 that the vice-principal of St Edmund Hall was instructing his brother, James, in philosophy and spent the evenings teaching him grammar and classics of which he 'knows little.' The principal, Dr Mill, like Wesley at a later date, instructed his pupil on Sundays, reading Grotius' *de Veritate Christiani Religionis* with him after the morning sermon. When George Whitefield began to associate with the Methodists, the master of his college, Pembroke, threatened him with expulsion, but his tutor was more sympathetic. 'He lent me books, gave me money, visited me and furnished me with a physician when sick. In short he behaved in all respects like a father.' William FitzMaurice, later Lord Shelburne, who matriculated at Christ Church in 1753, described his tutor, William Holwell, as 'not without learning and [he] certainly set himself out to be serviceable to me in point of reading. I read with him a good deal of natural law, and the law of nations, some history, part of Livy, and translated some of the Orations of Demosthenes with tolerable care.' Likewise Richard Edgeworth, who entered Corpus Christi as a gentleman commoner in 1761, paid tribute to his tutor, John Russell. 'I applied assiduously not only to my studies, under my excellent tutor Mr Russell, but also the perusal of the best English writers, both in prose and verse. Scarcely a day passed without my having added to my stock of knowledge some new fact or idea; and I remember with satisfaction, the pleasure I then felt, from the consciousness of intellectual improvement.'

In his statutes for Hertford Dr Newton laid down a tutor's duties in precise details. The undergraduate had to call on his tutor with his weekly exercise every Saturday afternoon at 4pm. The tutor was to return it properly corrected, observing what 'expressions are not grammatical, what words not classical, where the Latin is not full, and where not clear . . . where they have not taken the sense, or not approached the spirit' and so forth. The tutor was required to visit his pupils in their own rooms, and to direct them 'in proper methods of studying, that they may not give in to a desultory, wandering, fruitless Application; he shall discourage them from reading light, vain, trifling prophane and unprofitable Books, to the loss of their Time and of their Innocence.' Whether these regulations were put into operation we may doubt, but other college rules passed in the eighteenth century show concern for the proper fulfilment of the tutorial task, and for the regular performance of college lectures.

In his mature years Jeremy Bentham wrote caustically of the university and its 'Protestant monks'. 'Mendacity and insincerity—in these I found the sure and only sure effects of an English university education.' 'I learnt nothing. I played at tennis once or twice. I took to reading Greek of my own fancy, but there was no encouragement; we just went to the foolish lectures of our tutors, to be taught something of logical jargon.' The letters which he wrote after his entry at Queen's at the unusually early age of 12 provide a somewhat different picture. 'We have,' he told his father, 'lectures twice a day from Mr Jefferson, at 11 o'clock in the morning and 9 at night, except on Tuesday and Fridays (when we have publick lectures by the Greek lecturer, Mr Hodgekin) and Holidays. Mr Jefferson does not intend beginning with me in Logic yet awhile. On Saturday we all received the Sacrament; upon which account we were lectured in Greek Testament 3 days before. . .'. 'I have sent you a declamation I spoke last Saturday, with the approbation of my acquaintances', he wrote to his father at the close of his freshman's year, '. . . I have disputed too in Hall once and am going to again to-morrow. There also I came off with honour, having fairly beat off, not only my proper antagonist with arguments, the in-validity of which I clearly demonstrated. . . . Indeed I am very sorry it did not come to my turn to dispute every disputation day: for, for my own part, I desire no better sport.' As much importance should surely be attached to Bentham's early reactions to Oxford as to the reflections of an ageing man, who remembered the humiliations he had once suffered as a young boy at the hands of his seniors but forgot the apparatus of learning and logic which stood him in such good stead in later life.

But was what was taught of any intrinsic worth? Disputations remained, as Bentham's letters show, the basis of instruction. An early eighteenth-century tutor of Queen's, 'old Smug', Joseph Hunter, whom Hearne dismissed crisply as a 'drunken old sot', was so effective and enthusiastic a teacher of logic that he sometimes kept his classes after the dinner bell had sounded 'And Logick spew as potently—as Ale.' For many, the skills of the disputation formed the best possible mental training. 'One advantage all of them', Mr Salmon wrote in *The Present State of the Universities* in 1744, 'have in an Academical Education, which is not to be met with else-where, is the coming up in the Schools, and disputing publickly. There are some Lads, who are not to be mov'd by other Arguments, to apply them-selves to Study, who will take true Pains to qualify themselves for these Encounters, lest they should be recorded Blockheads, hiss'd and despised in all companies.' Whatever the virtues of the disputation, it was, however, not easy to refute the charge that the character of education was changing, and that Oxford was slow to adapt itself to new ideas. The syllabus remained conservative: the old text books, Eustachius, Baronius, Scheibler (whose *Metaphysics* remained on the reading list until 1744), Burgersdicius, Heerboord, Suarez, Stiesis, Brerewood and sundry others. These names, together with the works of Sanderson, Dionysius, Longinus, Zabarella, and Casus, appear on the reading lists of the Flemings in the late seventeenth century. 'At my first arrival', Fleming wrote on 4 May 1689, 'my chief studies was Logick, for the obtaining of which my Tutor read unto me Sanderson's and Du Treu's *Logicks*; over and above which I myself read Aristotle's *Organon* and Crackenthorp's *Logick* with others of the same subject which my Brother furnished me with; but at present my study is Moral Philosophy concerning which I read myself Aristotle's *Ethiccs* and Curcaellaeus, as for exercise we have Disputations, Declamations, Recitations and other exercise very constantly.' In July of the same year he reported that 'I have read the never to much to be praised Moral Philosophy . . . and now by the direction of my Tutor . . . I have read most part of Justinian's *Institutes*, being an Epitome of the Civil Law.' It was probably true, as David Gregory, the first professor of modern history, told Lord Townshend in 1728 that 'the old scholastic learning had been for some time despised, but not altogether exploded, because nothing had been substituted in their place.' John James, who went up to Queen's in 1778, said of his tutor, Thomas Nicolson's lectures: 'He does not explain a single term, and were I only to rely on the instruction I receive from him, I should find myself very deficient.' 'I wish much', he wrote on his departure in 1780, 'I must confess, to bid adieu to the force of discipline, and the freezing indifference of this College and its governors.' Nor was James alone in his estimate of Oxford's instruction.

It is, however, not enough to measure the content of a university education at any period of history by its set books. Young Henry Fleming enquired of his father whether he had 'any Geography books that you can spare.' His brother asked for money to pay for the tuition that he had received from his Hebrew tutor and from the professor of botany. Contemporary letters and diaries show that some undergraduates were aware of the studies in the new philosophy.

Although there may have been some decline in the middle and later years of the eighteenth century, the university continued to house scholars of originality and distinction. Dr John Mill of St Edmund Hall, who collated the chief manuscripts in England and the Continent, produced an epochal edition of the Greek New Testament in 1707. John Fell, the dean of Christ Church, was author of a critical edition of St Cyprian. Henry

Aldrich, his successor, achieved fame as an architect and musician as well as the author of a text book on logic which was still in use in the middle of the nineteenth century. John Potter, fellow of Lincoln and regius professor of divinity, was a notable patristic scholar.

The range of Oxford scholarship in the late seventeenth and early eighteenth century was astonishingly wide. Edward Bernard, who edited the great catalogue of manuscripts published in 1697, was Savilian professor of astronomy and prominent in the development of scientific studies at Oxford, but he edited Josephus and aspired to the chair of oriental literature at Leyden. Hody of Wadham controverted Isaac Vossius' criticism of Aristeas and refuted the non-jurors' interpretation of Byzantine history. The non-juror, George Hickes, ransacked patristic literature to vindicate the 'Dignity of the Episcopal Order.'

In particular, the pioneer work done in Anglo-Saxon and medieval texts demonstrated Oxford's vitality in the closing years of the seventeenth century. The basic dynamic of this movement may have been simply a passionate enthusiasm for antiquity; but it was stimulated both by a fundamental patriotism, a desire to exemplify the glory of the British race, and by the wish to find in the medieval and Anglo-Saxon past the prototype of the contemporary established Church. 'Between 1660 and 1730', Professor David Douglas has written, 'a long succession of highly distinguished Englishmen brought to its proper culmination the best sustained and most prolific movement of historical scholarship this country has ever seen.' Through their encyclopaedic knowledge and careful editing of texts these scholars laid the foundation of studies in medieval history and in Old English.

While the movement, if it can be so called, had its adherents at Cambridge, and ultimately came to be focussed on London, Oxford was chiefly though not exclusively, its fountain head. There Francis Junius the younger studied for many years, using Anglo-Saxon manuscripts to develop the understanding of comparative philology. He had an apt pupil in Thomas Marshall, fellow and rector of Lincoln, a singularly talented linguist and a pioneer in Anglo-Saxon philology. His colleague, George Hickes, elected a fellow of Lincoln in 1664, was the most distinguished of these Oxford scholars, though the great part of his work was to be produced after he had left the university. Deprived of the deanery of Worcester for his refusal to take the oath to William III, a political fugitive, living in some penury, Hickes found time to produce the first Anglo-Saxon grammar in 1689 and the incomparable *Thesaurus*, which did so much to shape the future understanding of Anglo-Saxon culture, in 1703.

If Lincoln produced two of the ablest Anglo-Saxon scholars of the age, Queen's was the most highly reputed 'profluvium of Saxonists.' For the first time what may be termed an organised school of English language and literature came into existence. William Nicholson, later bishop of Carlisle, was 'so well skilled in the Saxon language', as Fleming explained in 1679, 'that Sir Joseph Williamson has founded a Saxon lecture in our College which he reads every Wednesday in term time.' Nicholson's friend and contemporary, Edmund Gibson, subsequently bishop of Lincoln and London, was himself to produce a text of the *Anglo-Saxon Chronicle* in 1692, a revised edition of Camden's *Britannia* in 1695 and the indispensable *Codex Juris Ecclesiastici Anglicani* in 1713. The promotion of Anglo-Saxon studies at Queen's, however, owed most to Edward Thwaites, elected a fellow in 1698 and made preceptor in Anglo-Saxon. An exacting tutor, he became professor of Greek, but until his death in 1711 he continued to stimulate interest in Anglo-Saxon scholarship among his pupils. Deploring the lack of Saxon lexicons, he declared that he 'had fifteen young students'; with one of these, Thomas Benson, he assisted in the compilation of the compendium of Somner's Anglo-Saxon dictionary; with another, Christopher Rawlinson, he published an edition of Alfred's Boethius. Another graduate of Queen's, Thomas Tanner, who became a chaplain of All Souls and eventually bishop of St Asaph, a post which he combined with a canonry of Christ Church, was an immensely industrious and learned scholar whose *Bibliotheca Britannico-Hibernica*, 41 years in the making, was published in 1748, 13 years after his death.

By the first decades of the eighteenth century London rather than Oxford seemed to take the lead in Anglo-Saxon studies. The greatest scholar of all, Humphrey Wanley, was an Oxford man but so averse to scholastic learning that he never took a degree. He won, however, the patronage of Thomas Tanner and Dr Charlett of University and was appointed to an assistant keepership at the Bodleian. With the encouragement of Hickes, he moved to London to become Lord Oxford's librarian and to engage in the great work of cataloguing the Harleian manuscripts. But Oxford still had its notable scholars. Humphrey Hody, author of the learned history of *English Councils and Convocations* (1701), based on a wide reading of medieval sources, was subwarden of Wadham. Most notable was the lonely, atrabilious figure of Thomas Hearne, expelled from his assistantship at the Bodleian for his refusal to take the oath in 1715. Hearne was a man of prodigious industry and profound learning. At his death in 1735 he left no less than 40 volumes of scholarly publications and 145 manuscript note books. With acid pen, he described in unique fashion the academic atmosphere of the period; but he was no mere gossip. His passionate love of antiquity led him to edit medieval chronicles with exemplary accuracy.

No such proliferation of original research was to occur until the middle years of the nineteenth century. Yet if the flame of Oxford scholarship sometimes grew dim in the eighteenth century, there were always some notable scholars to keep it alive, Bradley and Halley in astronomy, Sibthorp in botany, Kennicott in Hebrew and Blackstone in Law. Thomas Warton of Trinity was a pioneer in English medieval literary studies. Sir William Jones, a former Fellow of University College, was the father of Sanskrit studies and one of the foremost orientalists of his day. Martin Routh, who became president of Magdalen, was an erudite patristic scholar. Benefactions were still being made to further learning. The earl of Lichfield left money for a lectureship in clinical medicine in 1780, having previously endowed prizes for Latin verse and English prose. In 1798 professorships of Anatomy, Medicine and Chemistry were founded through the generosity of George Aldrich. In 1806 Sir Roger Newdigate provided a permanent endowment for an annual prize in English verse.

In fine, the university, regarded with real affection by many of its old members, provided an adequate classical education, fulfilling its task of educating the future clergy with fair success. If its reputation as a home of scholarship was in decline, it may well have been, as is the case with most unreformed institutions, very much better than its critics made out. Moreover, bound as it was in law by the Laudian statutes of 1636, it could not make fundamental changes, either in its administration or in its curriculum, without grave difficulties. It was nonetheless impossible to refute entirely the charge that the university was magisterially slow to adapt itself to the changing conditions of the society which it was there to serve; in the age of the Enlightenment its scholarship and purpose seemed to its critics medieval. The two universities were, in the opinion of the wit and cleric, Sydney Smith, who was elected to a fellowship at New College in 1790, like 'enormous hulks confined with mooring-chains, everything flowing and progressing around them', whilst they remained immovable and decaying in mid-stream.

Such complaints, to which, as we have seen, the Whig politicians were very ready to listen, re-echoed throughout the century. The Whigs' inbred suspicions of the university as a house of Tory, even of possible Jacobite, reaction and of entrenched and privileged orthodoxy had been given a stimulus by a stream of criticism released by the Hanoverian succession. Nicholas Amhurst, who had been a fellow of St John's until his deprivation therefrom, allegedly for libertinism, in his *Terrae Filius* denounced Oxford not merely as the home of high Toryism and conservative churchmanship, but of indolence, low living, corruption and potential treason.

Amhurst had many followers in the early decades of the eighteenth century. In 1730 a young graduate of Wadham, James Miller, wrote a satirical play, *The Humours of Oxford*, in which the debaucheries and senilities of the dons were demonstrated. 'Why', wrote the author, 'should a poor undergraduate be called an idle rascal and a good for nothing blockhead, for being perhaps but twice at Chapel in one day, or for coming into college at ten or eleven o'clock at night . . . whilst the grey-headed doctors may indulge themselves in what debaucheries and corruptions they please, with impunity and without censure.' One of his main characters, a don called Haughty, is described as 'an imperious, pedantick, unmannerly pedagogue, of a vile life and vicious principles.' 'I have finished my Studies . . .', the undergraduate comments, 'I have been a downright drudge to them . . . what between Dressing, Dancing, Intriguing, the Tennis-Court and Tavern, I am so completely taken up my first two years . . . I had a good-for-nothing, musty Fellow for a tutor, who made me read Latin and Greek.'

> 'What Class in Life,' Haughty sang
> 'Tho' ne'er so great
> With a good fellowship can compare?
> We still dream at our old rate
> Without perplexing Care . . .
>
> An easier Round of Life we keep
> We eat, we Drink, we Smoak, we sleep
> And then, then, then
> Rise and do the same again.'

The impression was thus widely circulated that the university was, in the words of Miller's vice-chancellor, 'a Nursery of Ignorance and Debauchery.' 'These venerable bodies of Oxford and Cambridge', as Edward Gibbon asserted in his often-read *Autobiography*, 'are sufficiently old to partake of all the prejudices and infirmities of old age.' 'The silence of the Oxford professors, which deprives the youth of public instruction, is imperfectly supplied by the tutors . . . of the several colleges.'

Oxford's decline was reflected above all in its falling numbers. Whereas there had been an average intake of 500 or more in the 1630s, by 1700 it was no more than 300, and it slumped to 182 by the middle of the century. An annual entry of 220 by 1800 and of 219 by 1835 reflected a slow recovery. The most striking feature of this phenomenon was the dramatic decline in the admission of the children of the nobility and gentry; for them Oxford, so clerical and parochial in its outlook, had evidently ceased to provide, as it had done in the first half of the seventeenth century, the fashionable training which the man of quality desired. Yet, equally, the expense of an Oxford education, rising fees and battels, the fall in the value of scholarships and exhibitions, all reflecting current inflation, as well as the relative difficulty of acquiring a good classical education at school, had a deterrent effect on the admission of the poorer scholars, the sons of the less affluent country clergy, yeomen farmers and tradesmen. As class lines appeared to harden, poorer undergraduates sometimes found the society in which they lived unduly snobbish, while their chance of lucrative employment after graduation was relatively slim. The reduction in the number of church livings, a result of increasing pluralism, condemned many a poor university graduate to a penurious and prolonged career as a curate.

Consequently colleges tended to become closed oligarchies, their revenues largely expended on maintaining the head and fellows (many of whom were non-resident), and on new buildings. Although colleges classes continued, university lectures, with a few notable exceptions, lapsed. The tutorial function was confined to one or two fellows instead of being divided among many, the tutor no longer selected by the parent but appointed by the head (thus adding to his not inconsiderable store of patronage). Nonetheless, strong vested interests existed side by side with a growing realization that reform was essential if the university was to fulfil its function in the national life. 'I consider the sending a son thither at present, as a most dangerous measure, a measure which may probably make shipwreck of his learning, his morals, his health, his character and his fortune'. Vicesimus Knox, a fellow of St John's and headmaster of Tonbridge, wrote in 1781, adding, however, that 'when the discipline shall be restored, and the obsolete exercises abolished, no places in the world will be better adapted to a studious life, than our noble universities.'

VII

Oxford life in the late seventeenth and eighteenth centuries

After the Restoration Oxford began to assume something of its present shape architecturally, for there was a remarkable florescence of building, as much a tribute to the good taste of the dons as to the skill of the masons and craftsmen. In the first instance, it reflected the genius of Christopher Wren, fellow of All Souls and Savilian professor, who was responsible for the bell tower of Christ Church, and the Sheldonian Theatre, and to whom has been attributed the chapel of Trinity College (ascribed by some to Dean Aldrich), to which Grinling Gibbons contributed the splendidly carved screen and reredos. The Sheldonian Theatre, which was commissioned by the chancellor, Archbishop Sheldon, as a place for the 'enactment of university business', was finished in 1669. Wren's quadrangle at Christ Church was erected in the 'Gothick to agree with the founder's work', antipathetic as he was to the style, at the request of Dean John Fell. One of Oxford's most beautiful buildings, the Old Ashmolean, was built between 1679 and 1683 to house the collections of the naturalists and travellers, the two John Tradescants, and the antiquary, Elias Ashmole.

Gothic had in general given way to the all-pervading classical style, represented by the Clarendon Building which was built in 1713 to accommodate the university press. It was so-called because it was paid for out of the profits of Clarendon's *History of the Great Rebellion*. The press had been put on an organised basis by Laud who did not wish Oxford to be inferior to Cambridge in this respect. In 1632 the university had been empowered to appoint three printers and booksellers who could print all books not forbidden by law, subject to the consent of the vice-chancellor and three doctors. In practice the university failed to exercise its right, allowing itself to be bought off through 'covenants of forebearance' by interested parties. But types and matrices carefully garnered by Provost Langbaine of Queen's were stored in the Old Congregation House which became a *Domus Typo-*

graphica in 1662. At the initiative of Dean John Fell, a paper mill was established at Wolvercote. 'I hope', Daniel Brevint wrote to him jocularly, 'to see before your lease be expired all sort of Learning swarme and throng out of your Shop (if you give me leave to make use of this mechanicall word).' But Fell and his associates had over-reached themselves and the press, having fallen foul of the Stationers' Company, was absorbed in litigation and turmoil. The appointment of a special Delegacy for oversight of its business in 1691 betokened better times which the move from the Sheldonian to the Clarendon Building helped to promote further.

Another new university building was the Radcliffe Camera, a rotund and massive masterpiece by James Gibbs, which was opened as a library in 1749. Its creation was made possible by the benefaction of a physician of Queen Anne's day, John Radcliffe, whose '*Genius*', as a contemporary put it, 'being averse to the Laborious and Serious Study of Divinity, and carrying him to that of Physick, in the practice of which he was afterwards so Successful and Renown'd, by means whereof he acquired a vast Wealth.' The Observatory, begun in 1772, also owed its existence to the generosity of the Radcliffe Trustees.

The colleges were even more active, demolishing their medieval buildings and replacing them by new ones. 'Our forefathers', Dr Tatham stated in 1773, 'seem to have consulted petty convenience and monastic recluseness, while they neglected that uniformity of Design, which is indispensable to magnificence, and that elegance of Approach, which adds half the delight.' At Queen's, Sir Joseph Williamson had given money for a new block of rooms facing Queen's Lane in 1671-2, and had started a new quadrangle which was finished by 1707. The handsome new library, built to take the books bequeathed to the college by its former provost, Bishop Barlow, was complete by 1695-6. It is uncertain whether Wren was responsible or not; some have seen in it the handiwork of Dean Aldrich (who designed All Saints Church in the High Street, though Hawksmoor was responsible for the tower, which is shortly (1973) to be converted into a new library for Lincoln College). Queen's had more grandiose plans still; the old college was to be replaced by a grand new building in the classical style. The principal progenitor of the enterprise was Hearne's *bête-noire*, 'old smoothboots', Provost Lancaster, who contributed some £5,000 from his own pocket towards the costs of rebuilding. The library and north range were to be incorporated in a new plan which brought the college a frontage in the High Street, a west range, designed by Hawksmoor, a new hall and a chapel (for the ceiling for the apse Sir James Thornhill painted the

Ascension), which the archbishop of York consecrated on 1 November 1719, two years after Lancaster's death. In his sermon the new provost exhorted his listeners to regular worship, reminding them that 'piety was generally attended by promotion in this world.' Although there had been generous benefactions, the cost of the new buildings was so high that appeals for funds had to be issued in 1718–19 and again a decade later. The splendid new buildings had transformed the aspect of the High Street.

> That here, at once surpris'd and pleas'd, we view
> Old Athens lost and conquer'd in the new.

Other colleges followed Queen's example. All Souls was beautified by new buildings, if at the cost of the old cloister, hall and part of the chapel; the library, a result of a benefaction of £6,000 from Christopher Codrington, twin towers, a central block containing a senior common room, a new hall, buttery and kitchen, all designed by Hawksmoor but not complete until 20 years after his death. Magdalen had a grand plan for complete reconstruction, but, fortunately for posterity, the fellows had eventually to be content with the New Buildings, begun in 1733, designed by Townshend but bearing the marks of Gibbs' influence, which were intended originally to form the north side of a great classical quadrangle. At Worcester, which had been founded as a result of a benefaction from Sir Thomas Cookes in 1714 on the site of Gloucester Hall, new buildings were begun in 1720, though these were not finished until 1746; the hall was opened in 1784 and the chapel was consecrated in October, 1791.

The culmination of this building activity was the Oxford Mileways Act of 1771, the first of five such acts passed before 1848, which provided for the building and rebuilding of bridges and the removal of the market from the streets. Magdalen Bridge was rebuilt; Cornmarket Street and St Giles were opened by the removal of the North Gate and the Bocardo prison. The conduit was removed from Carfax. In his *Oxonia Explicata et Ornata* (1773), Dr Tatham was warm in his appreciation of the changes: 'Neatness and regularity in Streets, Areas, Market-places and Avenues constitute the beauty and elegance of every town: and Oxford will enjoy, above all others, the particular advantage of the Colleges and buildings of the University, so justly noted and admired for their sumptuousness and magnificence.' But there was, he added, still ample room for further improvements: the widening of St Giles with a carriage road and a foot path bordered by a sheet of water or a grass plot with shrubs; an avenue to create a new approach to Worcester marred as yet by 'obstruction and filthiness'; the replacement of St Mary's, 'not equal to so venerable and august an assembly as that of this University', by a Grecian temple. Dr Tatham's hopes were for the most part unfulfilled; but, by the end of the eighteenth century, the skyline of Oxford had been modified and its beauty enhanced.

Colleges were still predominantly clerical societies. But there was a greater degree of non-residence among the fellows as young dons served curacies outside Oxford. The majority of fellows waited their turn for a college living which would provide them with the opportunity for matrimony as well as preferment.[1] In the *Student* for 1750 young Thomas Warton, on the eve of his election to a fellowship at Trinity, justly summed the situation up:

> *These fellowships are pretty things,*
> *We live indeed like petty kings;*
> *But who can bear to spend his whole age*
> *Amid the dulness of a college;*
> *Debar'd the common joys of life,*
> *What is worse than all—a wife!*
> *Would some snug benefice but Fall,*
> *Ye feasts and gaudies, farewell all!*
> *To offices I'd bid adieu*
> *Of Dean, Vice-Praes,—nay Bursar too,*
> *Come tithes, come glebe, come fields so pleasant,*
> *Come sports, come partridge, hare and pheasant.*

Although their Freedom was restricted by the Mortmain Act of 1736, colleges used surplus revenue to purchase advowsons of livings, and improved those in their gift. Fellows eagerly discussed causing vacancies. At Queen's the fellows sometimes lifted their glasses to 'Hampshire rot', signifying their hope that senior members of the colleges, in possession of Queen's livings in that county, might soon die and leave the livings free for the fellows.

Yet, if most of the dons looked forward to marriage and preferment, their lot was not unenviable. They enjoyed a satisfactory stipend; at Lincoln, in 1765, a fellow received, if non-resident, £60 18s 2d. If he were resident, his stipend amounted to little less than £100. The sum varied according to the amount of money brought in by the renewal of farm

---

[1] In 1851 the colleges had some 372 livings at their disposal.

leases. In 1773, a resident fellow, Dr Hallifax, earned £83 4s 1d; he owed the college for battels £43 5s 8d. These were not princely sums—though in richer colleges the amount would be appreciably greater—but they allowed a fellow to live in comfort. College accounts testify to growing, though not excessive, luxury. Rooms were panelled and the furnishings improved, often at the cost of the fellow. Another amenity, a product of post-Restoration Oxford, was the provision of a senior common room (at Lincoln it dates from 1662). Common rooms constituted private clubs. Their affairs were regulated by the members, who defrayed the expenses, not by the College. Common room accounts record the purchase of candles for lighting, of pit coal and sea coal for heating, of punch ladles, clay tobacco pipes, the Oxford Almanack, journals and newspapers. It was there that the fellows foregathered to gossip, drink, play cards and make wagers.

While few Oxford dons were given to research in the modern meaning of the word, time did not necessarily hang on their hands. Some, as we have seen, were conscientious tutors; even in the eighteenth century a fellow of Queen's felt obliged to say 'I have scarce an hour to myself. . . . My place of tutor is a very toilsome and anxious employment.' Accessions to college libraries make plain that many dons were assiduous readers.[1] What with attendance at chapel and the university sermon, reading the journals in the coffee houses, playing cards and gossiping after dinner, the day passed agreeably enough, even without recourse to tuition. For exercise they walked, as Waldegrave did with his pupil, Edward Gibbon, up Headington Hill or in the countryside around Oxford, or rode or, if they were rich enough, hunted. In summer they went, as Woodforde and Wesley were to do, to the races in Port Meadow, and, if the winter was a severe one, as was that of 1763 when a sheep was roasted whole on the ice near High Bridge, they went skating. Music played a greater part in their lives than hitherto. Handel and 'his lowsy crew, a great number of forreign fidlers', as Hearne described them, was invited by the Vice-chancellor to perform at the Act in 1733. 'This is an innovaion', Hearne wrote disapprovingly, 'The Players might be as well permitted to come and act'. It was, however, undoubtedly popular. Nine years later the Music Room was opened in Holywell. 'A taste for Musick, Modern Languages, and other polite Entertainments', an observer commented in 1750 'have succeeded to the Clubs and Bacchanalian Routs.'

[1] Lucy Sutherland has shewn recently that at Exeter in 1786 16 Fellows, and five other members of the college, borrowed 233 books from the library.

But the observer may have been too sanguine. Increasing luxury led to a greater consumption of strong drink, more especially port wine.[1] The 'deep potations', upon which Gibbon remarked censoriously, and which form so inescapable a part of Woodforde's diary, were characteristic of eighteenth-century Oxford life. Such was the impression of a German visitor, Pastor Moritz, in 1782. Finding himself at the Mitre Inn at midnight, he was astonished to find 'a great number of clergymen, all with their gowns and bands on, sitting round a large table, each with his pot of beer before him.' Moritz introduced himself, mentioning that there were sometimes disturbances at German universities. 'O we are very unruly here too', said one of the clergymen, as he took a hearty draught out of his pot of beer, and knocked on the table with his hand. There ensued a long argument about the validity and interpretation of Scripture, whereupon a waiter was called to fetch a Bible. 'The conversation now turned on many different subjects. At last when morning drew near, Mr Maud suddenly exclaimed, d – – n me, I must read prayers this morning at All Souls.' It is hardly surprising to learn that when Mr Modd was chaplain of Corpus, he was to be reproved for drunken behaviour. Nothing could be learned at Oxford, Francis Jeffrey, the future editor of the *Edinburgh Review*, exclaimed on his departure from the university in the 1790s, 'except praying and drinking.'

Dinner in hall was for many dons the principal function of the day. As the century wore on, so its hour became steadily later. Several colleges, Hearne remarked in 1722, had moved their dinner hour from 11.00am to 12.00, 'occasioned from people's lying in bed longer than they used to do.' Dr Newton nominated 1.00pm as the dinner hour in Hertford with supper at 7.00pm. At Trinity in 1792, supper, consisting of boiled fowl, salt herrings, sausages, cold beef, brawn, bread and ale, was at 9.00 pm. Dinner was an occasion both for don and undergraduate. At Balliol, as at other colleges, where dinner by the end of the century was timed for 3.00pm, the young men wore swallow-tail coats, knee breeches, silk stockings and pumps, and their hair was prepared by the college barber, who started his work with the junior freshmen and worked steadily until some hours later he reached the senior fellow.

If the don's life was relatively care-free, so too was that of the contemporary undergraduate. He was naturally subject to college regulations and proctorial discipline. Even John Wesley was once 'progged' for not

[1] In Queen's S.C.R. the annual consumption in 1811 was 1470 bottles of port, 171 of sherry and 48 of madeira in addition to considerable quantities of gin, punch and rum.

wearing an academic cap, while Woodforde was set impositions by his college dean. There was, though to a lesser extent than in the seventeenth century, considerable violence in both town and gown. An undergraduate of Worcester, Mr Gower, was 'mugged' in January, 1756 in a dark passage near the King's Arms; but his assailant turned out to be a young girl, Maria Houghton, who was sent to do six weeks hard labour in Bridewell. Woodforde tells us that on 2 November, 1760, he engaged in fisticuffs with his friend, Macock of Lincoln in the High Street, and two years later 'Webber and myself had a quarrel in the BCR and fought in the garden where he . . . beat me unmercifully.'

But, more or less freed from the demands of university exercises or examinations, the undergraduate could read what he liked, indulge in scholarly study when the inclination suited him or merely pass the time in recreation. There were some industrious youths who spent their time well. Richard Graves of Pembroke found his friends among a 'very sober little party who amused themselves in the evening with reading Greek and drinking water'. 'There is', Dr Sutherland has said, 'ample evidence of diversified intellectual activities among undergraduates both as individuals and groups, some of them intense and having lasting effects.' But others were too easily tempted into idleness. 'Did I tell you the manner of our living here?' Francis Jeffrey, fresh from the astringent atmosphere of Glasgow University, wrote on his arrival at Oxford in 1791. 'We occupy, each of us, our separate apartments, and lock ourselves in at night. At seven o'clock we repair to prayers. . . . That detains us half an hour, after which most of us choose to talk till 9 o'clock, at which hour a George (that is to say a round penny roll) is served up, with a bit of butter, upon a pewter plate, into each of our chambers, where we provide our own tea and sugar. . . . From this time till 3 we do what we please, unless there be any lectures to attend; but, at three, the trumpet's martial voice proclaims the hour of dinner, to which we all repair in the Common Hall, after having ordered, on our way through the kitchen, whatever part of the bill of fare we may choose.' Moralists shook their heads over the possibilities of self-indulgence as well as of idleness. A well-meaning writer addressing a young man of fortune about to enter Oxford in 1784 feared that he might be tempted to join the ranks of those who go seldom 'to [their] tutor's lecture, to hall, and to chapel, who sleep often out of college, who most frequently make schemes to town; who spend most time at tennis, at billiards or on horseback, in shooting or in going up the water; who seldom wear a band and wears all his cloths, but particularly his gown, in the most slovenly fashion.' Bernard Blackmantle, the hero of one of the earliest novels of Oxford life, *The English Spy*, is constantly tempted to go on 'a good prad for a bolt to the village', that is to make for the gay life of London. For Tom Warton it was the joy of the ale-house:

> *My sober ev'ning let the tankard bless,*
> *With toast embrow'nd and fragrant nutmeg fraught;*
> *While the rich draught with oft-repeated whiffs*
> *Tobacco mild improves.*
>
> *Meantime not mindless of the daily task*
> *Of Tutor sage, upon the learned leaves*
> *Of deep* Smiglecius *much I meditate*
> *While ALE inspires, and lends its kindred aid*
>
> . . . .   *But if friends*
> *Congenial call me from the toilsome page,*
> *To Pot-house I repair*
>
> *Nor Proctor thrice with vocal heel alarms*
> *Other joys secure, nor deigns the lowly roof*
> *Of Pot-house snug to visit; wiser he*
> *The splendid Tavern haunts, or Coffee-house.*

At an earlier date, young Harry Fleming of Queen's, had been caught by the vice-chancellor, Dr Halton, the provost of the college, visiting an ale-house and with his companions given the choice of 'whether they would be whipt or turn'd out of their places, and they all chose the latter.' Harry Fleming was pardoned and spent ten years in assiduous study at the university for which he had, in spite of his failure to win a fellowship, deep affection. But his brothers, Roger and James, spent too much money on 'brandy, pipes and tobacco' and were tempted, until they learned she had the *morbus Gallicus*, by the company of 'Eastgate Ginny'. Intellectually the eighteenth-century undergraduate lacked the stimulus, which was so marked a feature of the Scottish universities of the period (except for St Andrews), but he was at least free from some of the competitive pressures which haunt his twentieth-century successor.

The society in which he moved was a strictly stratified one. If the nobleman, splendid in his gold-laced gown and golden tuft, free to get a degree without recourse to university exercises, was a comparative rarity outside Christ Church, there had been a significant increase in the number of fellow and gentlemen-commoners, who in return for higher fees received privileges similar to those enjoyed by the fellows. 'Be pleased to know', Provost Barlow of Queen's wrote in 1670 to Sir James Lowther, advising him to send his grandson as a gentleman-commoner, 'that we have two ranks of gentlemen in the College,[1] (1) Those we call Communars, which are gentlemen of inferior quality usually ... (2) Upper Communars, which usually are Baronets, or Knights sons, or Gentlemen of great fortunes: these have some honorary privileges above ordinary Communars.'

The gentleman-commoner was tempted to adopt a style of living which was both the envy and sometimes the example for men of lesser birth and wealth. Sir Erasmus Phillips, a fellow-commoner of Pembroke in 1720, listened to university declamations occasionally and learned the violin, but much of his time was spent in fox-hunting, cock-fighting, going to horse-races, and riding to Woodstock, Godstow and Nuneham. 'He goes as well-rigged', William Morgan wrote to Wesley of his son, Richard, 'and with as great a quantity of all sorts of apparel as I believe a Gentleman Commoner needs to be furnished with.' Contemporary accounts show that a gentleman-commoner's annual expenditure could be on the high side. Arthur Annesley, admitted at Lincoln in 1750, spent no less than £176 5s on a year's stay at Oxford. His accounts show that he paid £6 for the rent of his room, £12 12s for tuition, £4 4s for the laundress and £41 15s 6d for his battels. Among individual items he expended £4 10s 6d on wine, £3 on ale (previously he had bought a quarter or a hogshead of port for £4 9s 6d), £5 8s at his tailor's, £2 14s on silk hose, £5 1s 6d at the grocer's, £4 14s 6d on a gun, £13 5s on horse-hire, 18s on tea and 3s 4d on two night-caps. The bursar gave him £40 19s out of his allowance for pocket money. He spent £8 7s 4d on books, including 14s for a bible and 10s for a book by Voltaire, and £9 on prints. Another gentleman-commoner, John Robinson, who had matriculated in 1739, spent some £191 in a year, including a payment of £2 10s to his tutor, John Wesley, for tuition.

It was from men of this sort that the university 'smart' was drawn, 'bucks of the first head', as Richard Graves remembered them 'who keep late hours and drank their toasts on their knees.' They had 'not abundance of wit ... but very rich lace, red stockings, silver-buttoned coats, and other

---

[1] At Queen's, which admitted two or three a year in the late seventeenth century, there was a marked increase in the eighteenth century; 7 in 1720, 1725, 1728, 1741, 1771 and 9 in 1732. At Balliol 70 gentlemen-commoners were admitted between 1701 and 1717.

things which constitute a man of taste in Oxford . . .', and indeed only rarely proceeded to a degree.

Doubtless these well-heeled young men formed only a minority in every college. The majority of undergraduates consisted of scholars, drawing a small emolument from the college, and commoners, children of merchants, country-gentlemen and clergy. Graves recalled that at Pembroke there were two sets of men, in addition to the 'bucks', a 'set of jolly, sprightly, young fellows . . . who drank ale, smoked tobacco, punned and sung bacchanalian catches the whole evening', and a 'flying squadron of plain, sensible matter-of-fact men' who 'had come to the university on their way to the Temple, or to get a slight smattering of the sciences before they settled in the country.'

While their expenses would be considerably less than those of the average gentleman-commoner, there were indications that the cost of being at Oxford was rising rapidly. College rooms were often in so poor a state that to make them habitable an undergraduate might have to spend good money, even though the college would later recompense him for a third of the cost. In the 1730s one undergraduate paid an upholsterer's bill of £5 10s. While many rooms remained derelict and uncomfortable, as the *English Spy* makes clear, undergraduates were tempted to spend money on improving their furnishings. When Mr Plomer left his rooms at Lincoln, the inventory showed that his furniture, valued at £12 14s included half a dozen chairs with Spanish leather bottoms, a steel grate, a press and chimney glass, a mahogany table, a mahogany stand, teaboard and music desk, two other chairs, a sugar box and a tea-pot. Contemporary social conventions made many an undergraduate spend money that he could ill afford on dressing his hair—Wesley wore his own hair long to save the expense of a wig—on the hire of horses and on clothes. Mr Black, who paid the barber 12s 6d for shaving him in 1728, spent £1 13s on buckskin breeches and on his shoes. Mr Charlton paid £7 8s for a horse and £1 11s on saddlery. Mr Ryder paid £1 10s for a wig. Samuel Johnson, who went up to Pembroke in October 1728, found that Christ Church men smiled at his tatty shoes and clothes, and lack of money may have caused his premature departure from Oxford.[1]

The situation of the bible-clerk or servitor was the least agreeable of all. In return for reduced fees—it was reckoned that he could save up to £8 a

[1] A commoner, Charles Browne, who matriculated in 1731, spent £90 2s in a year at Oxford. This included £26 3s on his battels and room rent, £17 7s 2d on pocket money, £1 1s on a grate, £1 1s 6d on boots and shoes, £2 12s 6d on breeches and £13 6s 6d to his tailor.

year—he performed menial tasks, calling fellows and undergraduates before morning prayers at 6.00am, waiting at table, lighting fires in fellows' rooms—Wesley once admonished one of his pupils who was bible-clerk for his failure to perform this task—and doing other sundry odd jobs. He was often treated contemptuously by his fellow students. Thomas Brockbank, who became a 'poor boy' at Queen's in 1687, tells us in his diary that it was the 'custom at Queen's for the Seniors to turn the Juniors about the great charcoal fire, and I was so roasted that one of my legs was sore for a long time.' The principal character in Thomas Baker's comedy, *An Act at Oxford* (1704) was a servitor at Brasenose called Chum whose father is described as a 'chimney-sweeper' and his mother as 'a ginger-bread woman'. A poem of similar date (1709), describes the servitor's poor state:

> *Like* Cheesy-Pouch *of* Shon-ap-Shunkin
> *His Sandy Locks with wide* Hiatus,
> *Like Bristles seem'd Erected at as*
> *Clotted with Sweat, the Ends hung down;*
> *And male Resplendent Cape of gown*
> *His coat so greasy was, and torn*
> *That had you seen it, you'd had sworn*
> *'Twas Ten Years old when he was born.*

His room:

> *A Room with Dirt and Cobwebs lin'd*
> *Inhabited, let's see—by Four;*
> *If I mistake not, 'twas no more*
> *Two Buggy-beds*
> *Their Dormer windows with Brown-paper,*
> *Was patched to keep our Northern Vapour.*
> *The Tables broken Foot stood on,*
> *An old* Schrevelius *Lexicon*
> *Here lay together, Authors various,*
> *From* Homer's Iliad, *to* Cordelius
> *And so abus'd was* Aristotle,
> *He only serv'd to stop a Bottle.*

Yet, like Thomas Brockbank, he might learn to ape the tastes and manners of his wealthier contemporaries and, in time, be elected to a fellowship of his college; the famous Hebraist Kennicott, matriculated as servitor at Wadham in 1744. For, once an undergraduate had been admitted, Oxford continued to provide a career open to talent.

VIII

Two Eighteenth-century clerical dons: John Wesley and James Woodforde

Although Wesley and Woodforde were Anglican clergymen and fellows of colleges, their lives were ultimately to follow very different paths. Wesley, never beneficed, became the principal personality in the religious revival. In the formality of his religion, Woodforde epitomised the type of Anglican parson and Oxford don whom Wesley so often criticised. Yet, though so different in character, their Oxford careers have certain common features.

The historian is struck by the sociability of the society to which they belonged. As an undergraduate and young don, Wesley, like Woodforde, rarely breakfasted by himself; he was regular in his attendance at hall dinner and in the senior common room. Woodforde was regularly at the local tavern and spent many evenings in the Bachelors' Common Room at New College. Both took their exercise walking in Oxford and its immediate neighbourhood. They made expeditions on the river, to Binsey, Iffley (where Woodforde played skittles) and Godstow, and rode to Rousham and Blenheim where Woodforde paid 2s 6d to look round the house. Sometimes Woodforde went shooting on the New College estate at Stanton St John, but Wesley confined his more sportive activities, such as hunting and shooting, to visits to his friends, the Kirkhams and Tookers, in the Cotswolds. There were occasions on which Wesley played tennis, and Woodforde was, as the entries in his diary show, an early enthusiast for cricket: 'Peckham', he noted, 'laid me that his first Hands at Crickett (i.e. scoring the first stroke) were better than Bennett, and he was beat.' Both found pleasure in cards, though Woodforde was a daily player at piquet, quadrille, brag, cribbage, beat the knave out of doors, lansquenet—and Wesley eventually gave them up as a waste of time. At Epworth Wesley went dancing, while Woodforde engaged a dancing master at Oxford, Mr Orthman. In his early days Wesley was an avid reader of plays and occasionally visited the theatre in London, and his brother, Charles, seems to have been for a brief period entangled with a designing actress. Both men greatly enjoyed music. Wesley took lessons on the lute and Woodforde, who attended oratorios in the Holywell Music Room, paid the professor of music, Phil Hayes, to give him lessons on the harpsichord. Woodforde, like so many of his contemporaries, was fascinated by unusual exhibitions; a conjuror, a mimic, a man who played 'upon glasses with his fingers' at the King's Arms. With Poor of Oriel he went to the Cross Inn on 18 June 1761, to see 'Thomas Heyne, an Hanoverian, show tricks on cards . . . and a very curious root (viz. a mandrake) found in water, representing a human body.'

While Wesley made the occasional wager in his early years, Woodforde was an assiduous gambler, even if the stakes were small. With his friend, Williams, he bet Peckham five shillings that he would be unable to walk around the Parks in less than half an hour; but he lost, for Peckham accomplished the feat in 26 minutes. On 4 November 1761, Woodforde recorded that another of his friends, Dyer, 'laid Williams 2s 6d that he drank 3 pints of wine in 3 hours, and that he wrote 6 verses out of the Bible right—but he lost. He did it in the B.C.R., he drank all the wine, but could not write for his life—he was immensely drunk about 5 minutes afterwards.'

Neither Wesley nor Woodforde were averse to feminine company. Wesley, an essential romantic, engaged in gentle flirtation with Kitty Hargrave in Axholme, and dallied affectionately with his Cotswold lady friends. Woodforde tells of walks with the Bignall sisters, Nancy and Betty, the daughters of the New College steward, and of the small gifts he made to them, silver thimbles and pairs of scissors. When he was drinking ale in Holywell, a man made some verses on Nancy and himself. Was this the saddler's apprentice, Crozier, whom, five days later, with the help of three college friends, he thrashed for 'franking verses upon me'? Later he courted and hoped to marry a Somerset girl, but 'my dear Betty White' jilted him. After a series of abortive romances, Wesley resigned his fellowship when he married the widow, Molly Vazeille, in 1751, a union that was to prove disastrous for both of them. Other undergraduates were less refined in their choice of female company. When he was pro-proctor, Woodforde apprehended two men in the company of the ladies of the town; and it seems possible that Wesley's protégé at Lincoln, Johnny Whitelamb, was enmeshed with Molly, the Medley lockkeeper's daughter.

Wesley and Woodforde were both to be ordained on the titles of their fellowships as ministers of the Church of England. Wesley's first sermon was preached at South Leigh; he was to hold a curacy at Pyrton near Wallingford and often rode to villages in the neighbourhood of Oxford. Woodforde preached his first sermon at the Buckinghamshire village of Newton Purcell of which he had charge for nine Sundays (as the incumbent, another fellow, Dr Sale, was then acting as proctor), and later he took duty at Chesterton.

It is perhaps at this point that the lines which have so far been parallel begin to diverge. Woodforde's religion was of a formal character. He was a conscientious and kindly pastor, but the tensions which disturbed and enriched Wesley's spiritual life passed him by. He takes the sacrament on the infrequent occasions when it was celebrated in New College chapel, sometimes plays the chapel organ, attends prayers regularly and goes to the university sermon. Nothing in his approach to his ordination suggests that he made any special preparation for it, whereas Wesley engaged in intensive reading and purposeful prayer.

Clerical life hardly changed the monotone of Woodforde's existence. Less than a fortnight after he had preached his first sermon, he was sconced a bottle of wine for throwing some wine in Bedford's face in the B.C.R. (though Bedford had provoked the attack by throwing a cap at Woodforde); next day he took the service at Newton. Perhaps as a young cleric he played cards and wagered less than he had done in his undergraduate days. By the time he was subwarden he was certainly more sober and went to bed at more regular hours. An unfortunate incident, he tells us, had served as a cautionary tale: 'Had three bottles of wine out of my room in the B.C.R. this afternoon', he wrote on 7 September 1763, 'and Waring had another, out of his room. Waring was v. drunk, and Bedford was but little better . . . I was very sober, as I had made a resolution never to get drunk again, when at Geree's rooms in April last, when I fell down dead, and cut my occiput very bad indeed.' The pleasures of the table, however, had already established themselves as one of the main objectives of his day.

With Wesley even as a young man it was far otherwise. He was often depressed by his seeming inability to overcome the sins by which he believed himself to be beset: idleness, intemperate sleep, occasional bouts of ill-temper. He was constantly making vows to overcome them, regretfully noting his failures, underlining his resolution. He followed an ascetic régime that would have appalled Woodforde, resolving to rise at an early hour in the morning, to devote himself to works of religion and scholarship, to diminish the time given to recreation, the amount of food and wine taken at meals.

In 1729 Wesley was called back to be a tutor at Lincoln College. Lincoln was a poor foundation, very different from the wealthy New College where, as in Magdalen and Corpus, before 1854, there were no commoners at all, only scholars and gentleman commoners apart from the numerous fellows, many of whom were elected to their fellowships, like Woodforde, before they completed the course for their degree. At New College the society was governed by the thirteen senior fellows, who would, as Woodforde himself did later, take on the responsibility of college office. All undergraduates, as we have seen, were allotted a tutor who had oversight over his pupils; but non-residence made the appointment of a tutor in the smaller colleges sometimes difficult. Woodforde's tutor at New College was Henry Layng whose fees he paid with some reluctance. Wesley's tutors at Christ Church, George Wigan and Henry Sherman, clearly took their duty seriously, and it was to Sherman that Wesley owed the information that Lincoln was likely to call him back to be a tutor. He had a firm but kindly letter from the rector of the College, John Morley, summoning him from his curacy at Epworth, where he was helping his father, to undertake tutorial duties at Lincoln.

During his tenure of this office, which lasted six years, he was to prove the most conscientious of tutors. 'In the English colleges', he was to write in 1776, 'everyone may reside all the year, as my pupils did: and I should have thought myself little better than a highwayman if I had not teached them every day in the year but Sundays.' He saw his pupils, originally 11 in number, every day, usually either at ten in the mornings or at two or five in the afternoons; even on Sundays and holydays he summoned them to his rooms, probably to give them instruction in religion. He corrects declamations, sets logical problems and advises them on reading matter, drawing up lists of books for them to read. Nor did he confine his attention to purely academic or religious matters. We find him accompanying two of his pupils, Joseph Green, a Bible Clerk whose father lived at Shipton-under-Wychwood where Wesley sometimes took services, and Joseph Goodwin to the *Bear*. One summer's day in August, 1732, he went with another pupil, Richard Bainbridge, to visit Cottisford and Rousham, breaking their journey to call at Middleton Stoney on the rector's son, Benjamin Holloway, who was to enter the college at the start of the following Michaelmas term.

So far Wesley and Woodforde may simply seem to represent two different types of Oxford don, but the evangelistic impulse made Wesley a unique figure. The initiative for founding the Holy Club, which was to enable Wesley to give expression to this motive force, came from his brother, Charles, then a student at Christ Church, who had found the religious complacency of contemporary Oxford more and more frustrating. With a few friends he tried to make his spiritual life more real. They vowed to take Communion more often, to meet together to pray and to read the Scriptures and to foster charitable activities, all things which led their more secular-minded contemporaries to mock them. Whether, without John Wesley, this manifestation of piety would have accomplished very much may be doubted. It was Wesley's return to Lincoln which gave the society a dynamic which made it a vital as well as a much-criticised force in the life of Oxford.

Religious societies had for some time been a not unfamiliar aspect of English parochial life. Why then were the activities of the Holy Club so consequential? Partly because of John Wesley who was to give the society a solid theological foundation, scriptural but also traditional and patristic. Under the guidance of the Holy Spirit genuine Christians could return to the practices of what he and his friends fondly imagined to be the unpolluted apostolic age: regular and frequent acceptance of the sacraments, daily prayer and bible reading, fasting, early rising and acts of charity. The combination of faith and works in this fashion made an immediate impact on the serious-minded young don and undergraduate.

So the scope of the society's work soon expanded. 'I hope to God', John Clayton, a high churchman who was a fellow of Brasenose, told Wesley in 1732, 'we shall get an advocate for us, if not a brother and fellow-labourer in every College in town.' Wesley formed a group in Lincoln, Clayton in Brasenose. They were reinforced by Patten, a young don in Corpus, Watkins, a fellow of Wadham (much concerned to see that justice was done in the case of the unfortunate Warden Thistlethwaite), Kirkham in Merton, Broughton in Exeter and by Clements, a pupil of Wesley's who was elected to a fellowship in Magdalen. They had other sympathisers in Queen's and Jesus, even though the original members of the Holy Club probably numbered no more than five. In spite of growing support, Wesley wrote gloomily to his father of his 'ill-success' which seems to have 'frightened every one away from a falling house', an unduly pessimistic comment at the time that it was made in 1733.

The Holy Club represented an attempt to reawaken the conscience of what seemed to its adherents a sleeping university. Under the enthusiastic guidance of William Morgan of Christ Church, its members visited the prisoners in the Oxford Castle and in the debtors' prison, the Bocardo. 'On Sunday', John told his father on 11 December 1730, 'they had prayers and a sermon at the Castle; on Christmas Day we hope they will have a dinner; and the Sunday after a Communion.' They helped the prisoners to get legal advice and brought them food and fuel as well as religious tracts. 'We c'ant compass Thomas Burgesses liberty yet, though it seems to have a fairer show than formerly.' They tried to raise money to help pay the debts of those who were languishing in the Bocardo. They taught the prisoners and their children how to read. They held services and gave religious instruction; one prisoner was confirmed by the bishop at Cuddeson at Wesley's instance.

Such activities were increasingly criticised. They showed a degree of enthusiasm which reminded some Anglican dons of the sects. Their social concern had unfortunate undertones. Wesley became deeply involved in the case of one Thomas Blair who had been charged in the autumn of 1732 'for an assault on the body of Hugh Sanderson(?) with intent to commit sodomy.' Mr Horn, a friend of Wesleys, 'and I', Thomas Wilson noted in his diary on 22 November 1732, 'had rather a warm dispute about the Methodists taking the part of Blair who was found guilty of Sodomitical Practices and fined 20 marks by the Recorder. Whether the man is innocent or no they were not proper judges, it was better that he should suffer than such a scandal given on countenancing a man whom the whole town think guilty of such an enormous crime.' But such a view would have shocked Wesley. He continued to show an intense interest in the unfortunate Blair, who had pleaded not guilty and who was now incarcerated until his fine was paid, only to endure persecution from his fellow prisoners. In addition to seeking legal advice, he visited the vice-chancellor, perhaps principally to explain why the Methodists were interesting themselves in the case. Blair languished in gaol until he was discharged early in the New Year, 1733; but entries in Wesley's diary for some months reveal the deep compassion by which he was moved. Perhaps he recalled that the chaplain of Merton, Mr Pointer, 'long suspected of sodomitical practices', had in November, 1732, only been required to leave the college to t ake duty at his Northamptonshire living.

It is interesting to compare Woodforde's attitude to crime and punishment. He regularly attended the assize sermon and the subsequent trials. When in 1761, the well-known highwayman, Dumas, was up before the court, Woodforde and his friends tried to be present at the trial, and when they discovered that the vice-chancellor and proctors had forbidden gownsmen to attend, they 'hallowed and hissed' the offending university officials. In March 1762, he made a special visit to the Castle to see 'Shadrach Smith, a Gipsy . . . condemned' to death, but was evidently so little moved that in the next entry in his diary he comments on the high prices charged by his tailor. In February 1768, he went with his friends to the Castle to visit a highway robber, Mr Cartwright; 'he drank with us the last bottle, and smoaked a pipe with us, and seemed very sorry for what he had committed.' But when, on 13 March 1775, he went to watch the execution of a murderer, it was partly as a pro-proctor, for he rebuked two undergraduates 'for wearing different capes to their coats', and partly as an observer of a spectacle. 'He confessed . . . the Crime for which he suffered, . . . A Methodist prayed for him in the cart some time under the gallows.' 'I think', Woodforde confessed, 'I never saw such Sullenness and Villainy in one Face' but, once it was over, he quickly forgot it in the routine activities of the day.

It is easy to understand why the Methodists' activities seemed to contemporaries to smell of hypocrisy. They pretended, as one said, 'to be more religious than their neighbours . . . they put a gloomy and melancholy face upon Religion, and affected greater Austerities and Exemplariness, than the Doctrines of the Gospel requir'd.' Although they had initially enjoyed the goodwill of the bishop of Oxford, the vice-chancellor and the rector of Lincoln, the courteous Dr Euseby Isham, they found criticism growing steadily. When a young protégé of Wesley's, William Smith, was elected to a fellowship at Lincoln, Clayton declared exaggeratedly that he went in danger of physical assault. Nor did the tragic history of one of the original members of the Holy Club, William Morgan, augur well for the society's future. His actions became more and more unbalanced, his health deteriorated and eventually he died. In his last illness, it was reported, 'he spoke often of the Wesleys: "Oh religious madness!" that they had hindered him from throwing himself out of the window.' To blame the Wesleys for what happened was unjust, as even the boy's father admitted, but two of Wesley's colleagues at Lincoln, Hutchins and Farrar, told John of the sinister rumours that were circulating about the Holy Club. At once he wrote a lengthy letter to Morgan's father, explaining fully what the Holy Club was seeking to do, and sought interviews with the bishop of Oxford and the vice-chancellor. A hostile letter appeared in the local newspaper, *Fog's Journal*, 9 December 1732, which produced a vigorous rejoinder, defending the Oxford Methodists, probably from the pen of William Law.

But it would take more than a tract, however well written, to remove the slur. Even in the last decade of the century the unpopular rector of Lincoln, Dr Tatham, got drunk at a college gaudy to prove, as he put it, that 'he was no damned Methodist!' A cloud of suspicion was to engulf the Methodists for years to come. Wesley's colleagues could not rid themselves of the belief that he was using his position as tutor to indoctrinate his pupils. His diary, it must be admitted, does something to justify the charge. It shows Wesley recommending the reading of pious books, early rising, and attendance at Holy Communion; and it indicates how firm Wesley could be with recalcitrant pupils. Remonstrances gave rise to emotional scenes ending in reconciliation and new resolutions.

The elder Morgan, convinced of Wesley's rectitude, had somewhat ingenuously consigned his younger son, Richard, to his care. Unlike his brother, Richard wanted to be a 'smart' and soon tired of his tutor's kind but vigilant supervision. Wesley tried to ensure that Richard made the right friends, introducing him to his devout pupils, taking him to Blenheim in their company and laying down a course of good books for his edification. 'Mr Morgan', he told Richard's father complacently, 'usually rises about six. . . . He seldom goes out of College unless upon business or to walk for his health. . . . He loses no time at taverns or coffee-houses.' But Richard was increasingly frustrated by his tutor's presence at his shoulder, and, in a moment of depression, wrote a virulent letter to his father, complaining of Wesley's over-religious attitude. 'By becoming his pupil I am stigmatized with the name of a Methodist, the misfortune of which I cannot describe.' Unfortunately Wesley visited Morgan's rooms in his absence, saw and read the letter and wrote straightaway to the father. The elder Morgan responded sensibly and coolly. 'What Dick', he told Richard, 'did you so soon forget our stipulations and conditions on your going to the university, as to carry a greyhound with you to Oxford, and to attempt keeping him in your college, contrary to the rules of it? Did you not promise to stick to your studies and be as subservient to your tutor as if you were a servitor?' After some tearful, emotional scenes, Morgan agreed to conform to his tutor's wishes. He had, as Wesley put it feelingly in his diary for 17 March 1734, 'overborne' him. Richard Morgan was to be among those who went to Gravesend to bid the Wesleys farewell when they left for Georgia, and he wrote from Oxford, where his ostentatious habit of fasting annoyed the rector of Lincoln, that he only wished that he could join the brothers.

Wesley's decision to leave Oxford was a decisive event in his career, reflecting that persistent feeling of dissatisfaction which was not to be over-come until the conversion experience of 24 May 1738. 'Primitive Christian-ity', as his friends in the Cotswolds so appositely called him, had not really found spiritual happiness. The Holy Club had had too meagre success. He was depressed by the failure of his essays in love: Kitty Hargrave, Sally Chapone, the beautiful and cultured widow, Mrs Pendarves. His father suggested that he might succeed him as rector of Epworth, but the thought of that bleak but well-loved terrain filled him only with foreboding, nor had he any wish to resign his fellowship which would cut his links with the university. And so he sailed for Georgia to become a chaplain for the Society for the Propagation of Christian Knowledge in succession to the Rev Mr Quincey whose pastoral work suffered from the disadvantage of his having seduced his serving-maid.

In a sense Wesley's departure from Oxford brings the story of Oxford Methodism, in so far as it was a significant force in the university, to a close. The Holy Club continued to have the support of young dons, like Charles Kinchin of Corpus and Broughton of Exeter, and was maintained for a time by the enthusiasm of George Whitefield of Pembroke; but its impact was fading. Wesley was to remain a fellow of Lincoln until his marriage in 1751; but his visits to his university and colleges became increasingly in-frequent as his preaching found a wider and different audience. 'There is', he wrote to his former pupil, James Hervey, from his college on 21 November 1738 'a general shaking of the Dry Bones; and not a few of them stand up and live.' Hervey wrote back, urging Wesley to settle in a parish, only to evoke a passionate response. 'I cou'd not serve . . . a cure now. I have tried, and know it is impracticable, to observe the Laws of ye English Church, in any Part of England. . . . Set the matter in another Light, and it comes to a short issue. I everywhere see GOD's People perishing for lack of knowledge. I have power (thro' GOD) to save their Souls from Death. Shall I use it, or shall I let them perish—"because they are not of my Parish".' He preached one final sermon before the university in 1744, almost sensationally critical of the shortcomings of contemporary Oxford, and was never to be asked to preach in St Mary's Church again.

Yet one further episode in Oxford Methodism requires mention. In 1768 a small group of pious undergraduates at St Edmund Hall, sub-sidised by Lady Huntingdon, fell out with their vice-principal, John Higson. The men had been admitted by the principal, Dr Dixon, with whom Higson's relations were strained. When Higson remonstrated with Dixon for admitting the men because of their Methodist affiliations,

Dixon replied that 'if there were Methodists, or had preached in Methodist meetings, he thought none the worse of them.' Higson determined to secure evidence to support his suspicions in the hope that he could get them expelled from the university. He was helped by a former member of the college, a Mr Blackham of Newport, Salop, where one of the young men, Thomas Jones, lived, having made for Blackham a 'very good periwig which I now wear.' Artfully Higson tried to suggest that the men were not literate enough to make a successful use of the university course.

The principal was displeased at Higson's zeal, aware that it was in some sense directed against himself; but he advised Higson to put on a series of lectures on the Thirty-nine Articles at nine in the evenings 'that he might satisfy himself whether they held any erroneous opinions.' Nor were the young men better pleased, since this was the hour when they usually met to read the Bible at the house of a townswoman, Mrs Durbridge. Although one of the young men, Erasmus Middleton, told Higson that he would absent himself from the lectures, urging that it was 'like being sent to the Gallies', Higson at least had the satisfaction of knowing that the men held extreme Calvinistic views on the doctrines of election, reprobation and grace.

The tutor was a determined and ill-balanced man. He thought himself, as he said, 'obliged in conscience, both to the Church of England and the University to lay the whole of this affair before the vice-chancellor as Visitor of the Hall.' He managed, without difficulty, to show that the men were neither very literate nor learned; but it was less easy to demonstrate that they were inimical to the Church of England. The evidence was ill-assorted and of dubious reliability. One undergraduate declared that one of the accused, Mr Matthews, never made responses in Chapel. A Mr Bromehead remarked, a trifle reluctantly, that another, Mr Grove, had been heard to say that the prayers of the Church of England were 'cold and dead letters'. The testimony of one hostile witness, Mr Welling of St John's, became suspect when it was learned that he had himself asserted that he would preach any doctrine, Methodist or Deist, for £500 a year, murmuring 'This hum of religion! this hum of religion!' Later, on 10 May 1768, Welling was obliged to make a public apology in the presence of Congregation, explaining that what he had said was uttered 'in liquor' after St John's Gaudy.

The vice-chancellor's action in expelling the six Methodists from the university provoked an outcry. Dr Johnson, like Horace Walpole, approved. 'Sir', Johnson thundered, 'that expulsion was extremely just and proper. What have they to do at an University who are not willing to be taught, but will presume to teach.' But for many it confirmed their belief that the Church's monopoly of higher education was disadvantageous for the nation.

None of these events find any mention in Woodforde's diary, but there can be little doubt where his sympathies would have been. He bought a copy of a sermon preached by Dr John Free at St Mary's on Whit Sunday, 1758, strongly critical of Methodist preachers. 'Pity', he had told his congregation, 'that such an *inspired* APOSTLE should prove so extravagantly foolish and ridiculous.

> *He sends his wanton lambs, a* thousand *kisses*
> *Pray! to the* Masters? *Sir, or to the* Misses?

'The name', said Free of Methodism, 'was first given to a few particular Persons, who affected to be so uncommonly Methodical as to keep a Diary of the most insignificant and trivial Actions of their Lives such perhaps, as how many Slices of Bread and Butter they eat with their *Tea*, how many *Dishes* of Tea they drank, how many *Country-dances* they called at their *Dancing Club* or after a *Fast*, the Number of *Pounds* they might devour in a Leg of Mutton.' Could any quotation more aptly describe Woodforde's own diary? But he was apparently not deterred, for Free's views were similar to his own, and he went to listen to the Assize sermon which Free was to preach in March 1762.

In effect Oxford's religious life was to be determined by its Woodfordes rather than by its Wesleys. In spite of the immense attraction of his diary, his native charity and kindliness, Woodforde was basically a dull man, unimaginative, self-indulgent, conventional, and in his very mediocrity he mirrored an age in Oxford's history.

IX

Reaction and Reform, 1789-1878

State of the university in the early nineteenth century

The French Revolution, finding few sympathisers in Oxford, helped to consolidate the alliance between the university, the Church and the crown which had re-emerged in George III's reign. It did not need French émigré priests, granted hospitality at Oxford, to stress that revolutionary politics were anti-religious and were designed to destroy ancient institutions. Senior members who volunteered to defend their city and university against possible French invaders were reviewed by the Duke of York on Port Meadow and received their colours from the chancellor. Once peace was re-established in 1814, Oxford honoured Britain's allies against Napoleon, bestowed honorary degrees on their leaders with becoming pageantry, flattered them in poor verse and dined them in solemn panoply in the Radcliffe Camera.

The alliance between the government in power and the university was to be maintained during the first three decades of the nineteenth century. Oxford was anxious that Catholicism and Nonconformity should be contained, that the control which the Church of England exercised over its life should remain inviolate.

> *Why blame the dons, who never yet gave way*
> *To upstart theories of modern day,*
> *They prize what ages past was held in fame,*
> *And ages hence shall find them still the same.*
>
> *No—rather prove how England's Church must fall*
> *When toleration pours her balm on all;*
> *With good old maxims rear the Mitre's hope,*
> *Teach him to address the Monarch, curse the Pope;*
> *With bless'd 'No Popery' make each College ring,*
> *And pray for Stalls, and Tythes, and Church, and King.*

The university of Oxford, William Sewell of Exeter asserted in 1834, 'has been for years the recognized minister of the Christian Church as existing in this country before the corruption of Popery.' The close alliance between the university and the established Church was therefore an essential bulwark against the intrusion of 'false doctrine and heresy'.

> No, Oxford—secure from apostacy's stain,
> Thou hast been, thou art, and thou shalt be, our pride
> And if she must fall, ye fall side by side!
> Whoever their faith and their honour fight
> Old England shall say, Oxford stands by me yet!

It was, however, an open question how long Oxford's love match with the government would last, and how long too the Anglican monopoly of its life could remain intact. The university's choice of Grenville as its chancellor in succession to Portland in 1809 had been unfortunate since the great Whig noble was already a spent force. Suspect of favouring Roman Catholic Emancipation, Grenville's dilute liberalism made little appeal to the Oxford residents. They were better served by their parliamentary burgess, Sir William Scott, distinguished as a former tutor, Camden professor and friend of Dr Johnson, and his colleague, Charles Abbot, the Speaker, both Tories of unimpeachable integrity. But the conversion of Abbot's successor, Sir Robert Peel, once the darling of Christ Church, to the cause of Roman Catholic Emancipation, was regarded by many as a betrayal of the principles of protestantism. His critics found a fitting opponent at the next parliamentary election in the sincere Evangelical, Sir Robert Inglis, formerly Sidmouth's parliamentary secretary, who emerged victorious by 755 votes to 609. The university's rejection of Peel marked the close of the understanding which had for the past half century bound together government and university in a common cause. Henceforth Oxford was likely to be on the defensive against the government rather than working in collaboration with it.

In a rapidly changing England, full of the groundswell of political reform, its trade burgeoning as a result of industrialisation, Oxford seemed to many to be tied to an earlier age, affluent, idle, Anglican, aristocratic, having, in the minds of its radical critics, none more astringent than Sir William Hamilton in the authoritative pages of the *Edinburgh Review*, all the defects of moribund privilege. Fellows were still elected because of their regional qualifications and family connections and with too little regard to scholarship. Once elected, the majority had no obligation to pursue either a course of study or research, retaining their positions until a college living offered an opening for preferment and the opportunity of marriage. At most colleges many fellows were non-resident and one or two sufficed for the instruction of undergraduates. In default of adequate college teaching, men, who were keen on getting a good degree, employed at their own expense a private tutor, 'the crutches of our lame system', as Whately described them. Even Charles Larkyns in *Verdant Green*, that entertaining novel of Oxford life, sought a private tutor in the hope of winning a First in his finals. 'Within the last three or four years', G. O. Morgan said in 1850, 'there have been few instances of undergraduates obtaining a Pass Degree, and scarcely any other obtaining high honours, without having previously received assistance from a Private Tutor.'

The teaching provided by the university was negligible. Edward Nares, who was told by Lord Liverpool on his appointment as regius professor of modern history that he was expected to lecture, tried to fufil his duties with moderate conscientiousness, but lack of an audience, the difficulty of securing a room in which to lecture, led him to retire more and more to the comforts of his country rectory. 'For some time', he told the vice-chancellor in 1832, 'I complied with all the rules, and at so great expense, by the removal of my family, hire of expensive lodgings, and payment of a curate at home, as to exceed the income, and certainly without any material benefit to any member of the University, being sometimes unable to procure any class, and at best so uncertain a one that long before I could get through 20 lectures, many were called away to college collections, public examinations, or to attend upon private tutors.' The professors of science lacked laboratories, and even the most elementary apparatus with which to conduct experiments. Dr Daubeny, the professor of chemistry, was allocated the lower room of the Ashmolean Museum for his use in 1817, and, when he requested additional accommodation, he was offered a share of the keeper's kitchen with the use of the common pump. After rejecting the offer as 'humiliating to science', he equipped some rooms at his own expense.

Even Oxford's claim to be the 'nursery of the Church of England', whence, as Henry Wilberforce put it in 1835, 'a succession of men may constantly issue ... with minds well stored with the wisdom of former times', was criticised. Oxford was still a predominantly clerical society. In 1851, some 18 out of 19 heads (Merton was the exception) and 349 out of 542 fellows were in Holy Orders, at Queens the entire society, at Lincoln 11 out of 12, at Magdalen, 33 out of 40, at Corpus 16 out of 20, at

Worcester 20 out of 21. A very high proportion of undergraduates were ordained.[1] But the university's critics underlined the worldliness of the dons and the inadequacy of its instruction in theology. Worse perhaps, was the narrow sectarianism, as it seemed to the critics of the university, which obliged all members of the university to subscribe to the Thirty-nine Articles, both at matriculation and on taking degrees. This, they said, was a requirement which the Church of England did not even demand of its lay members.

A senior common room was still very much like what it had been in the eighteenth century, a pleasant, masculine, clerical club, sometimes split by wrangles among the fellows, but for the most part a congenial society, comparatively youthful, respectable and plain-living. While no fellow's stipend could fairly entitle him to be called affluent, many colleges had large revenues which, their critics held, were not efficiently used to promote education. After 1812 the number of undergraduates increased rapidly, though the entry still remained very small in some colleges. Besides, though there were scholarships and exhibitions, the cost of Oxford education remained high.

There were other publicised grounds of complaint. Oxford seemed given over, less so than a superficial survey might at first suggest, to the children of the relatively rich. Save in exceptional circumstances, it seemed difficult, if not impossible, for a poor boy to attend the university. The religious qualification which confined its membership to Anglicans, barring Nonconformists, Jews and Roman Catholics, was bitterly criticised. If the graduates of Oxford constituted an élite, it was determined less by intellectual excellence than by the hazards of birth, religion and wealth. Towards the new university of London Oxford adopted a patronising, hostile attitude. Moreover, as Adam Smith had remarked long ago, Oxford's learning seemed ill-adapted to the needs of an increasingly industrialised and commercialised society. There were probably few thoughtful men who held that the university should change its curriculum to serve the mechanical arts, but its narrow courses, its reluctance to admit the existence of Science, let alone Modern Languages, English, History and

[1] The number of Oxford ordinances was slightly below those from Cambridge; between 1850 and 1870, varying from 215 in 1851 to 120 in 1862, averaging *c.* 170. At Brasenose between 1868 and 1877 some four-ninths of the men took Orders. The figures for Lincoln may be regarded as representative. Of 130 entrants between 1830 and 1839, 80 became clergy; 1840–49, 92 out of 150; 1850–59, 61 out of 125; 1860–69, 59 out of 180; 1870–79, 50 out of 177; 1880–89, 72 out of 198. The close connection between the university and the established Church was underlined by the number of sons of clerical families among the entrants: 75 out of 370 in 1835, 118 out of 394 in 1860 and even in 1885 175 out of 749 matriculands came from clerical homes.

Law, diminished its claims to train undergraduates even for those careers for which they were likely to be destined.

Oxford residents were, however, not merely aware of these problems but in their own cautious way were setting their house in order. The atmosphere of Oxford in the 1820s was neither obscurantist nor indifferent, even though pockets of deep conservatism existed in some colleges, but surprisingly buoyant and optimistic. The Hebdomadal Board had already —in 1801—introduced an Honours Examination, in Literae Humaniores and Mathematics, taken by only a small percentage of the finalists, but constituting a major change, for this was the seedbed of the modern examination system.[1] Professors began to take their duties more seriously. 'We, about 20 fellows sit all about in his library', Hurrell Froude wrote of the lectures of Charles Lloyd, the professor of divinity, in 1826, '... and he walks up and down in the middle, sometimes taking his station between one fellow and sometimes before another asking them questions quite abruptly to catch them being inattentive and amusing himself with kicking their shins. .... Sometimes he pulls the ears of the man he is very intimate with. Most of the class are first and double firsts, the greater part of them are masters of arts and a pro-proctor contributes his dignity to the honours of the august assembly.' The scene is not perhaps wholly impressive, but it was an augury of the future.

Individual colleges took greater care over admissions and elections to fellowships. The reputation of Christ Church, under the princely rule of Cyril Jackson, mounted steadily, not merely because it was the home of the aristocratic *jeunesse dorée* but because it was a nursery of true scholarship and good tutors. Oriel, under provosts Eveleigh and Copleston, threw open its fellowships to competitive examination, making its elections on grounds of promise rather than achievement. Its senior common room became the most highly reputed in the university, not merely because the future Tractarians, Keble, Newman, Froude, Pusey, were numbered among its fellows but because in the group of dons known as the Noetics, it promoted the spirit of rational enquiry. The Oriel common room became not a 'mere place of resort for relaxation and recreation, but a

[1] The examination for the first Honour School was still mainly oral (in 1802 2 candidates, in 1805 1 candidate were given honours), but became a written examination. In 1807 it was split into two parts, Classics and Mathematics, both of which had to be taken for a degree. Class lists were introduced, first and seconds, a third class in 1809 and a fourth in 1830. In 1808 Responsions or 'Smalls' (by contrast with Greats, the final examination) was instituted and taken between the third and seventh terms. Moderations, taken between Responsions and the final examination, was introduced in 1850.

school for sharpening the argumentative process.' The leader in this was the colourful Richard Whately, good-humoured but rough, to be seen striding in Christ Church meadow before breakfast, accompanied by his huge dog whom he taught to climb the trees and drop into the river below. Whately, later archbishop of Dublin, argued for an entrance examination into the university. 'Unless we secure men's coming here tolerably grounded in elementary knowledge', he said, 'we must ever remain as is too much the case now, in great measure a school, and a bad school too, rather than a university.'

Such was the impact which the new look made that it became difficult to secure immediate entry at the more highly reputed colleges. Gladstone had to spend nearly a year after leaving Eton before he was admitted to Christ Church and even so found that a grim, dirty and dark set of rooms was the only set available. Pattison had to wait before a place was vacant at Oriel. At Balliol there was sometime as much of a wait as four years. Other colleges could not ignore the signs of the time. Even a modest conservative college like Lincoln introduced some sort of examination for its fellowships. For the first time in university history, college tutors began to pride them-selves on the distinctions which their pupils gained in the examination lists. 'You would', Edward Hawkins, provost of Oriel, told Lord Radnor in 1835, 'congratulate the country, that the University has, within the present century, carried so many serious reforms with effect (and that before reform was at all in fashion), rather than express surprise that matters of inferior moment yet remain to be considered.' 'Only', he pleaded, 'leave us to ourselves.'

Such changes were cautious and moderate; to the radical critics of the university they appeared trivial and niggling. The university still remained a bastion of the Church of England; its studies still seemed only partially relevant to the age. In effect the gradual changes in the syllabus and the system of examinations created new problems. Colleges which had hitherto managed with one or two tutors no longer found it possible to provide adequate instruction for their men, in both classical and mathe-matical studies. The replacement of oral by written examinations meant that there was a greater emphasis on composition, less on construing. Many colleges, more especially the poor ones, found that they had too many fellows who were unable to take their part in the additional teaching load, nor, educated as many had been under the old system, were they necessarily competent to do so.

The Tractarians

In any case the movement for reform was to be overshadowed, and in some cases deflected from its objects, for two decades, by the onset of religious controversy. The Tractarian movement, taking its name from the tracts with which its leaders propagated their religious views, was principally a reaction against the seeming sterility of the university's religious life. Nourished in a scholarship that seemed often to be romantic rather than profound, rooted in the writings of the fathers and the Caroline divines, the Tractarians looked back towards the Church in apostolic and later times before its unity was fractured by the Reformation. They wanted a theological and spiritual revival, founded on apostolic and catholic teaching, which would combat the infidelity and rationalism of the age. As far as the university was itself concerned, they desired, as Wesley had at an earlier period, to purge the senior common rooms of their worldliness and to persuade tutors to fulfil their moral and spiritual responsibilities. They mistrusted reform as likely to reduce the religious ethos of Oxford and to promote some degree of secularism.

The Tractarian leaders were men of intelligence and ability, capable of evoking enthusiasm among young dons and impressionable undergraduates. Although in 1833 the movement's doyen, Keble, was 41, his colleagues were still comparatively young men, E. B. Pusey, 33, Newman, 32, Froude, 30, Isaac Williams, 31. Keble was a gentle saint, highly moral and very devout, a popular if overrated poet, with a good if unadventurous mind; he had withdrawn with some relief from Oriel where he had been a fellow since 1811 to a rural pastorate. Hurrell Froude, the son of the formidable Archdeacon of Totnes, was essentially a Romantic, a man of intense feelings for whom Tractarianism seemed an emotional as well as an intellectual catharsis. 'One of the acutest and cleverest and deepest men in memory of man' was Newman's comment after his election to a fellowship at Oriel in 1826. His charm and good looks made him widely liked and an early death gave him a haloed image. His posthumous *Remains*, so critical of the teaching of the reformers, confirmed the fears of the movement's Protestant critics that its inclinations were papistical.

J. H. Newman, a softer flame, sensitive, intelligent, refined, a spellbinder in words, devout yet, as so many contemporaries felt, in some indefinable way devious, was the prophet, the nonpareil of Tractarian Oxford. Impressionable young men copied his every movement. But it was Pusey, canon of Christ Church, regius professor of Hebrew, who gave Tractarianism solidity and scholarship. Scion of aristocratic stock, brought up, like Newman and Gladstone, in a fervently Evangelical background, Pusey found his proposed marriage to Maria Barker forbidden by his father. His frustration found expression in hard work and travel. He acquired an unrivalled knowledge of contemporary German theology, passed through a liberal phase, but a liberalism quickly stemmed by the 'deadly breath of infidel thought.' His eventual marriage brought personal happiness, but his deep seriousness was transmitted to his wife who became as devout as her husband. Austere and guilt-ridden, Pusey seemed to many, not wholly without justification, curiously inhumane. His son, Philip, was constantly chastised. His daughter, Mary, was once tied to a bed post for mispronouncing a word in a lesson and lashed, sometimes four times a day, until on the eleventh day she got the word right. His wife's death left him narrowly entrenched in a pietist position, preoccupied with sin and salvation. Yet, for all his shortcomings, Pusey was a man of great integrity, with an overwhelming, deep and abiding faith in the catholicity of the Church of England, passionately concerned to preserve her from all enveloping Erastianism and infidelity.

Politically the Oxford movement was a protest against the political and social reforms introduced by Lord Grey's Whig government, which seemed to many to harbinger future attacks on the Church (and it was the government's interference with the Irish bishoprics which led Keble to preach his famous assize sermon at St Mary's in 1833) and the universities. They protested vigorously at Lord Melbourne's attempt to appoint a liberal theologian, the dull Dr Hampden, to the regius chair of divinity, and managed to persuade Convocation to pass a motion deleting Dr Hampden's name from the committee for the nomination of select preachers before the university. The proctors at first vetoed the move, as they were entitled to do, but when it was put forward again in May, 1838, it was passed by 474 votes to 94.

In its initial stages Tractarianism's opposition to liberalism was regarded sympathetically by many Evangelicals. Together they managed to defeat a sensible proposal of the Hebdomadal Board to substitute a general declaration of belief for the subscription to the Thirty-nine Articles required at matriculation. The proposal seemed to them a direct challenge not merely to the Church of England but to the Christian faith itself, a 'deliberate attempt', as Sewell of Exeter asserted, 'to undermine the foundations and bulwarks of our religion.' The Thirty-nine Articles, Eden of Oriel said, were 'beacons scattered over a dangerous coast which the perversity of human mind and human will has invested with danger', more especially dangerous to impressionable youth. In 1865 the proposed declaration of assent found only 57 votes in its favour to 459 against.

> *This vile declaration, we'll never embrace it,*
> *We'll die ere we yield—die shouting 'Non Placet'.*

But the Catholic theology of the Tractarians soon drove a wedge in the conservative ranks. As a result the Evangelicals made common cause with the 'high and dry' clergy, so strong in the senior common rooms, to bring pressure on the Hebdomadal Board in the hope that it could find a means of stemming a movement that seemed Romeward in direction.

It was against such a background that the seemingly unwise and un-justified policy of the Hebdomadal Board has to be placed. When Newman's *Tract XC* was published, purporting to show that the Anglican formularies were not out of line with the Tridentine decrees, there was a furore which the heads could not ignore. Golightly persuaded four Oxford tutors to confute Newman's arguments and pressed the heads to state that they were 'inconsistent with the due observance of the statutes of the university.' Even more indiscreetly, they suspended Pusey from preaching before the university for two years for a sermon on the Eucharist which one of Pusey's fellow canons, the Lady Margaret professor, Faussett, delated to the vice-chancellor as heretical. Unjustified the heads may have been, but they were not improbably correct in estimating that Tractarian-ism was a failing cause in Oxford. The Tractarians had failed in 1842 to get one of their number, Isaac Williams, elected to the chair of poetry. Newman's resignation of the vicarage of St Mary's and his retirement to the semi-monastic community at Littlemore grievously weakened the movement. Two years later, in 1845, the publication of W. G. Ward's ponderously learned *Ideal of the Christian Church* again promoted an outcry, resulting in the condemnation of the book and the deprivation of the author of his degrees. But an attempt to associate with this a condemnation of *Tract XC* was foiled by the proctors' veto to the tumultuous cheers of juniors and seniors alike. On 9 October 1845, the Passionist, Father Dominic, received Newman into the Roman Catholic Church.

It was not the end of the Oxford movement which was to re-invigorate the life of the English Church at parochial level, but, as far as Oxford was concerned, the religious crisis was past. 'It was a deliverance', as Pattison recalled in his *Memoirs*, 'from the nightmare which had oppressed Oxford for 15 years. For so long we had been given over to discussions unprofitable in themselves, and which had entirely diverted our thoughts from the true business of the place.' Oxford had, however, re-emerged from the time-absorbing controversy in a dazed state. To many the heads of houses had demonstrably displayed their inability to cope with the situation. To others it seemed as if a decade or more had been lost, for in the interval comparatively little had been achieved in the way of academic reform.

University reform

Although the Whig governments had abstained from interfering with the university, the chorus of criticism grew steadily stronger. It was with the knowledge that it needed a sure defender that the masters chose Wellington to be chancellor on Grenville's death in 1834. The duke, who was no scholar, had no particular liking for Oxford. Christ Church had recently rusticated his son Lord Charles Wellesley, and the duke had promptly sent him to Cambridge—and he was at first reluctant to stand. Yet his great reputation, his intrepid opposition to parliamentary reform, the hope that he would stand firmly in defence of the Church and university, made his election a foregone conclusion. His installation was a great personal triumph, attracting many who would otherwise have been at Ascot for the races.

The conservative temper of Oxford made major reforms unlikely. When in July 1835, a parliamentary bill providing for the abolition of subscriptions (to the Thirty-nine Articles) was defeated by 163 votes to 57, Oxford opinion greeted the outcome warmly. The more radical of the university's critics, not much convinced by the modest reforms already achieved, were becoming more sure that the university had neither the will nor the capacity to reform itself and began to clamour for parliament to intervene. In the spring of 1837, Lord Radnor, alleging that the colleges misinterpreted their statutes and misused their endowments, unsuccessfully demanded the setting up of a royal commission. For a while Wellington readily defended Oxford's privileges and sought to protect its interests, but he was sufficiently realistic, as a soldier and politician, to foresee that there was no point in seeking to defend indefensible positions. If the university was to continue to enjoy a privileged position, it must demonstrate its efficiency. How many college statutes, he enquired, were in fact obsolete? To what extent had genuine abuses been remedied? Could subscription to the Thirty-nine Articles at matriculation really be justified?

The Hebdomadal Board took the hint but found their constituents, many still immersed in theological discussion, unresponsive. The heads suggested that colleges should revise their statutes and proposed to set in train a revision of the statutes of the university. The colleges' response was an angry one. They repudiated the action of the university in seeking to dictate what they should do as interference with their independence. They urged that the reform of the statutes of the university was itself a prerogative of the Convocation and threw out such modest proposals, as the setting up of two new schools, of Natural Sciences and of Political Sciences, each to be taken as an option after Greats—as the Board presented to Congregation. The only outcome of a decade of discussion was the establishment of two new professorships, of ecclesiastical history and pastoral theology, in 1842, and the institution of a voluntary theological examination for ordinands.

Although the university was after 1845 freed from the deep religious tensions which had mastered it during the previous decade, the situation was confused. The Tractarians were still influential under Pusey's lead, but their forces were in disarray. The lead in university politics had passed to the Evangelicals, led by Ben Symons and Pusey's brother-in-law, Dr Cotton of Worcester, and to the Liberals. The latter formed a strong minority group, headed by able and intelligent men, Vaughan, A. P. Stanley, W. C. Lake, Liddell, Goldwin Smith, Mark Pattison, H. B. Wilson and Francis Jeune, the master of Pembroke. Halford Vaughan, much influenced by contemporary scientific and advanced intellectual ideas, was developing strong views about what should be done. He had been elected to a fellowship at Oriel, but his unwillingness to take Orders and the college's refusal to transfer him to a fellowship which could be held by a layman had led to his deprivation in 1842. That experience, coupled with his growing distrust of the Tractarians and his failure to be elected to the chair of logic, in part as a result of the suspicions with which his religious views were regarded, helped to convince him that the university could only be effectively reformed if clerical influence was eliminated and the power of the colleges reduced, and that this could only be done by government interference. In 1848 he was appointed to the regius chair of history and began to propagate his views more vehemently. Naturally enough what he and his associates urged was regarded with deep distaste by the more conservative clerical dons. Both Evangelicals and Tractarians were alarmed by the liberals' rational theology and even latent infidelity. The year 1849 had seen the publication of J. A. Froude's novel, *The Nemesis of Doubt*, pointing to the growing erosion of faith, and Sewell had the book publicly burnt in Exeter College hall.

But the liberals, though themselves somewhat divided, found a sympathetic hearing outside the university, especially among the dissenters. The *Edinburgh Review*, reflecting liberal feeling, declared that the university was characterised by an 'utter absence of all spirit for investigation of every sort, except in polemic theology' and by an unwillingness to sponsor scientific pursuits or to forward literary studies. The *Times* commented on the inadequacy of professorial teaching. The chairman of the parliamentary committee on legal education queried Oxford's facilities for the teaching of law. James Heywood, dissenter and M.P. for North Lancashire, discussed Oxford's shortcomings in a paper read to the members of the British Association in September, 1846.

Only a diehard of deepest die—and there were some in Oxford common rooms—could believe that major reforms would not have to be introduced immediately if parliamentary intervention was to be staved off. There was, however, considerable disagreement, even among those who favoured reform as to what exactly should be done. The high churchmen still wished to ensure that the Church should continue to control the university and suggested that to provide a cheaper education for future ordinands a new college or hall should be established. The Hebdomadal Board commented crisply that it was ridiculous to set up a new college while many had empty rooms. The confusion was reflected in the parliamentary election of 1847. The Hebdomadal Board favoured the candidature of Edward Cardwell, a moderate conservative not averse to reform. He was opposed by Gladstone who had the joint support of the Tractarian remnant, attracted by his religious sympathies, and by the academic liberals who liked his politics. But many of the residents pushed the claims of a more ardent conservative, C. G. Round. In the event Cardwell withdrew and Gladstone strode into second place to Inglis with 997 votes to Round's 824. His victory, which analysis showed had been made possible by the support of the younger and more distinguished scholars, was seen by many as a triumph for liberalism.

The Hebdomadal Board pushed ahead with proposals for further reforms. A draft statute proposed that there should be three new honour schools in the future; candidates who graduated in Greats would be free to study mathematics, natural sciences or history. Although the principal objects were approved in Convocation, they were subject to amendment in detail. A later proposal to establish a school of history and jurisprudence was passed by 14 votes. After four years of hard discussion the new examination statute was accepted; but the time and the grind made it painfully clear that it would take years, if not decades, to implement the full programme of liberal reform. The institution of the new Schools, far from helping to resolve, as the moderate reformers hoped, some of the problems of university reform, actually made them worse since they made demands on the teaching facilities of the colleges which the present tutorial system could not well bear. 'It is quite impossible', R. W. Browne of St John's was to tell the commissioners, 'to expect that any individual College and Hall could supply men qualified to teach all the subjects of study introduced by the New Examination Statute.' The new statute had made government intervention much more likely. On 23 April 1850, James Heywood once more asked for a commission on the universities. The Whig prime minister, Russell, while deprecating Heywood's motion, agreed to set up a royal commission of enquiry, and, in spite of opposition from Gladstone, the proposal was approved in the Commons by 22 votes.

The die was surely cast. The Hebdomadal Board, the liberal Dr Jeune being absent, indignant at government interference, refused to collaborate in the appointment of the commission. Many heads of colleges were as adamant in their opposition, pleading that it was against their conscience to co-operate in an illegal invasion of their rights. The commissioners were however, an able and distinguished group, liberal in temper; headed by Samuel Hinds, the shrewd if unpunctual bishop of Norwich (whose 'liberalism' was perhaps to find its ultimate expression in his marriage to his cook), they included Tait, Jeune (who, as master of Pembroke, agreed not to attend meetings of the Hebdomadal Board while acting as a commissioner), J. L. Dampier, the loquacious Baden Powell, H. G. Liddell and G. H. S. Johnson, later dean of Wells. Their sentiments were liberal, but they were not wholly at one, Tait and Johnson being moderate in their sympathies, Liddell and Jeune more radical. A. P. Stanley acted as secretary with Goldwin Smith as his assistant. Although they met with a good deal of opposition and their own powers were limited—they could not compel witnesses to testify and they had no authority to investigate college finances—the commissioners eventually produced an epochal report.

Working with what in the light of more recent royal commissions must seem surprising speed, they produced a series of important and radical recommendations for reform. To provide a more democratic machinery of university government, they proposed to revive Congregation and to endow it with wider powers. The Hebdomadal Board (in its revised form) would continue to be the university's executive, but Congregation would be able to initiate measures and to discuss those proposed in the Hebdomadal Board. Convocation retained its right of vetoing new legislation.

The commissioners suggested that the professorial body should constitute a delegacy to superintend studies, examinations and libraries. To make it possible for poor students to use the university's facilities, they proposed the foundation of private halls or halls attached to colleges. More immediately they advised that students should be allowed to live in lodgings; they also proposed the admission of non-collegiate students. To improve the standard of entry to the university they suggested a compulsory matriculation examination.

They confirmed many of the criticisms recently made of the colleges, more especially their failure to fulfil their statutes. They held that the colleges did not provide properly for poor students, and that their fellows did not effectively live a common life or devote themselves to learning and research. Only 22 out of 542 fellowships were fully open to competition. But since a fellowship could serve a useful purpose in assisting a man in his career outside the academic world, they did not wish to insist on residence. They disapproved of the obligation on most fellows to take holy orders, believing that it encouraged intellectual dishonesty. A number of witnesses had argued that the rule requiring celibacy should also be relaxed, but the commissioners were unwilling to go that far, holding that there was insufficient accommodation in college for married fellows, and that consequently the latter must live away from college to the neglect of their pupils. 'The gross absurdity of allowing marriage to ordinary Fellows', the historian, E. A. Freeman commented complacently, 'has happily found no favour in the eyes of the commissioners.'[1] The commissioners suggested that there were far too many fellowships—some 30 a year fell vacant—creating heavy expense without proportionate return. The money saved could be better expended in maintaining professors and lecturers.

The reaction to the report was what might have been expected. 'There were', Gladstone wrote, 'but a very few of those persons who *are* attached to our institutions that did not regard it as (in an academical sense) revolutionary.' There had been an election at Lincoln in 1851 which, because of

---

[1] W. Sewell, a fellow of Exeter and later warden of Radley, satirised the proposal in a letter addressed to Lord John Russell: 'According to your Lordship's wish, I proceed to inform you of my arrival at Oriel College. I arrived by the 5 o'c train last night from Rugby, accompanied by my wife, six children and three nursery maids, and drove immediately to our new apartments in the first quadrangle. They occupy one half of the south side, and the other half is appropriated by the residence of the Professor of Conchology ... My wife .... complains that there is no second drawing room, which I fear it will be necessary to provide ... I have spoken to the new Provost, who ... has suggested that, by taking into my house, three more undergraduates' rooms, this improvement may easily be made' and much more in a similar vein.

the scandal to which it gave rise, reinforced the Liberals' convictions that the commissioners had not gone far enough. But most heads remained intransigently opposed to its findings. At Magdalen the aged president Routh remained an immovable obstacle to reform until death at the age of 99 paved the way for an almost equally conservative successor in Frederick Bulley.

While the clerical diehards continued to oppose all reform, and few liked the findings of the commissioners, there was a growing realisation that some kind of reform was probably unavoidable. But how radical were such reforms to be? This was a basic and critical question. Would they mean simply the adaptation of existing institutions to new needs, and the introduction of some new but not revolutionary measures, or would they involve radical changes which would transform the university totally? The moderate Tutors' Association, recently revived, was averse to the proposals for increasing the power of the professoriate and to the introduction of unattached students into the university, and it believed that what was wanted was the elimination of abuses so as to make the colleges more efficient as centres of instruction. Such views were regarded sympathetically by the more moderate liberals (under the lead of Francis Jeune, the reforming master of Pembroke), though they favoured some increase in the power of the professors.

But the moderates were regarded with growing intransigence by Halford Vaughan and the radical dons, among them J. M. Wilson, the positivist Richard Congreve, Goldwin Smith, Mark Pattison and Conington. They wanted not merely the ending of the Anglican control of the university and its virtual secularisation, but they insisted that the university should be placed under the control of a learned professoriate (whose prime duty was to be scholarship and research rather than instruction). Vaughan argued for institutional changes which would have revolutionised the university. It was not sufficient for colleges to reform their statutes and to open fellowships. They must be brought under the control of a university which had opened its doors to the new forces in society. He recommended that the Hebdomadal Board should be replaced by a revived and strengthened Congregation in which the professors would be in a permanent majority. This professorial aristocracy would control also the educational and disciplinary system of the university. Vaughan favoured the admission of students without any college association. Such advanced views, so unfavourable, not simply to clericalism but to the colleges, fortunately found only a minimal following. Pusey argued forcibly

against Vaughan's recommendations, finding in them all the more dis-
agreeable features of the German universities, and evoked a powerful
response from Vaughan in his *Oxford Reform and Oxford Professors*.

Yet one surprising and important convert to the cause of university
reform had been made. This was Gladstone, whose appointment as chancellor of the exchequer in the coalition government led by Lord Aberdeen,
had already aroused considerable disquiet among his constituents. He had
now become convinced that the heads were unlikely to carry through the
reforms that the university needed. His conversion made many uneasy.
Nor did the appointment of Lord Derby as chancellor in succession to
Wellington appear a very effective bulwark against government intervention.

For it was clear that parliament must intervene. The Hebdomadal Board
reacted to the publication of the commissioners' report by requesting
members of Convocation to give written evidence on its contents. If they
hoped to forestall government action by instituting further reforms themselves, time was running short. Meanwhile Gladstone turned his attention
to drafting a bill in consultation with Jowett and other Oxford friends.
The bill, introduced by Russell on 17 March 1853, provided for a reformed
constitution, a Congregation comprised of the teaching members of the
university which should be able to discuss proposals sent down to it by
the reformed Hebdomadal Board (now to be called the Hebdomadal
Council) and to suggest amendments to it (it had no powers to amend by
itself), for the establishment of private halls, for the opening of fellowships,
more of which should be available to laymen, for restrictions on non-
residence, for the revision of college statutes and, if possible, for some
redeployment of college revenue for the support of professors.

'Not merely inexpedient but unjust and tyrannical' was Dean Gaisford's
predictable response to these proposals, but though many were critical,
others held that in some respects the university had got off lightly. In
particular many liberals thought that the bill was too moderate and had
conceded too much to the university clericals: it restricted but did not
abolish clerical fellowships, retained celibacy and left college revenues
practically untouched. Although the more extreme liberal dons had few
supporters inside Oxford, they had followers outside the university, in
particular three M.Ps., James Heywood, Edward Horsman and J. F. B.
Blackett, a former fellow of Merton. Gladstone realised that it would be
folly, however, to impose radical reforms on an unwilling university.
Besides his personal sympathies were with the more conservative

reformers, his aims dictated, as he told Bonamy Price, by the 'principle of working with the materials which we possess, endeavouring to improve our institutions through the agency they themselves supply, and giving to reform in all cases where there is a choice the character of return and restoration.' Though this was surely what the moderates, who were represented in the Tutors' Association, wanted, the more extreme radicals, working with the dissenters, were determined to base the bill, if they could, more firmly on the commissioners' original findings. They were critical too of the seemingly conservative character of the commission which the bill was to set up to implement the reforms. 'Various causes', Gladstone told Jowett, 'among which stand most prominently forward the strength of private interests, the infusion of religious jealousies into our debates, the indifference of most of the Dissenters to the mere improvement of the University, and the actual opposition offered by the *London* portion of the Oxford Reformers, have given obstruction such a power that to pass the Bill in its present form would require nearly the whole Session even if all other public business were abandoned by the Government.'

Aware of the storms ahead, he prevailed upon Russell to agree that the only way to ensure success was to delete the clauses relating to the colleges and to give the commission more powers to deal with this aspect of the problem. Ultimately the opposition weakened, for the dissenters under Heywood's lead turned their attention to the question of subscription and were partially satisfied with the success they achieved on this score. Heywood introduced a motion for the abolition of the religious test at matriculation (which the commissioners, though critical of the obligation, had been unwilling to touch) which passed by nine votes; Pusey and his fellow Tractarians let out a howl of anguish, fearful of the onset of infidelity to which this would open the way. Consequently, to the disappointment of the extreme liberals, the Oxford Reform Bill became law. 'All the while, I bore about with me', Vaughan wrote to Edward Twisleton, 'the sense of that heavy blow which the Bishop of Oxford, in conspiracy with Gladstone, dealt to Oxford Reform—by an utter subversion of the Constitution as given and settled by the House of Commons, and by the establishment of a clerical democracy, in its place.' But Oxford opinion had more or less come round to the inevitability of moderate reform. A petition against the bill promoted by the Hebdomadal Board, but opposed by the Tutors' Association, passed but narrowly in Convocation, by 193 votes to 191. The changes had come to stay.

The sequel to the University Reform Act

As a result Oxford found itself with a revised constitution, and the colleges confronted with a requirement to revise their statutes for the approval of the commissioners. The Hebdomadal Council would consist henceforth of the vice-Chancellor and proctors, six heads, six professors and six members of Convocation elected by Congregation, that is, by the teaching masters of the university. The new Council was respectable, scholarly and in the main conservative (Wilson and Jeune were virtually the only liberals; Pattison had tied for last place with Marriott and in a new poll Marriott was victorious by five votes, the liberal vote having been divided by the nomination of Thomson of Queen's.) It drafted a statute permitting the admission of dissenters and for the regulation and setting-up of private halls.

The University Reform Act of 1854 was thus a watershed in Oxford's history. College life was to experience a steady reorientation as senior common rooms slowly lost their clerical character and received infusions of fresh blood. A fellowship could no longer be regarded as a prize which the fortunate recipient could hope to enjoy for the remainder of his life without serious duties. Henceforth it became more and more a responsible tutorial office whose holder was expected to engage in advanced study and research. Major changes occurred with the creation of new honour schools, with a more effective professoriate and with a more efficient, theoretically more democratic, form of self-government. The liberal-minded Liddell succeeded the conservative Gaisford as dean of Christ Church in 1855, though as the years passed Liddell's liberalism proved to be very much a milk and water affair. Another supporter of university reform, Mark Pattison, though not by unanimous vote, was elected rector of Lincoln in 1861. Benjamin Jowett, a candidate for the mastership of Balliol in 1860, had to give way to a dull but impeccable scholar, Robert Scott, and only on Scott's preferment to the deanery of Rochester in 1870 did he become master and establish the liberal-rational tradition which was to dominate the college's history for the next century. Among liberals who became professors were Jowett, as professor of Greek, Stanley as professor of ecclesiastical history and Goldwin Smith, more effective as a propagandist than as a scholar, as professor of modern history, who succeeded Vaughan in 1858.[1] Conington, a man of liberal sympathy, a friend and associate of

[1] Vaughan's resignation was forced by his refusal to comply with the university's requirements for residence, an odd stance for a reformer. The remainder of his career, as Mr Bill has shewn, was an anti-climax; apart from an important role on the Public Schools Commission, he spent his last 20 years in south Wales, a valetudinarian and near recluse, increasingly irritable and neurotic, working on his *magnum opus*, a history of morality, which was never completed.

Goldwin Smith, became the first Corpus professor of Latin in 1854, though lured, much to Pattison's disgust, to a narrow form of evangelical belief, Max Müller, whose teutonism aroused distrust, was appointed Taylor professor, 'Everything', he asserted blithely, 'cannot go exactly as we wish, but the avalanche rolls in the right direction.' Whether it was in fact an avalanche may be doubted, but at least a stream was in full flood.

The colleges revised their statutes, eliminating anomalies, reducing the number of clerical fellows and throwing fellowships open to wider competition. Among the colleges Christ Church's position was unique. It had had no statutes since its foundation but was ruled by the dean and chapter. Its students, the equivalent of fellows in other colleges, did not share in the government of the college and, with a few exceptions, were nominated to office by the dean and chapter. The latter owed their appointment to the crown. This system had worked tolerably well for 300 years, in part because the chapter and the students were joined by a strong bond of sentiment. But the introduction of the honours examination system, the strain which it imposed on the tutorial system of the college, and its decline in performance created grounds for unsettlement, the more marked as non-Christ Church men were intruded into the chapter.

The university reform act of 1854 left Christ Church untouched, but brought the problem of its future government to the fore, more because the issue was one of power and influence (since the dean and chapter enjoyed very considerable powers of patronage, appointing to no less than 90 livings, and controlled the purse strings) than because the question was educationally very significant. Apart from some conservative members of the chapter, the majority of the students, among them the senior censor, Osborne Gordon, favoured the recent reforms in the university and wanted statutes for the college which would give the students some share in the college's government and in the disbursement of its finances. The commission drew up ordinances for Christ Church in 1858, which, though unacceptable to the dean and chapter, were eventually approved by a committee of arbitration headed by the archbishop of Canterbury, to which they had been referred. The new statutes introduced some financial reforms and brought the senior students more actively into the educational administration but they did not as yet bring them fully into college government. The statutes thus failed to satisfy either students and the chapter. These grievances were to be eventually remedied by the statute of 1867.

The apparent victory of liberalism did not, however, mean that the liberals were by any means dominant. In the elections to the new Heb-domadal Council they had at first made some headway (though in a further candidature Pattison was beaten by J. E. Sewell of Christ Church); but in 1857–8 they lost to conservatives. That neither Jowett nor Pattison acquired a place could be accounted for in part by the antipathy with which many regarded them, but the same could not be said of another liberal, Henry Smith, the Savilian professor of geometry, a man of the greatest charm and integrity, who failed to be elected in 1866. To many, not all of whom were necessarily reactionary conservatives, the liberals seemed both arrogant and doctrinaire. With the exception of A. P. Stanley, who left Oxford to become dean of Westminster in 1854, their spokesmen had only a restricted following. Their close association with *Essays and Reviews*, in the condemnation of which Tractarians and Evangelicals were at one, lost them further favour with the more conservative clericals.

After an initial period of frustration the conservative forces in the university rallied, checking the movement for further liberalisation. They managed to delay the rescinding of the religious tests (until 1871), retaining after that the tests for graduates in divinity, and they blocked (until 1919) the demand for the abolition of compulsory Greek. The strength of academic conservatism lay in part in its entrenched position. Only steadily did death—and Tory heads of colleges were certainly gifted with long life—remove its more intransigent adherents, Dr Wynter of St John's in 1870, Ben Symons, 40 years warden of Wadham, in 1878, Montague Burrow of All Souls in 1905. Dr Pusey continued to wield con-siderable influence for, solitary and introverted as he was, he remained profoundly interested in political and social issues. In the Hebdomadal Council he was invariably listened to with respect and sometimes proved persuasive.

Strong among the majority of the residents, the conservatives could make a bid to control elections to the Hebdomadal Council, and they were able, through the medium of the more consequential Congregation, to frustrate some radical proposals. And behind Congregation there was a further court of appeal, Convocation, consisting of all masters who had kept their names on the books of their colleges. Since a majority of masters had graduated before 1854, they were unlikely to be sympathetic towards change. The country parsons, so a critic averred, formed a 'trusty phalanx' 'rallying at the well-worn cry "The Church is in danger", and flocking to the Sheldonian in overpowering numbers.' An improved postal service and the greater ease of travelling which the railways made possible enabled the more conservatively-minded masters to travel easily to Oxford to cast their vote against radical proposals.

There was then still much to underline the liberals belief that, in spite of outward changes, the spirit of the place remained the same. Oxford's rejection of its loyal son, Gladstone, for the part he had played in the University Reform Act, testified to this. The intrepid Archdeacon Denison organised the non-residents outside the university in support of Gathorne-Hardy and, in 1865, Gladstone emerged bottom of the poll, with nearly 200 votes less than his opponent. Conservatives were reinforced at Oxford by the appointment of William Stubbs as professor of modern history in succession to Goldwin Smith, and of another high churchman and Tory, William Bright, to the chair of ecclesiastical history. After prolonged opposition the conservatives had reluctantly accepted the setting-up in 1870 of an honour school of theology, insisting successfully, however, that the school and its examiners should remain fully under orthodox clerical control.

The powerful influence which the clericals continued to exert over Oxford reinforced the progressives' conviction that something more was needed to oblige the university to fulfil its national function. There was an obvious case ready to hand, that of religious subscription which was disliked by many moderate conservatives as well as by the liberals. Goldwin Smith, typically belligerent, publicised the harmful and unjust effects of the tests which, he declared, prevented the universities from fulfilling their role as 'centres of science and progress.' The supporters of the tests replied that the tests were designed to vindicate the faith of the established Church (which they identified with the Thirty-nine Articles), itself a dogmatic system, supernaturally provided, without which society, let alone the university, must inevitably decline or perish. But their critics argued that the tests inevitably promoted intellectual dishonesty, and confined membership of the university to a religious group which could no longer pretend even to represent a majority of the population. In demanding an abolition of the tests, the Oxford liberals had the support of the national party, more especially of the free churchmen among its supporters. Gladstone was personally reluctant, but he realised the force of the argument and was content to see the abolition of religious tests included in the liberal programme for the next general election. Once the Liberals were returned to office, the government drew up a bill in 1870 proposing the abolition of tests for all degrees save those in divinity and for university posts. The conservative churchmen petitioned the archbishop, urging that

the 'battle is for Christian faith and Christian morals. It is for very life.'
Pusey gloomily scented disestablishment as the likely sequel to the abolition
of the tests, with consequential secularisation of church property, and was
sufficiently moved to seek an abortive alliance with the Methodists. After
a series of complex political manoeuvres, in the course of which Lord
Salisbury tried desperately to find a compromise, Parliament passed the
bill.

Although the abolition of religious tests was a major reverse for the
conservative die-hards, they did not easily accept defeat. The foundation
of a new college to commemorate the memory of John Keble who had
died on 29 March 1866, was itself a reminder of the strength of the high
church tradition. Many liberals were vehemently opposed to the new
foundation, which appeared to be not merely sectarian but the instrument
of a party; though its first warden, E. S. Talbot, was more liberal minded
than his sponsors. Without avail H. A. Pottinger tried to establish its
illegality. He argued that the university had no legal powers to admit
Keble College to its membership, the decree being 'a most crude and
indigestible piece of legislative perversity.' The College 'was designed', so
a writer in the *Daily News* asserted on 10 December 1870, 'to be the
embodiment of the denominational principle and even to perpetuate that
principle which the new legislation had swept out of all the older colleges
and out of the governing bodies of the university itself.' Contrariwise
Keble's proponents saw in the new college a counter to the dechristianisa-
tion of the older societies. 'Shall we live', one of them asked, 'to see the
time when *our* grey walls are deserted by the mighty spirits of the past and
your buildings alone affording them a refuge?'

There was thus a growing feeling that what had so far been achieved
affected only the peripheries, not the heart of the place. 'It is, I think',
wrote the pertinacious H. A. Pottinger, 'clear that it is hopeless to expect
that the University, as at present constituted, will ever carry out in a
hearty spirit the intentions of Parliament. Nearly all the abuses which
require reform arise from the predominance of the clerical party, and they
have been enabled for twenty years to evade the manifest intentions of the
legislator. Oxford ought to be a national institution but is bound hand and
feet by the clergy of one sect.' The Liberals welcomed the relaxation of
rules relating to residence in college, permitting students to live in lodgings
and providing for the admission of non-college students; but they attacked
the inequitable distribution of wealth in the colleges and the continued
dominance of conservatism and clericalism. Some of these criticisms were

voiced in one of the most compelling literary fruits of the movement, Mark Pattison's *Suggestions on Academical Organization*. Yet interesting and forward-looking as were many of his recommendations, pertinent as were his criticisms of the existing regime, what he really wanted the university to be, a home of genuine research and scholarship, was not wholly in line with the aspirations of his liberal-minded colleagues. They emphasised university education as a preparation for public service, the need to adapt the university to the requirements of the contemporary world, rather than as a society concerned with the pursuit of knowledge. Pattison, idiosyncratic, increasingly suspicious of Jowett and the image which he sought to give to Balliol, became misanthropic both in his private and public life.

The liberals concentrated on demands for further reforms in the government of the university, among them a reduction in the powers of Convocation with its large number of non-residents. They wanted further changes in the statutes of the colleges, the removal of most of the remaining clerical restrictions which C. S. Roundell had already tried vainly to achieve in his own college, Merton, the elimination of the requirement for celibacy and the abolition of fellowships, such as prize fellowships, which could only be regarded as sinecures; they demanded further improvements in tutorial and professorial teaching, the promotion of new subjects, more especially in the sciences, and a redistribution of college revenues with advantage to the poorer societies. There were some reformers, like Sir Benjamin Brodie, who believed that the colleges should relinquish a part of their autonomy as well as of their wealth to the university; but, as there was a Tory government in power until 1868, the reformers were not especially anxious to call for a royal commission to be set up under its aegis.

In fact a number of reforms, if minor in character, continued to reshape the life of the university. Colleges co-operated together to appoint joint lecturers, and opened what had hitherto been college lectures to members of other colleges; this was first done in the school of modern history and jurisprudence, whose severance, in 1872, into two separate schools was to the advantage of both subjects. The modern system of faculties and faculty boards started with the decision that the six honour schools should be governed in future by a board consisting of professors and other teachers. An attempt to do away with compulsory Greek failed; but moves were made to create a faculty of natural science, which would enable candidates to take their degrees in science alone.

The rate of growth depended, however, on the financial resources available to the authority. The need to expand teaching and to provide new buildings strained these to the uttermost. The Bodleian Library could no longer house all its books, and it was decided—a plan to rebuild the library in the Parks was rejected because of its remoteness from the university—to take over the ancient Schools, which could no longer accommodate the growing number of examinees. A new Examination Schools were to be built, designed by T. G. Jackson and costing £100,000, on the site of the Angel Inn in the High Street; they were finished in 1882. While the university hoped that colleges might contribute towards university costs, whether by a voluntary levy or decree, a questionnaire showed that in spite of this wealth, they were unwilling to do much in this way as their own revenue began to be affected by the prevailing agrarian depression. Nonetheless Balliol and New College had shewn their interest in the widening spectrum of national education by allocating £300 a year to the newly established university college at Bristol.

The movement for further reform had strong backing, in the university as well as in the country, and greeted warmly Gladstone's decision in 1871 to set up a new royal commission under the chairmanship of the Duke of Cleveland. In its report, issued in 1874, the commission showed how better endowed the colleges were than the university (which had an annual income of £32,000 to the colleges £830,000). While the commissioners paid tribute to the efficient way in which the colleges handled their revenues, they demonstrated that the university could not carry out a programme of necessary reform without their financial assistance. Even if the university raised its dues and fees spectacularly, a course which the commissioners deplored as likely to place an Oxford education outside the range of all except the wealthy, the increase in its resources would be insufficient to meet its rising expenditure. At this stage no financial help could be expected from the state. Nor could it be forgotten that there was a very uneven distribution of wealth among the colleges, for if some were very rich, others were poor. Although the figures at the commissioners' disposal did not always give a true picture of college finances—and they overestimated the likely increase in college revenues in the future since they had understandably not taken into consideration the impact of the coming agricultural depression—there was no doubt that the cost of maintaining their fellows was their biggest item of expenditure, amounting in 1871 to £101,171 4s. In view of the excess number of non-resident and non-tutorial fellows, it was felt that by economising in this respect colleges could assist the university.

The situation was complicated further by the fall of Gladstone's government in 1874 and its replacement by Disraeli's Tory administration, which caused dismay among the more fervent of the university's liberals. But the liberal ranks were not themselves united. The more moderate argued for cautious reform, holding that there had been insufficient time to judge the effectiveness of the first reform act, more especially as vested interests, in the shape of older, more conservative fellows, were only slow to disappear. Christ Church, for instance, had only recently been liberated from its undue subordination to the dean and chapter. There were thus many, even among the liberals, who would not press for radical reforms and were ready to accept the kind of proposals that a Tory government might formulate. In such an atmosphere the ministry decided to act before the Liberals were returned to power. Its proposals, put forward in the Commons by Gathorne-Hardy in 1877, gave the universities 18 months to reform their statutes for the approval of the commissioners.

The results of the royal commission were then less radical than the more extreme liberals would have wished, even if they were not conservative enough to please the Tory churchmen. To promote research and to improve teaching by the provision of more professors and lecturers, to create more and better laboratories, a Common University Fund was to be set up, maintained by contributions from the colleges in proportion to their wealth. This entailed a diminution in the number of fellowships,[1] but, to improve teaching facilities and to assimilate tutors and lecturers who could not be fellows because they were married, provision was henceforth to be made for married fellows.

There was fresh controversy over the extent of the proposed restriction on clerical fellowships. Arguing in support of clerical fellows, John Wordsworth, future bishop of Salisbury, then a fellow of Brasenose, declared that they had the 'great advantage of a fixed principle of authority on which to rest in the past, and a steady light of hope in the future.' He declared in forthright terms which his lay colleagues could hardly have appreciated that 'they were less likely to be affected by the self-centred indolence or melancholy, which is a pressing danger of academic life.' Moreover, he concluded, 'our contention is, that existing clerical fellows and headships are benefices in the possession of the Church of England which are rightly and justly the property of the national Church.' But critics of the system denounced not merely the way in which clerical

[1] It is ironical to observe, as Dr Pantin has suggested recently, that if the reformers had not insisted on the abolition of fellowships, some of the problems confronting the contemporary university, more especially that of providing all university teachers with fellowships, need never have arisen.

fellows enabled the Church of England to maintain its stranglehold over the university but their frequent intellectual inferiority; 'a stigma . . . now unmistakeably attaches to the whole order.' The more radical liberals headed by C. S. Roundell and James Bryce, argued that the colleges should be only obliged to ensure that religious instruction was available, and to maintain services in the chapels. On these issues the commissioners made very moderate recommendations.

The commission also brought to an end the remaining private halls, except for St Edmund Hall which was in any case in tutelage to Queen's. For some time, the halls had been financially precarious, and it was argued that the establishment of a society for non-attached students had done away with their principal *raison d'être*. Their defenders regretted the disappearance of societies which, they believed, could provide a cheaper education for future clergy than the colleges; and were angry at what they considered to be the imperialist policies followed by the colleges, as New Inn Hall became a part of Balliol (christened by contemporaries the Balliol Tap), St Alban Hall was absorbed into Merton and St Mary's was joined to Oriel.

Although the changes approved by the Commission went some way further to improve the university's function as a centre of education and research, the radicals were critical of what had been achieved. They held that too much had been done to mollify the conservatives, that colleges continued to have too much autonomy and that their wealth had been insufficiently tapped or redistributed. But they were in a minority. The majority, with Jowett as vice-chancellor, readily accepted the new statutes. Perhaps the most dramatic single rear guard victory was that of Bishop Wordsworth of Lincoln who greatly resented the attempts which Lincoln College (of which he was the Visitor) had made to reduce his visitatorial powers and to deprive him of the rights which as bishop he traditionally enjoyed to appoint to a fellowship. In the name of religion and property, he raised the question in the House of Lords and managed to get the college's new statutes annulled (with the result it continued to be governed by the statutes of 1854 until 1925). All in all the commissioners' work was not negligible. They had managed to create conditions for further progress and reform without embittering the majority of Oxford's residents. Moreover, as a result of the new situation which the second university reform act created, the heat had been taken out of the prolonged controversy over religion and politics which had absorbed so much energy in earlier decades.

Oxford was no longer to play so vital or determinant a part in either political or religious controversy. The brief essays that it was to make later into national politics, epitomised by the influence which Balliol men wielded in the early Imperial history of the 1900s, and in the prophetic exegesis of Lionel Curtis, and by the association of a group in All Souls with the doctrine of appeasement in the 1930s, shewed that while the university was not influential in national politics, both politics and religion were ceasing to be central to its existence. The university's attention was turned more and more to teaching and research.

X

The Statesman and the Don:
W. E. Gladstone and Màrk Pattison

Although at first sight Gladstone and Pattison would seem to have little in common, their Oxford careers illuminate university life in the first half of the nineteenth century. In the 1830s and 1840s Oxford was still a country town, its unpleasant suburbs not yet built and even its railway station to be constructed at a discreet distance from the colleges. Its principal streets were, however, often busy with traffic—some at least of its narrow and medieval lanes had disappeared after the face lift which the town had experienced in the 1770s—for Oxford was the junction of many coach routes. By such means the majority of undergraduates converged on the university. In 1828 Gladstone travelled from Liverpool by the *Aurora* coach, experiencing a hazard to which the traveller was often liable when the coach was upset near Walsall. Fortunately a hedge prevented it from turning over and no one was hurt.

Oxford's nearness to the countryside provided undergraduates and dons with ample opportunity for recreation. The 'foppish athlete of the arena', whom Pattison was later to despise so much, had hardly made his appearance, though there were hard-riding and hunting men who paid little attention to their books. The days of athletic clubs and organised sports may not have been so far distant, for Gladstone went to watch the first Boat Race at Henley on 7 June 1829, and on occasions played cricket, but most undergraduates made their own exercise. The river held its perennial attraction. Gladstone noted in his diary that he had gone boating with his friend, Doyle. For Pattison, who fished in the fast flowing streams of his native Wensleydale, the Isis and Cherwell formed a source of much-needed tranquillity. For relaxation from the strains set up by the condemnation of *Tract XC* he went skulling in a wherry down to Nuneham— 'and I do not know when I have had so enjoyable an excursion—Hannah, Gregory of CCC and myself—fancy us lying on the grass, inhaling the divine weed, and imbibing much "Rhein-wine"—and producing the most ingenious extravagances in the way of talk that our imagination could suggest.'

In winter frost—and the Victorian winters seem to possess an authentic Dickensian patina—Gladstone and Pattison became enthusiastic skaters. 'Yesterday', Pattison wrote to his sister, Eleanor, in December, 1842, 'I went skating upon the Isis . . . most unpoetically thronged with cads.' He remembered wistfully the solitariness, the ducks and the pine-trees around the frozen Newfound England pond of Wensleydale.

Like the majority of contemporary dons and undergraduates, Gladstone and Pattison thought nothing of covering considerable distances on foot, though few undergraduates in the 1830s would have emulated the Wesley brothers who regularly walked home to Epworth, some hundred miles or so from Oxford. But Gladstone would walk to Abingdon to hear the Bishop of Calcutta preach an 'admirable' sermon, or walk over to Cuddesdon to dine (with his mathematical tutor who was vicar there). Once he set out for Leamington, got as far as Steeple Aston where, overtaken by a thunderstorm, he took refuge for the night in the local inn, probably *Hopcroft's Halt*, before covering the eight miles to Banbury for breakfast. Then he set out to complete the remainder of his journey. Pattison would readily walk out to the village of Combe, a college living eight miles from Oxford.

For more distant journeys both men had their own horses; Gladstone told his father 'that a horse will materially assist me in preserving my health during my hard reading.' 'I must have my horse up at once. Be so kind', Mark told his sister, 'as to consult T[homas] B[owes] on the best mode of conveyance i.e. whether by R. way or by road.' Pattison never lost his enjoyment of field sports, so pleasing a feature of life at Hauxwell before it had been soured by disputes with his father. As late as December 1847, he recounted how he had gone hunting with Coxe and Kerslake, intending simply to 'see the break-cover and then jogging back to our books.' But when the fox broke away, 'the grey was so keen on the sport that I found field and field and fence after fence going away beneath me, and the company gradually becoming more select, to nobody's surprise more than to my own.'

If most dons were more sober than Woodforde and his contemporaries, cards, wine and billiards were prominent in daily recreation.[1] Gladstone

[1] Cf. a comment made by Sir Frederic Madden in his diary for 7 May 1825: 'Walked again in Chr. Ch. meadow with Mr Young. He told me he had been in St. John's Gardens, the most

regularly breakfasted and dined with his friends and attended and held 'wines' of his own. Yet sociable as he undoubtedly was, Gladstone was of an economical and abstemious disposition, purchasing his own tea because it was cheaper than that which his scout provided. The death of a Christ Church undergraduate, Lord Conyers Osborne (to whose father, the Duke of Leeds, the elder Pattison was chaplain and who had shown young Mark some courtesy on his first visit to Oxford), in a drunken scuffle seemed to Gladstone an horrifying object lesson which, he feared, made an insufficient impact on his Oxford contemporaries. 'If this hath not a voice', he commented gloomily on 16 February 1831, 'all things are dumb to us', noting three days later that his death 'seems forgotten' as he had seen one of Osborne's friends, Boscawen, drunk before seven in the evening.

For Pattison, coming from a narrow and predominantly female society in the remote Yorkshire countryside, Oxford social life was something from which he recoiled with horror. His first 'wine' was, as he remembered it long afterwards in the *Memoirs*, an unremitting disaster. Throughout life a weak stomach made excess of food and drink unpalatable. He found college feasts repugnant, though as he told his sister he found some pleasure on one such occasion. 'After the punch had been flowing freely for some time it began to tell upon some of the party—the Subrector, in particular was thoroughly sold up—I never saw him so completely done for before. Somehow or another it so happened that I was not in a state to be affected, I kept on till a very late or rather early hour putting down glass after glass without being able to produce the slightest effect, and afterwards went and sat and talked with Hannah, and walked up and down in the quad enjoying the lovely moonlight night.'

Social life at the university, still interspersed by drinking and betting, meant cards and billiards and, for the more studious, interminable discussion about religion, politics and life. Gladstone played cards, but with dilute enthusiasm. As an undergraduate at Oriel, Pattison regularly played cards with Kensington and his other friends. As a young don he told his

---

beautiful spot in Oxford and had *witnessed* a curious scene in them about *one o'clock in the day*, namely in a sly corner he surprised one of the very revd. fellows of – – – – – College *in flagrante delicto* with Miss Brown, eldest daughter of the *Rev. Proctor* ! ! So much for Oxford morals! He said the man was old enough to be her father, and the girl, a very pretty, fair creature! Oh shame! The old fellow buttoned up his inexpressibles and set off with his *inamorata* to Trinity gardens, where he probably renewed his games.' It should, however, be added that there was no proctor called Brown at this time; the proctors for 1825 were William Dalby of Exeter and John Watts of University, neither of whom was likely to be married.

sister how he had left the senior common room early to play whist. 'I had Driffield and Adamson dining with me, and Walesby was there, but not withstanding these fascinations at home, at 8 o'clock I pleaded an engagement to my two guests, and left them sitting there under the suspicion that it was Thos. Aquinas, at best with whom my engagement was—while I stole off to a certain upper room in High Street where Courtney, Baker and Nichols awaited me.' Later he came to regard cards as a 'waste of time': 'perfect quiet preferable.' Although as an undergraduate and young don Mark Pattison was very far from being the taciturn and aloof, not to say rebarbative, scholar of later years, he yearned already for the solitary life. Excusing himself from visiting his home at Hauxwell at Christmas 1842, he spoke of the appeal of the 'long unbroken mornings and the still solitary evenings when one can wrap oneself in visions of past times and of great and good men. I am quite in love with the desolation—though as far as have yet gone there has been nothing worthy the name of Xmas solitude —and next week we have two audits with their accompanying feast, a domus dinner on Xmas day and I don't know how many other things to break one's seraphic visions.'

Gladstone was fundamentally more sociable, though almost equally serious. With his Etonian friends, he formed an essay club, known by the initials WEG, which met to discuss serious questions. Gladstone became secretary and president of the Oxford Union Society, founded some five years previously, taking a prominent part in debates, ardently espousing the Tory cause.

Ambitious and conscientious, Gladstone was determined to win a good degree. If Pattison could confess that he was 'almost in too vigorous a state of mind to read novels', Gladstone too abstained for the most part from the fiction which had once delighted Woodforde (though he too found *Pamela* enjoyable reading), and fastened his attention on his classical texts. At Oxford he strengthened that love of classical literature which was to abide with him throughout life, though, like Wesley, he read into the ancient poets themes and feelings which were more Christian than pagan. Although he failed to win the Ireland scholarship, he had been made a Student of the college on the dean's nomination, and crowned his academic career with a first class in both classics and mathematics.

Pattison's undergraduate career had been far less satisfying. He essayed only once to speak at the Union. He lacked the scholastic discipline that Gladstone had received at Eton. He had been educated by his father, the eccentric rector of Hauxwell in Wensleydale, with the result that while he

had a wider range of intellectual interests than the majority of his contemporaries, his training had been irregular and his knowledge was patchy.
At Oriel, which he entered a year after Gladstone went down, he found the
tuition stereotyped and the college lectures dry and uninformative. He was
so apprehensive about his work that he came to the conclusion that he
must supplement his college tuition by employing a private coach, but he
only achieved a Second in the schools, a bitter disappointment as he had
already set his heart on a fellowship.

For students as serious-minded as Gladstone and Pattison a fellowship
and ordination seemed a natural sequel. If Gladstone had wished to become
a resident Oxford tutor, nothing could have been easier. 'After lecture', he
recorded in his diary on 23 November, 'my tutor asked me whether I was
going into the Church, and whether there would be any chance of my
wishing to remain here and take pupils.' The possibility of ordination,
fostered by his mother, had long been in his mind. When he was staying
at Cuddesdon, studying mathematics with Mr Saunders, he wrote to his
father in 1830, deeply convinced that 'a fearfully great portion of the
world around me is dying in sin', to tell him that he intended to take
orders. The elder Gladstone urged delay, and persuaded his son to wait
until graduation. Although, for Gladstone, as for Pattison, his time at
Oxford was a period of religious unsettlement, it was to be in the fields of
politics rather than of religion that he found an opening for his
vocation.

Pattison's future was more open to doubt. He experienced a number of
disappointments before he was elected to a fellowship at one of the lesser
colleges, Lincoln. He had first noticed the vacancy in an advertisement in
the *Herald* and though 'deep in the Fathers' was persuaded by his friends to
send in an application. With seven other candidates, he was examined for
three days 'not very hard in comparison with Balliol, the main point being
two English Essays—An Historical one on the "The influence of the discovery of the New World on the State of the Old at the time" and a
Theological one on "Prophecy".' His friend, Mozley, brought him news of
his success. 'Then I had to call on the Rector and each of the Fellows to
return thanks, and fork out to the ringers and finish all by dining with the
Rector and Fellows, at a most sumptuous banquet, to have my health
drunk.'

If Christ Church was the most highly reputed college in Oxford, Oriel
the intellectually most distinguished, Lincoln was dim. 'Every College',
Pattison wrote, describing the election to his sister, Eleanor on 10 Novem-

ber 1839, 'has its peculiar character distinct enough to those who have seen, but impossible to convey by words. If you divide the Oxford Common Rooms into three classes, the first containing those whose members are Scholars and Divines—the second, which are fashionable, aristocratically inclined men of the world—the third unfashionable good homely squires, barristers, country parsons—Oriel may be the instance of the first—Merton or All Souls of the second—and Lincoln will represent the third. To be more particular, the corporeal stature of the Fellows is large, their intellectual small, with the exception of Mitchell [Michell], the new Professor of Logic, one of the first men in the University according to Oxford estimates of men—also one or two of the Junior Fellows, who have been elected since strict examinations came up. But the studies and thoughts of the older ones are rather of the good old days of "Tory ascendancy" than of the reform era—the days of O'Connell, Mr Frost and Newman. They are of the Port and Prejudice schools, better read in Hawker on Shooting, Burn's Justice, or "Every Man his own Butler", than in Hooker or St Augustine. To explain the Gilbert Act, to get near partridges in January, to effect a tithe Composition, and to choose a pipe of wine, to anathematize Ld Melbourne and Co, none surpass them. A competent knowledge of (at least English) History, and a moderate taste for antiquities are general accomplishments, and the Rector's collection of Engravings is the first in Oxford, a praise which is extended with still greater unanimity to his stock of wines. However, I never was inclined (and am less so now than ever) to think all men fools who are not philosophers—let those study and theorize who have the turn for it—but the world must be carried on, and mere intellect is accordingly justly rated in the world as a qualification very secondary to those of station, fortune, knowledge of the world, businesslike habits, power of conversation etc. I never remember to have felt so happy as I do now; the first shock of surprise is over, and the excitement has subsided with a calm and equable satisfaction undisturbed by a single feeling of a contrary kind.' Was there ever to be a time again in Pattison's remaining years when he could speak with such confidence?

Lincoln was certainly not the college to which he would have gone had he had a free choice. 'I confess I had rather have been Fellow of University with the prospect of [the college livings] Arncliffe or Melsonby in the distance than anything else in the world . . . next to that Oriel with an eye to Aberford would have been my ambition. . . . And if I have not got into one of the most brilliant Colleges in the University there will be the more room for me to exert myself for its benefit.' And this is what the young don was to do in the next 12 years, with so high a degree of success that the intellectual tone of the place was raised, its reputation in the university and the world at large improved.

The task was no easy one. The rector, John Radford, courteous and old-fashioned, was a strong conservative, distrustful of change; and the other fellows would have seemed familiar figures to Woodforde. Every new election to a fellowship was thus a matter of major importance to Pattison. He had become identified with the group of young liberal fellows who favoured reform of the university's antiquated machinery and who were concerned to make the college a home of true scholarship. In a small college it was vital to try to seek to turn the balance in favour of the liberals by the election of liberal-minded fellows. The first elections which took place after Pattison's own admission were moderately satisfactory: the younger Kay, too Evangelical in religion for Pattison's taste but an excellent scholar, John Hannah, otherwise too worldly for Pattison but his stay was short and in 1844 he became headmaster of the Edinburgh Academy; G. G. Perry, later eminent as a Church historian. But Pattison was bitterly opposed to some of the other elections, more especially of Bousfield, Metcalfe and Washbourne West. When Bousfield was elected, the election was to a fellowship reserved for candidates from the diocese of Lincoln. Since Magdalen had recently made an election from the same area, there were only two candidates, 'very incompetent, but the cleverest of the two, of very doubtful character, being a commoner of our own—just the material to make another Thompson out of—On Thursday evening, the Rector, by appointment, met us in the C.R. and we had a grand fight, and, of course, when it came to voting, we were well beaten.' So 'a dis-agreeable associate' was 'forced on us by a tyrant-majority'. 'Kettle fought well and did good service, though I don't (in my own mind) like any of his arguments, we voted (the minority) of 5—Kettle, Kay, Hannah, Perry and myself—Green, I'm sorry to say, as I had long foreseen, deserting to the cause of the old Regime'. Although Pattison was then college bursar, he 'absented myself from the dinner for the purpose of marking my sense of the impropriety of the election.' The election of J. C. Andrew, 'a man of fair abilities, but not anything very superior', in 1846 was recorded as a victory since it prevented the intrusion of an unsuitable candidate to a close fellowship, and in T. E. Espin, elected in 1849, whose second name Espinelle has been perpetuated in one of the lunar craters, he had a friend and ally. All things considered Pattison could reasonably hope that there were enough liberal-minded Fellows to secure his election as rector when John Radford died in 1851.

In spite of what some of his colleagues held to be a disagreeable reserve and unsociability, Pattison had enormously improved the college's intellectual standing. He was a most conscientious teacher, taking great pains to prepare his lectures and to master the relevant material. 'I have taken,' he wrote on 26 November 1842, 'more pains this Term with my Lectures than I ever did before, and have been besides looking over compositions with more attention.' 'My second Lecture day is Friday. The men are beginning to get impertinent, now the novelty is over, and now begins the tug of war—if I can manage them just now, I shall keep the whip hand, but if I bend it will be a second edition of Johnny (Calcott). I can tell pretty well by the way in which they listen to me that I have got their ear on certain subjects—the most important certainly—such as relate to conduct moral and religious—but I have got to find out how far I could get them to depend on me intellectually. . . .' Of Pattison's conscientiousness there could be no question. 'Wherever I am', he confessed, 'I cannot afford to be idle.' To find time for reading, he came less and less to the common room. 'I have eschewed C.R. except during the audit and Christmas week', he wrote one vacation, 'I have shunned our College parties as much as possible, so that most of my evenings have been spent in my own rooms.'

Nor can it be doubted that the better undergraduates responded well to the challenge of his astringent, powerful intellect. His relations with those in his charge were friendly, void of the sarcasm which later made him so remote and so repugnant. His men admired him and developed a genuine affection for him. The death of one of them, young Stilwell, by drowning filled him with grief, and brought a 'week of so much anxiety and distress.'

In college meetings he sought to represent a more liberal attitude on disciplinary questions. 'At the College meeting', he wrote indignantly to his sister, '. . . we perpetrated one of the most unjust acts that ever a despotic oligarchy was guilty of—rusticating one man, and giving a heavy punishment to another, for nothing in the world, but because some person or persons unknown had lately been making rows in College which it was necessary to put a stop to, and as Johnny [Calcott] was too inactive to find the real author, he settled matters by knocking on the head the two who happened to be near him.' Yet on indolence he took a hard line. When one Grainger was charged with idleness, Pattison argued for taking away his exhibition and rusticating him for a term. 'Like everything else it occasioned a fight, and so we had a good set to from 9 till 2—5 hours—lectures and everything else went to the dogs. Fine amusement in a close C.R. with the thermometer at 80°. Strange scenes such meetings had they only a Dickens to analyse them, and draw out men's motives and characters in the words and arguments they use.' There is ample evidence to show how deeply the undergraduates appreciated Pattison's interest.

In college too he took his turn in the rota of offices. He became bursar and noted gloomily that there was a £100 deficit for which he could not account which he would have to pay out of his own pocket, an experience remarkably similar to that which Newman had had when bursar of Oriel. He was elected subrector and so became responsible for presiding in Common Room, not a job which he particularly liked . 'You know', he wrote on 8 November 1846, 'how I have been occupied this week, in eating and drinking with . . . ardour worthy of a better cause—after five days incessant labour of this description I find myself, somehow or another, elevated to the subrectorial seat—this took place on Friday—Green retires from the scene to the privacy of his parish, to renovate himself for his proctorship in April next. My first public exhibition was on Friday— I have not for some years shown myself in Hall on that day—but I could not avoid it on this occasion and I had to preside on the Rector's left hand —and to make a fool of myself in the usual way in proposing toasts etc. Beyond this chairmanship in Hall and C.R. I have to present for degrees, and the entire regulation of the discipline.' When his time came up for re-election he was not enthusiastic. 'They', he wrote home on 5 November 1849, 'have got up a party to oppose me. Andrew is going to offer himself! He will have the support of Metcalfe, West and Ogle certain, and of others perhaps. My position is certainly a hard one. I had much rather not be Subr, and could a creditable substitute be found wd. not be. It is not at all to my taste to have to fill the chair in C.R. and to drink wine when I don't want. Nor is it at all agreeable for a Tutor to have to haul men up for trifling breaches of discipline, such as missing Chapel etc. It creates a little irritation necessarily in their minds, wh. indisposes them to listen to yr. instructions. So that I am really sacrificing greatly my own comfort to the respectability of the College in being willing to become Subr as we might as well be governed by Jim Crow as by Andrew.' In the university Pattison had a growing reputation. He acted as examiner. He won the Denyer Prize two years running; 'I am the first,' he proudly told his sisters 'who ever got it twice'. He was known to view the movement for university reform sympathetically.

Yet the opposition to his re-election as subrector was ominous for the future. He had not concealed his dislike of the 'old gang'. His contempt for wagers and cards was riling. To avoid the Common Room dinner he had been known to dine an hour earlier. 'We have a bit of mutton roasted, hot the first day, and cold the 2nd. The old fogies do not quite like our cutting them so dead, but it is much nicer to dine early that we e'en let them growl.' There was, however, a more deep-rooted cause of the dislike with which Pattison was regarded by his seniors.

To understand this we must return to the religious scene of contemporary Oxford which made so powerful and continuing an impact on both Gladstone and Pattison. Both men were passionately aware of their shortcomings, idleness, impure thought, too much sleep, insufficient devotion and so forth, and they repeatedly resolved to do better in the future. They had little opinion of contemporary religion in the university. Gladstone wrote bluntly that the 'state of religion in Oxford is the most painful spectacle which ever fell to my lot to behold.' He commented on the small attendance at Communion and found the College service (which at Christ Church took place in the cathedral) often 'lacking in decency.' 'Had,' he commented, 'to go to Veysie about a most disgraceful disturbance in Chapel last night.' 'I am sorry to say,' he wrote home 'that the matter appears to me to be more shamefully profaned here than at Eton.' Attendance at College chapels was still compulsory, and even Gladstone, having stayed up too late talking the previous night, overslept and, like Woodforde, had to do 'an imposition' for missing Chapel, 'third time in five days, of which I am really ashamed.' As a junior Student, it was one of his duties to act as 'prickbill', that is, to take a note of the men attending chapel. The current state of religion in Oxford, to which Pattison's experience also bears witness, explains how well fertilised was the soil for the onset of Tractarianism.[1]

But Gladstone, brought up in a strongly Evangelical tradition, was an essentially religious man. He was an extremely conscientious church-goer, rarely missing morning and evening chapels, taking the sacrament whenever the opportunity presented itself, going to the university sermon and attending services in the city churches. Yet his time at Oxford was to be a period of religious unsettlement. He not only began to question some of

---

[1] Cf. the comment in *Academical Abuses Disclosed* (1832): 'After the doors are closed the reader commences the Church of England service, which, stopping only for want of breath, and being ably seconded by the responder, (the rest being totally indifferent) he generally succeeds in running through, in fifteen minutes and some odd seconds. Such is the mockery of religion which he is compelled to attend twice a day'.

the fundamental tenets of his Evangelical upbringing, notably the doctrine of predestination, but he was exercised by moral scruples, more especially by a feeling of guilt rooted in adolescent experience. His diary and letters, intensely introspective, were full of resolutions to overcome sin and temptation. 'This day', he wrote on 29 December 1828, 'by God's mercy I close my 19th year. Would that in looking back I could discern any decided features of improvement. Would that I did not on the other hand see many grievous crimes, many unlawful fears and objections.' The following year he noted that he had 'to thank God for many signal mercies. In one besetting sin there has been less temptation perhaps tho' not less readiness to be tempted—and though God has kept the temptation perhaps away there has been black sin on my part. Yet may I know who hath caused to be written "The Blood of Christ cleanseth me from all sin".'

He sought to find a practical expression for his Christian belief. Even in his undergraduate days there are references to the rescue work which was to cause so much anxiety to his friends later in his life. On a visit to Oxford in the summer of 1828, he 'met a woman and had a long conversation with her' and the next day 'at night met the poor creature again.'[1] On 24 July 1829, he 'had some conversation and business with two persons, both really, I believe, in some distress.' He certainly engaged in religious discussion with his friends. A curious incident later in his undergraduate career demonstrates Gladstone's attempt to apply the code of values which he had embraced to his own life. When he was set on and beaten up by a group of men (were they those whom he had reported for making a disturbance in chapel the previous day?) after midnight in his own rooms, he used the occasion to deduce what good lessons might be drawn from the unpleasant experience: 'a mortification of my pride'—"Christ was buffeted and smitten" an exercise of the duty of forgiveness.'

Gladstone left Oxford before the Tractarian movement got under way, but his religious sympathies were moving away from the Calvinistic Evangelicalism of his home towards a more Catholic position. He had already embraced the doctrine of baptismal regeneration. Unlike Pattison his faith survived the assaults of doubt and became the foundation of his political life.

Pattison's birthdays gave him occasions for reviews of past shortcomings and of resolutions for the future. On his thirtieth birthday he commented,

[1] The Proctors' Manual for 1887 asserted that 'it is one of the most important duties of the Proctors to keep the streets clear of prostitutes.' A special room was allocated in the Clarendon Building for their reception. One enthusiastic proctor in the nineteenth century is said to have chased one woman as far as Witney.

'Ripe and mature in age, but only beginning . . . Christian life—a child in knowledge and judgement . . . spent nearly two hours this morning in devotion and self-examination, with some fervency.' On 29 October 1843, he confessed: 'Did not get up to Communion this morning—find myself gradually slipping away from strictness and spiritual thoughts.' Nearly two years later on 29 July he reflected that he felt 'a sense of distance from God, and that I am leading a sensual life, devoted to my bodily comforts, and running away, as though for a respite, from religious thoughts.'

If Gladstone and Pattison were typical of their generation, the impact which Tractarianism made on Oxford becomes the more explicable. Gladstone left Oxford before the movement started, but it soon attracted his sympathy from afar. Pattison had lived on the same staircase as Newman, but only began really to know and admire him after he became a graduate. Had Provost Hawkins of Oriel mentioned the direction in which Pattison's religious sympathies were moving, it is extremely unlikely that he would have been elected at Lincoln. He was already involved in the movement, though perhaps never quite to the same extent that he later suggested. Nonetheless he became a devoted follower of Newman: at the Oriel Gaudy 'I luckily got next to J.H.N. and had a very nice snug talk— for nothing is so snug as a large dinner party—about Athanasius and the Benedictines.' 'To me', he wrote in September 1842, 'the greatest solace I have is my share in the little congregation at St Mary's, morning and evening, so that I feel, when I miss, quite put out.' Newman, who appreciated Pattison's qualities, asked him to contribute to the series of lives of the British saints which he had planned.

The infection spread from Oxford to his sisters at Hauxwell. 'Cast in your lot', he tells them 'with Nelson, Kettlewell, Ken, Patrick, Taylor, Hooker, Sanderson—with the great names of the English clergy under the Stewarts. . . . And embracing heartily, and with fixed purpose of *practising* accordingly this system, go to the N.T. and *then* and to *such a* mind, (and to such only) Scripture ceases to have that character of vagueness and ambiguity which seems to belong to it.' The sisters needed little persuasion. In their remote Yorkshire rectory Tractarianism gave them an interest which they badly wanted. They took a keen, if sometimes uninformed, interest in the saga of the Tractarians at Oxford, read the tracts, sought to adopt Tractarian ritual and ceremonial to their own lives—'Imagine breviaries in Drawing-rooms, and meditation on a sofa' was Pattison's somewhat acid comment—and wrote to their learned elder brother for advice. What should they read? What was the appropriate design for an altar frontal? In so doing they had to brave the wrath of their tyrannical, deranged father. They were repeatedly 'covered with disgrace, obloquy and dislike', as Eleanor told Mark. 'I sincerely hope', Mark wrote to her on Easter Day, 'your Easter has not *yet* been invaded by any attack or insult. . . . Nothing delights me so much as to find my dear Sisters so visibly walking with God. . . . E's account of your Lent is indeed cheering—it is truly "serving God with fastings and prayers night and day".'

It was through their brother's eyes that they watched the procession of events which led through the *Tracts* and the eager discipleship of young Oxford men to a revivification of Anglicanism as well as to a flow of converts to Rome. Pattison was himself involved in each of the crises that marked the fluctuating history of the movement. At first Pattison's attitude appears to be relatively detached. As he became more closely identified with the Tractarians cause, so his once sympathetic opinion of Dr Hampden hardened. When in May 1842, the heads tried to rescind the decision which prevented Hampden from sitting on the board to appoint select preachers, Pattison was among the signatories who sought 'to avert the mischief with which we are threatened.' 'In my eyes', he told the sisters, 'victory or defeat are unimportant in comparison of the lodging the protest in vindication of Catholic truth against the deepest and subtlest heresy of our day.' When *Tract XC* was condemned, the 'fulmen of Golgotha', Pattison commented, 'has fallen at last—a formal condemnation by the board of Heads of the mode of interpretation of the Articles inculcated in the Tract.' When the attempt to make Isaac Williams professor of poetry failed in 1842 (by 923 votes to 621), Pattison could assert: 'One thing is proved—that is, the astonishing fact that 621 members of Convocation, as Hannah says, have common sense!' In practice, the movement was already passing the climax of its influence in Oxford, its decline in part promoted by the steady flow of converts to Rome.

Of this development Pattison was at first highly critical. 'I suppose you have seen in the Papers', he wrote to Eleanor on 31 December 1842, 'this new Row about Bernard Smith. I do not know whether you remember him as a very early Undergraduate acquaintance of mine in the Belfield set. He was originally of Oriel, but had been elected to a Demyship at Magdl., a most amiable fellow—but I think the description in the O.H. tolerably correct "not very strong-minded." He is gone over to Rome. As to the action I have nothing to say. Every person of religious views must naturally prefer the acknowledged Fellowship of the Saints to our, at best, dubious position, but it is time and circumstance that are so annoying.' As more and more friends and pupils made the venture of faith, his judgment became more charitable. He could write of Seager's reception that 'he has been so long notoriously a Roman Catholic that people feel it's good riddance', but when Dalgairns came to bid him farewell 'before his departure for Langres, where is going to study for orders with a friend of his Abbé Lorrin', Pattison confined himself to the comment, 'Think of his being a Priest in a year's time!' His own visits to Paris led in time to interesting contacts with French Catholic scholars. He stayed there with the Seagers and found them very friendly.

The final crisis of the movement came with the publication of W. G. Ward's book, *The Ideal of a Christian Church*. Ward had originally entered Lincoln (before Pattison became fellow) but had rapidly passed on to Balliol of which he became a fellow and mathematical lecturer. The scene in which the book was condemned, and Ward was himself deprived of his degrees, though the condemnation of *Tract XC* was vetoed by the proctors, was described vividly by Pattison in a letter to his sister.

Such stirring events could not pass the college by. If some of the younger fellows were, like Pattison, drawn towards Tractarianism, the older clerics were either evangelical or high-and-dry and regarded the movement with scant sympathy. Pattison always insisted, as Wesley had done before him, that he never used his position as tutor to bring undue pressure to bear. But where he saw hints of Puseyism, he could not help feeling a thrill of pleasure. 'One thing I must tell you of', he told Eleanor on 26 March, 'which has mainly contributed to keep me at home [he had thought of visiting Belgium in the vacation]. I have got three of our own men (a B.A. and two undergrads.) who come every day to say Vespers with me—their own proposition you may be sure—I cannot express the joy with which I received it—or the consolation it has been to me—and the punctuality and evident pleasure they take in the service is most cheering. I can see very plainly too they are all making efforts to keep the fast (Lent)—and one of the three in particular is indeed a good and guileless soul that it is impossible to help loving. . . . How can I help thinking that it is God who has sent me these souls for my comfort just at the time when I was throwing up all in despair?'

He reverted to the theme in a later letter. 'I am much more gratified by your true sympathy, so heartily expressed, in my three friends, "my boys" I call them. The pleasure of this indeed takes up too much of my thoughts. . . . They are, in fact, four, but one is away, having been obliged to go down in the middle of term.' This was Guthrie, who had had to leave Oxford because of his father's financial difficulties. Pattison's first impression of this young man had not been especially favourable, 'simple-hearted and amiable' but not particularly religious: Pattison had visited him when he was recovering from small-pox but he 'never even asked me to pray with him, though I had a P. Book in my pocket always for the purpose.' A later talk proved a revelation. 'I perfectly astonished to find in one who seemed externally only an uneducated child so much depth of feeling —so much character—and sound understanding . . . you may imagine my astonishment when before quitting the room he knelt down and begged my blessing. . . . 'You see here enough happiness to make mine indeed a "calix irrebrians" this Lent. . . . What never happened to me in my life till now—for 6 weeks past I have been in such a state of mental happiness as sometimes almost to alarm me.' Of another pupil, F. B. Guy, later first headmaster of Bradfield, he observed: 'To my eye the mere manner, gesture, countenance of the boy is an unceasing source of gratification. The more having him coming into my room twice a day though I may'nt (often not) speak to him, is worth anything to me. . . . Ornsby, here for a few days on a visit, happened to say Vespers with us one day—he knows nothing of the party, not even their names—but asking about them when they were gone, he said "and they seemed such nice-looking men too, particularly that one in the Commoner's gown".'

The realisation that he had a group of friends among the undergraduates was most gratifying to Pattison. He found unfailing joy in their common religious purpose. 'One of four scholars had been a good part of the Vacation', he wrote in February 1843, 'Smith—you must have heard me speak of him as our crack man (i.e. to be a double first etc) and I am rejoiced to say that, from all appearance, he is advancing in a really religious course. To my surprise, he has been a regular attendant at daily prayers and the early communion all the Vacation—at Chapel during Term he has always been so, but that might have been out of obedience to Coll. discipline. This has given me a great deal of pleasure—for though I knew that the infection of Puseyism had lately penetrated even into L. and that there was a knot of our undergraduates more or less well-inclined, I had never in any way encouraged them, and have most scrupulously abstained from mentioning the subject in conversation with them.'

The undergraduates rejoiced to find one of their tutors of their way of thinking. Later a group of men founded an association to promote the principles of Tractarianism, to observe the fasts and to take part in works of charity. They wished to make Pattison their president, but Pusey warned them against this. Even so, Pattison was closely associated with them, and he sponsored their request to the governing body to place a brass eagle lectern designed by Butterfield in the college chapel; this, the one surviving expression of their works of charity, now rests in the church of Waddington, Lincolnshire, a college living.

The crisis of 1845 had not left Pattison unscarred. He certainly pondered following Newman into the Roman Communion, but no more than Gladstone was Pattison able to take such a step. Both were too rational in their approach to religion, too liberal in their attitude, to reconcile themselves to much of the traditional teaching of the Church of Rome. Gladstone, like Pusey, remained an High Anglican. Pattison's faith gradually cooled, the process continuing slowly over the years, baffling and distressing his friends, strengthening his critics. For if the fellows of Lincoln looked askance at his championship of Tractarianism, they thought his new-found modernism even more disconcerting. By 1851, the year of the election to the rectorship, no one quite knew where he stood. The more conservative fellows held religious liberalism to be as repugnant as the political liberalism, with its implicit demand for university reform, which Pattison had also championed.

He could still reasonably have hoped to be elected rector in 1851. He had done more than any other tutor to raise the college's intellectual standing in the university. He had won the respect and affection of many of his pupils. He had been prominent in the university reform movement, urging much-needed changes and the elimination of long-standing abuses. His gradual disillusion with Tractarianism should have worked in his favour with colleagues suspicious of any form of religious enthusiasm. Of the eleven fellows two were abroad, one in India, the other in St Helena. The remainder were evenly divided. Everything depended on the vote of a non-resident lawyer, J. L. Kettle, who promised to support Pattison. At the last minute, partly owing to the machinations of the clerical conservatives, Kettle changed his mind. As a result the election went in favour of a former fellow, Thompson, an incumbent of a country living, who, in the opinion of many, was certainly not a scholar and possibly not a gentleman. As a result of litigation arising out of the election the College soon faced unwelcome publicity, suggesting that many of the charges which the liberals made against the colleges of unreformed Oxford were demonstrably true. As for Pattison the shock was total. Seared by grief at his failure, he practically withdrew from College life nor was his election ten years later a sufficient compensation for the disappointment he had suffered. The experience was so traumatic as to make him emerge a sadder, even a changed man.

If Pattison had to endure rejection by his college, Gladstone had ultimately to undergo a similar, though less bitter, experience at the hands of the university electorate. As an undergraduate Gladstone had taken a leading role in drawing up a petition against the Reform Bill which had been signed by no less than two-thirds of the residents, some 770 in number. Although he remained a devout Anglican, he was to recede steadily from high Toryism towards an idealistic and reasoned liberalism. By 1847 some of the Oxford residents were already showing their disquiet at their learned member's doubtfully progressive opinions, even though, as we have seen, he at first emerged triumphant from the challenge.

Although Gladstone's political principles were liberal, he had resisted for some time the growing demand for a royal commission on the universities, but he came to realise that the university's attempt to overhaul its own machinery, dilatory and piece-meal, would not satisfy public opinion. So Pattison and Gladstone were brought together by their desire for university reform; nor was their liberalism unmarked by their critics. 'Gladstone's connexion with Oxford', Sir George Lewis wrote in March 1853, 'is now exercising a singular influence in the university. Much of his high-church supporters stick to him, and (insomuch as it is difficult to struggle against the current) he is liberalizing them, instead of their terrifying him.' Gladstone, supported by the younger and more intellectually distinguished members of the university, was returned without opposition in 1857. Two years later he had to compete, successfully, against Lord Chandos.

But he began to wonder whether the game was worth the candle. His affection for Oxford began to be strained by the intransigence of his opponents. Even Pusey, for long so loyal, looked askance at Gladstone's candidature. Defeated by Gathorne-Hardy in 1865, largely because of the introduction of the postal vote which enabled the clerical die-hards to change the balance of the election, Gladstone moved to another, very different, constituency. 'A dear dream is dispelled,' he commented in his diary, 'God's will be done.' Though Gladstone's association with the university became less intimate, the university never had a more loyal son; the faith which sustained him, and upon which his political idealism was founded, had been consolidated and enriched by his experience of Oxford, not least by the teaching of the Tractarians.

Gladstone died in 1898—his memory perpetuated by the foundation of a university prize—Pattison some 14 years earlier. In spite of his avowed liberalism in politics and religion, the latter demonstrated by his readiness to contribute to the controversial *Essay and Reviews* in 1860, he was elected, not without opposition, rector of Lincoln in 1861. The great disappointment which he had suffered as a result of his failure ten years earlier was wiped out but never forgotten. He became an Oxford character, no less so than his rival, Jowett of Balliol, whose career had followed a course in many ways so similar to his own. Although he only published one major work of scholarship, his life of *Casaubon*, he was commonly regarded as one of the most learned men in the university. He figured in contemporary literature, possibly, though very far from certainly, in George Eliot's *Middlemarch* as Dr Casaubon, plainly as Professor Forth in Rhoda Broughton's *Belinda* and as Roger Wendover in Mrs Humphrey Ward's *Robert Elsmere*. In the university he continued to champion liberal education, criticising not merely the still-existing abuses in the university but the methods which were being used to remedy them. For Pattison, the overriding purpose of the university was basically intellectual, to promote research and to break through the frontiers of existing knowledge. So he viewed with increasing contempt the way in which Jowett seemed to aim to transform the university into a superior public school, replete not merely with a classical education but with all the panoply of competitive games. On becoming rector he had married a clever, elegant woman, Frances Strong, years younger than himself, who became a recognised authority on the history of French art. As Liberal in her opinions as her husband, she made the rector's lodgings the centre of a salon.[1] All the luminaries of nineteenth-century Oxford, as well as those with a wider reputation in the outside world, among them George Lewes, George Eliot and Walter Pater, came to their dinner table. The college flourished. Its academic record was good. If the older type of fellow, the Wests and the Metcalfes, remained a constant and irritating reminder of the past, among the young fellows there were scholars of real distinction, Henry Nettleship, Warde Fowler, Samuel Alexander.

Yet for Pattison life became soured. Perhaps he had never really got over the bitterness of the election of 1851. Perhaps his relations with his

[1] She was in many respects a sophisticated and sociable woman. On one occasion she and some friends were entertaining undergraduates to charades in the Rector's lodgings, which involved the company dressing up in ridiculous costumes. Then the Rector arrived unexpectedly, advanced grimly into the drawing room and insisted on being introduced solemnly to all the participants, so bringing the party to a prompt and sad conclusion.

family had never recovered from the shock which his revulsion from Tractarianism had called forth at Hauxwell. Perhaps he could not cope with the fatal psychological taint which had so haunted his father and destroyed the happiness of his Yorkshire home. He found college affairs infinitely tedious, the company of the majority of his colleagues repugnant, that of undergraduates for the most part uncongenial. He was to them a remote and unattractive figure. His marriage ran into stormy waters, for his wife found the marital relationship increasingly abhorrent to her, while her poor health led her to stay for long periods in the south of France. Lonely, obsessed with the notion that his wife was spending too much money, Pattison did not improve matters by falling in love, or semi-falling in love, with a liberal-minded but prim young lady, Meta Bradley. He found serenity alone among his books, but there, too, he must often have sighed as he remembered the confidence of his earlier days and felt the strain of the uncertainty, the lack of faith, the agnosticism which had replaced it. 'I have so often told you,' he had written nearly half a century earlier, 'that it is not mere existence, not the outside shell, that constitutes a person; but that *excellence*, first and chiefly of heart and character and secondly of head that can qualify anyone for a *companion*, a *friend* or a *sister*.' If he had achieved the second excellence, the first had escaped him. On his death-bed, the aged Newman made a special journey to see his old friend. Pattison was touched but characteristically suspicious. The solitude of the study had become the solitariness of life itself.

In their century Gladstone and Pattison, unique personalities as they were, could be said to represent many of the significant features of Oxford. Oxford was still very much a place of religion, a place where religious issues were constantly discussed, where religious activity, soon to be reinforced by the appearance of Roman Catholics and Free Churchmen, played a vital part in the life of the place. Yet in Gladstone's firm convictions and Pattison's waning faith we seem to see the two sides of a picture, the emergence of tensions which were to condition study and life in the century after their death.

XI

A Century of Change,
1878-1973

Contemporary trends

In the century which followed the second university reform act the modern university took shape. Although the framework of the university and the pattern of its organisation remained comparatively unaltered, profound changes took place in its teaching and syllabuses, in the research undertaken there, and ultimately in its social composition. Such changes did not occur at once, though two World Wars acted as catalysts, but their cumulative effect was to make modern Oxford a very different place from what it had been a hundred years earlier. Adaptation to the real, or supposed, needs of contemporary society played an increasingly influential part in this process. As a consequence, though the university was often criticised, sometimes justly, sometimes with malice aforethought, its prestige as an international centre of scholarship mounted steadily.

The range of studies, both for junior and senior members, widened in these years. Many more new courses were made available to undergraduates. The joint school of Jurisprudence and History was divided into component parts in 1872; the school of Theology was set up in 1871. It became possible to take the honour school of Oriental Languages, a useful training for the Indian Civil Service, largely staffed by Oxbridge graduates, in 1872. Other new schools included English, instituted in 1893 after much controversy, Geography (1933), Agriculture (1939) and Forestry (1945). After the First World War the joint honour school of Modern Greats or P.P.E. (Philosophy, Politics and Economics), though criticised by some as 'one more nail in the coffin of Greats', was accepted by 95 to 58 votes in Congregation. A decree put forward in 1922 to set up a Science Greats, founded on philosophy and natural science, was, however, defeated by 66 votes to 38, and it was not until 1970 that a school of Human Sciences was established.

P.P.E. was the precursor, at some distance, of a number of other joint honour schools, P.P.P. (Philosophy, Psychology and Physiology), set up in 1949, Engineering and Economics, History and Modern Languages, History and Economics, Mathematics and Philosophy—and more were on the way. This diversification of study, contrasting with the predominantly classical and mathematical courses of the earlier nineteenth century, partly resulted from the findings of the Kneale Committee and was designed to overcome the deficiencies thought to result from over-specialisation in single subject schools.

Even more novel was the attention paid to graduate research. After 1918 two new degrees, the B.Litt. and the D.Phil., were introduced to enable foreign students, more especially Americans, to win some positive recognition of their studies. There was a steady increase in the number of research students, partly as a consequence of the award of the Rhodes scholarships; 145 in 1931, 257 in 1936. But it was only after 1945 that the increase was spectacular; in 1971–2 there were 3,098 post graduate students (by comparison with 8,011 undergraduates). As a result colleges had to provide new amenities in the form of special or middle common rooms. Another new degree, the B.Phil., was established in 1947, to provide a half-way house between the course for the B.A. and the intensive research leading to a thesis for a research degree, and soon won some regard as a measure of scholarly capacity.

Such changes were only made possible by the extent to which senior members contributed to the university's reputation for scholarship by writing, teaching and research. Oxford's prestige for classical studies had stood high in the late nineteenth century as the names of Pattison, Jowett, Nettleship and Ingram Bywater testify; in philosophy T. H. Green and F. H. Bradley attracted attention. In subsequent years the tradition was sustained and extended to other subjects. If Oxford lacked the mastery of the enigmatic Wittgenstein, it was, as the teaching of A. J. Ayer, J. L. Austin, Gilbert Ryle and Peter Strawson demonstrated, long to be in the vanguard of philosophical exploration. A catalogue of scholars can hardly prove illuminating, but a university which numbered among its professors, the classical scholars, Gilbert Murray, John Beazley and Eduard Fraenkel, the historians C. H. Firth and F. M. Powicke, the lawyers, Frederick Pollock, Paul Vinogradoff, A. V. Dicey and W. S. Holdsworth, the author Walter Raleigh, the chemists Robert Robinson and Cyril Hinshelwood, the neurologist Charles Sherrington and the pathologist Lord Florey, to name only a few distinguished senior members, could surely be said to compete favourably in scholarship with most other universities.

It is against a backcloth of scholarship and research rather than one of political and religious change that Oxford life has to be placed. Before the First World War the majority of undergraduates were drawn from the upper and middle classes. In many respects they were unlike their eighteenth and early nineteenth-century forebears. It was not merely that they dressed differently, though still soberly and neatly,[1] but, more important, their values were largely determined by the *mores* of the public schools, from which they came. The Junior Common Room, itself a recent innovation (established at Christ Church in 1832, at Lincoln in 1854) became the focal-point of their existence, the scene of debates and smoking concerts, the arena from which the now powerful *cultus athleticus* stemmed, and from which college literary and other societies proliferated.

Willie Elmhirst of Worcester, for instance, whose diary of his freshman year, 1911–12, provides an invaluable record of undergraduate activity, shared fully in nearly all spheres of collegiate activity, the river, the cricket field, the literary society and the college mission. His time runs smoothly enough, reading novels in the Union, taking part in amateur dramatics, celebrating the end of Torpids: 'Pierce was pretty well even in Hall and was most amusing. O. T. Jones had visitors about 12.15 last night who woke him by emptying 2 siphons of soda water in his bed and also smashed a picture and a walking stick.' He was a conscientious but not an inspired student, doing his weekly essay and finding the lectures dull. Only once apparently did he attend a debate in the Union when it passed a motion by 86 votes that 'the present Home Rule Bill is unworthy of support.' Mention of the Irish problem sends a cold breath through the summer air. Although Elmhirst never alludes to continental politics, he was an enthusiastic member of the O.T.C., preferring to drill rather than to watch the May Day ceremonies at Magdalen Tower. He would test his new army boots—with dire effects to his feet, on a route march. In such exercises there was an element of ominous predictability. He went down with a Third in Law in 1914, was articled to his uncle, a solicitor and was killed at the age of 24 on the Somme in 1916.

Undergraduate life was not necessarily without its moments of protest. When, in 1880, members of the University College Boat Club screwed up some of the dons' outer doors, among them that of the senior proctor, the

---

[1] Although, on his last visit to Oxford, Gladstone commented on the shabby appearance of the undergraduates, silk hats or bowlers were still universally worn on Sundays.

Rev. A. S. Chavasse, after their annual dinner, the governing body rusticated the majority of the college for the remainder of the term. Eight years
later, when the Hon L. J. Bathurst was rusticated by New College for
including some material thought to be offensive in a university magazine,
his contemporaries dragged his cab to the station and refused to attend hall
or evening chapel.

But the average undergraduate of the late Victorian and Edwardian era
was a conventional creature, suspicious of any departure from the norm.
In the 1880s Bohemianism had a momentary vogue. Oscar Wilde was at
Magdalen in 1874. Max Beerbohm graduated at Merton in 1882. But the
hearties often persecuted the aesthetes, even to the extent of breaking up
their rooms and furniture. One, who had been forced out of college by
this kind of behaviour, admitted that he had 'committed the unpardonable
offence of wearing ties of unusual tint, of using scent in chapel, and of
having made a speech at the Union with which his assailants did not
agree.' 'We are not', he continued, 'so narrow-minded as to believe that
to wear a tie of sage-green, to have an admiration for peacock-feathers, to
prefer soft shades and delicate tints to glaring colours, to dedicate a
college-room to the worship of Apollo rather than of Bacchus . . . are the
outward signs of affectation or lower powers.'

His cause was, however, that of a minority of undergraduates. The
majority, once they had graduated, 'wearing *spats*, remarkably short hair,
and collars and ties of uncomfortable stiffness', would follow a professional
career in medicine, in teaching, the law, politics, the Church, the Home
and Indian Civil Service. There was still a relatively small intake into the
commercial and mercantile world.

The personnel of the senior common rooms underwent a more radical
transformation. Oxford was still a very clerical society. In 1903 the
chemist, N. V. Sidgwick, bet the future clerical master of Pembroke,
Homes Dudden, that they would see at least 15 clergymen walking
between Wolvercote and the Turl and won his bet, for they saw 18.
Nonetheless the clerical don was slowly fading from the scene. Colleges
preferred to elect young scholars of promise, few of whom were in holy
orders. Although the majority were probably conventionally conservative,
there was a growing leaven of humanists, agnostics and radicals—such as,
for instance, Sidney Ball, the Fabian socialist of St John's—whose teaching
was regarded with some suspicion by their more traditionalist colleagues.
The elimination of celibacy as a necessary qualification for a fellowship—
though Worcester deprived its former dean, Truslove, for marrying

without leave of the College—helped to promote a major change in the character of the senior common room; and the growth of north Oxford, a fine field for the speculative builder, as Keble's steward, Walter Grey, future mayor and Tory M.P., discovered, represented not merely the extension of the university but the changed status of the don.

Even so, however many the signs of that steady erosion of faith, which continued to haunt Dr Pusey whose long tenure of the chair of Hebrew came to an end in 1882, religion in some shape or form long continued to be one of the principal activities of don and undergraduate. The virtual ending of the Anglican monopoly of the university had helped to release new energy. There was a flourishing school of theology, invigorated by the attempt of Gore and the *Lux Mundi* group to align high Anglicanism with philosophical idealism, for Gore realised, much to the pain of H. P. Liddon and the older Tractarians, that it was impossible to maintain the traditional ascriptions of the Old Testament books in the face of modern critical research. The termination of religious tests allowed the foundation of a number of new denominational societies: Mansfield College, founded to prepare men for the work of the Congregational ministry in 1886 (and given status as a permanent private hall in 1955); Manchester College, a Unitarian society originally established at Manchester in 1786 which moved to Oxford from London in 1888; Campion Hall, for the Society of Jesus, set up in 1896 and admitted as a private hall in 1918; St Benet's Hall in 1897, also recognised as a private hall in 1918. Local churches, like St Aldate's during the long ministry of Canon Christopher, flourished. Pusey House was founded as an Anglican centre for Catholic minded undergraduates. The O.I.C.C.U., and later the S.C.M., continued to have a large following; and university missions, such as those conducted by Dean Inge in 1924 and Archbishop Temple in 1935, drew large congregations of undergraduates. It was perhaps symptomatic of the continued strength of clerical opinion, at least among old members of the university, that the proposal to open examinerships in Theology and degrees in divinity to those who were not priests of the Church of England produced the largest meeting of Convocation on record; the motion was lost by 1,294 to 1,147 votes.

The development of science

If religion was still so much a feature of Oxford life, the university was affected in the century which followed the second reform act to an ever increasing extent by the intrusion of natural science into its curricula and common rooms. In general the Victorian don regarded science with suspicion, if not with contempt; and colleges were slow to elect scientists to fellowships. But Oxford could not in the long run resist the pressures which industry and technology, as well as intellectual enquiry, brought to bear upon its life.

The appearance of new buildings, the setting-up of new professorships, the formation of new departments and new honour schools all marked the outward development of this side of the university's life.[1] Buildings are, however, less significant than the men and women who work in them. The scientific achievements of Oxford, more especially since the ending of the First World War, have been of a varied character, in general representing less the initiative of a single individual than the collaboration of a group of research workers under his direction. Frederick Soddy's tenure of Dr Lee's chair of chemistry, lasting from 1919 to 1936, was in some ways unproductive, for he was too often diverted from research to vigorous and sometimes bitter arguments with his colleagues, and to the propagation of his individualistic views on currency reform; but he had played a significant part in the discovery and development of isotopes, more particularly in the formulation of the Law of Displacement. At a still earlier age he had been associated with Rutherford in the exposition of the theory of atomic disintegration. Soddy's successor, Sir Cyril Hinshelwood, so wide-ranging in his interests that he occupied the presidency of the Classical Association as well as that of the Royal Society, was responsible for pioneer work in the field of chemical kinetics. Soddy had read science at Merton in the late 'nineties; Henry Moseley, who graduated at Trinity in 1910, worked under Rutherford at Manchester where his analysis of X-ray spectra led to the first unambiguous assignment of atomic numbers, which might have augured well for Oxford science in the future had he not been killed at Gallipoli in 1915.

Another scientist of an older generation, N. V. Sidgwick, who astonished his contemporaries by taking a first class in Greats *after* he had been awarded a first, in 1895, in science, made an important contribution to the understanding of chemical valency, applying the theory of the Rutherford-Bohr atom and its later developments to the whole range of chemical compounds. Sidgwick's knowledge was exceptionally wide, his perceptions crisp, his tongue sometimes acid, and he represented in the universality of his scientific learning, a type of scientist that modern specialisation has virtually made extinct.

[1] I have to thank my colleague, Dr P. W. Atkins, for help with this section.

The Clarendon Laboratory has been more especially pre-eminent in the development of low-temperature physics, and in the development of magnetic resonance, more particularly electron paramagnetic resonance in solids. It was a small and ill-equipped institution when it was taken over by 'the Prof.', Frederick Lindemann, later Lord Cherwell, in 1919. Cherwell held Dr Lee's chair of experimental philosophy from 1919 to 1956 (and from 1921 two fellowships, one at Wadham and the other at Christ Church where he lived and to which he left some two-thirds of his considerable fortune). Later a close associate of Winston Churchill, who greatly valued his advice, Cherwell in his right-wing Toryism, snobbishness and egoism seemed an unattractive figure to many of his contemporaries, his vegetarianism an uncharacteristic aspect of an aggressive temperament, but, in spite of prolonged absence on government work, he did a fine job in creating the Clarendon Laboratory as a world-reputed department of low-temperature physics. His successor, Francis Simon, only survived his appointment a few months, but he had been working in Oxford since 1933, having left Germany on Hitler's accession to power (though as a Jew with a first class war record, including an Iron Cross, he was exempt at this stage from Hitler's anti-Semitic legislation), and had been professor of thermodynamics since 1949. He had a more original mind than Cherwell and was held to be the most distinguished low-temperature physicist of his time; he was largely responsible for the formulation of the Nernst heat theorem which became the third law of thermodynamics. It was in the Clarendon Laboratory that helium was first liquefied in Britain. Simon later played an important part in promoting Britain's development of nuclear energy.

Among the more recent scientists who have done much to enhance the reputation of Oxford have been W. Hume-Rothery, the first holder of the Wolfson chair of Metallurgy, who did original work on the theory and structure of metals and alloys; Sir Hans Krebs, Whitley professor of Biochemistry from 1954 to 1967, whose name is commemorated in the 'Krebs cycle' in biochemical studies; and Professor Dorothy Hodgkin, a Nobel prize-winner, whose intricate and exciting work on the X-ray structure of complex molecules, more especially Vitamin B_{12} and insulin, contributed greatly to the understanding of the structure of biologically important materials. The work of university scientific departments, liable to periods of occasional stagnation, is a continuous process. In 1966 the university established a chair in molecular biophysics. Subsequently a group of chemists and molecular biologists have undertaken research, with the object of throwing light on enzymes, in the process employing a wide range of techniques to explore the central problem of living systems, planned study that was likely to prove fruitful and important for mankind as well as interesting in itself.

On this canvas the figure of the late Lord Florey looms large, because of the world-wide implications of the work that he and his colleagues, E. B. Chain, N. G. Heatley, A. G. Sanders and E. P. Abraham (whose work on the drug cephalosporin has been of a similar character) did on penicillin. Appointed to the chair of pathology in 1932, Florey investigated the many ways in which the anti-bacterial properties of penicillin could be developed, first demonstrating its curative character by dosing mice successfully on 25 May 1940. Wartime conditions in Britain were not propitious for its full scale propagation, but it was produced, with American help, in the United States, so that in 1943 it was being used to cure war wounds in North Africa. While Oxford escaped the attention of the *Luftwaffe*, fear of a possible invasion led some of the research workers at the Sir William Dunn School to rub freely sporing mycelium in their pockets in the hope that, if the Germans did invade, they might escape to a friendly or neutral country and so continue their research work there.

The university and the admission of women
Another important development which was to change the life of the university, though it seemed at the time a hole-in-a-corner affair, was the admission of women. An Association for the Higher Education of Women in Oxford was formed on 22 June 1878, and in October of the following year, two residential halls, Lady Margaret Hall, its membership at first confined to members of the Church of England, and Somerville, an undenominational society as its somewhat bleak chapel still testifies, were founded. Subsequently Miss Wordsworth founded St Hugh's in a semi-detached house in Norham Gardens in 1886, with Miss Moberly as principal and 4 students. St Hilda's, founded by Miss Beale, the principal of the Ladies College at Cheltenham, started life in 1893. Non-collegiate girls were catered for by the Society of Oxford Home-Students, which was instituted in 1879 and which became, in 1952, St Anne's College.[1]

Many senior members resented the new development, believing that the feminine vocation was best promoted in the home, and fearing, not wholly

[1] From 1879 to 1893 the Oxford Home-Students were under the supervision of the Association for the Higher Education of Women; the university gave to the society the privileges of a recognised Society of Women Students in 1910. It was admitted to full college status in 1959.

unreasonably, that their entrance into the university might foreshadow a matriarchal society. Statutes permitting women to take certain university examinations (widened to include all in 1894) were passed in Convocation on 29 April 1884, by 464 votes to 321. Opponents of the measure stressed the 'more refined, delicate and domestic nature of women and the dangers of an unrestricted course of reading and study to the future mothers and teachers of our race, to the glare of publicity, and the excitement of un-wholesome rivalry.' Dean Burgon, preaching in New College on 8 June 1884, declared that the proposed statute was a 'reversal of the law of Nature which is also the law of God concerning women'; better that they should remain 'our modest mothers in their secret innocence of Physical Science and of a creedless Philosophy.' 'Inferior to us God made you, and inferior to the end of time you will remain. But you are none the worse for that!' But, even in 1884, the dean's weakness for ridiculous hyperbole evoked a titter from his congregation. Thomas Case, the President of Corpus, wrote to the *Times* on 27 April 1884 predicting that consequences of the statute could only be undesirable. 'Sound learning and the midnight lamp will be succeeded by light literature and the art of conversation at tea-parties. Young men will play at what young women like; the University Park will become a huge tennis-ground, and the river a series of expedi-tions to Nuneham.' The foundation of women's halls, in Pusey's view, was 'one of the greatest misfortunes that has happened even in our own time in Oxford.'

It seemed odd to the supporters of women's education that the university should allow women to take its examinations but refuse them the degree.[1] In 1896 a proposal was brought forward to approve the women's halls of residence and to allow the B.A. degree to be conferred on successful candi-dates in the examinations. After a debate in which Professor Dicey reminded the gathering that women constituted half the nation and that it was time Oxford took note of the fact, the resolution was lost by 215 votes to 140. The Oxford Union followed suit, rejecting a motion in favour of admitting women to the B.A. by 165 to 55 votes. *Punch* published a cartoon of Minerva finding her way blocked by an old clerical don with the caption, 'Very sorry, Miss Minerva, but perhaps you are not aware that this is a monastic establishment.' A. D. Godley reflected the tenor of the debate in humorous fashion:

[1] There was a curious anomaly in that Trinity College, Dublin, offered *an eundem* degrees to those who had qualified for degrees at Oxford and Cambridge, so that it was possible on payment of a fee for a girl who had passed the university examinations at Oxford to receive a Dublin degree.

Ye Somervillian students, Ye Ladies of St. Hugh's
Whose rashness and imprudence Provokes my warning Muse,
Receive not with impatience, But calmly, as you should,
These simple observations—I make them for your good.

Why seek for mere diplomas, And commonplace degrees,
When now-unfettered roamers—You study what you please,
While man in like conditions Is forced to stick like gum
Unto the requisitions Of a curriculum.

Initially the women's colleges were housed in Oxford's tall Victorian houses. The early principals were women of great, in some sense, masculine, character, accepting a minute salary and ruling their charges in an autocratic but paternalistic way. They were not distinguished academics; the first of whom this description could be used was Dame Emily Penrose, principal of Somerville. The girls' own regime was austere; characterised, as one of them recalled, by a diet of rice pudding, stew and Sunday observance. At first the Association for the Higher Education of Women took responsibility for the actual education of the girls and the halls were only concerned with residence. The Association, which was not dissolved until women were given membership of the university, made arrangements for the admission of women at inter-collegiate lectures, accompanied by a chaperone (even in 1919–20 the Association's expense sheet contained the item, £1 2s 6d 'for chaperonage'). The number of women attending university courses was for long so small that the average undergraduate probably never met his feminine counterpart nor, either because the undergraduate of the age was less mature than his successor or simply, and more probably, because customs were different, does he seem to have found the loss burdensome.

In spite of Oxford's conservatism of outlook, there was a steady shift of attitude, in favour of placing women on a less restricted basis. Magdalen, the last college to refuse to admit women to its lectures, gave way in 1906. Lord Curzon, who had been elected chancellor in 1907, in part to avert the threat of a royal commission, personally urged the university to undertake essential reforms. Mindful of his advice, in 1912, it had established a Board of Finance and reorganised the faculties, and in 1913–14 Congregation and the Hebdomadal Council were reconstituted in the interests of administrative efficiency. Curzon strongly advocated the admission of women to degrees, both in the interests of the university as of

the women, and a resolution to this effect had been accepted by the Hebdomadal Council on 22 June 1909.

But the stream of change, steady, if unspectacular, dried up with
rapidity as the First World War emptied Oxford of its students; a generation of young men went gaily, almost blithely, to the holocaust with very
little understanding of the dread catastrophe of which they were the
sacrificial victims. In October 1914, there were 1,400 undergraduates, in
1916, 550, 1917, 460 and in 1918, 369, many of the latter unfit or too young
to serve. The seniors who were too old to serve in the army were as committed to the seemingly patriotic cause as most of their less learned
contemporaries. The Examination Schools was turned into a military
hospital. Schools of instruction for young officers were set up in 1915 as
well as a school of military aeronautics.

The Armistice was greeted as warmly in Oxford as elsewhere, though, as
the editor of the *Oxford Magazine* commented, the city presented 'a
pleasing contrast to the scenes which disfigured one of London's historic
monuments, and which dragged patriotism into disgrace at Cambridge by
the wrecking of a newspaper office.' There was a special service of thanksgiving at St Mary's and fireworks at St John's; in the evening some
undergraduates celebrated the occasion by daubing the heads of the
Emperors outside the Sheldonian with red paint. By February 1919, 1,357
undergraduates were in residence.

Oxford between the wars

More important than the interregnum which war had created was the
dividing line which it represented. Many of those who returned to take the
shortened honour courses were mature men, some of whom had under-
gone a traumatic experience in the trenches. They were glad to be freed
from the carnage for study, but they did not always find it easy to adapt
themselves to a routine so different from that which they had recently
followed nor to obey the petty regulations typical of a society that was
still in some sense more of a school than a community of adults.

Although, in the course of three centuries, the rules had been modified,
undergraduate behaviour was still controlled by the statute *de Moribus
Conformandis* of 1636. Colleges exacted small gate fines from those who
were not in by a certain hour. Although tobacco could be purchased (its
sale banned in 1636), no undergraduate was allowed to smoke in academical dress. He could not keep a motor car without proctorial permission, a
rule only recently rescinded. He might not play billiards before 1.00pm or

after 10.00pm. He was forbidden to loiter at stage doors, attend public race meetings or take part in shooting, coursing or other sports. His opportunities for dancing, a craze with young people in the 'twenties, drinking and dining were carefully regulated. A male undergraduate could not enter the room of a female undergraduate, though a woman with special leave from the head of her college might enter a man's rooms with a chaperone. It was only slowly, and in some colleges not until after the Second World War, that compulsory chapel, gate fines and other minor restrictions disappeared. Yet such rules appeared already outmoded in the changing world of the 'twenties and 'thirties.

In no sphere was the change more marked than in that of women's rights. 'The war had made a peaceful change in the status of women which seemed incredible six years ago', Miss Annie Rogers, one of the most indefatigable campaigners, remarked on 30 January 1920. Oxford could now implement the resolution which the Hebdomadal Council had passed in 1909 and admit women to full membership of the university. From May 1920, women were allowed to matriculate and to take all degrees except those in theology, the latter a disqualification which was eventually removed in 1935. But a good deal of inbuilt resistance to feminine influence remained. The Union at once regretted the 'recent triumph of the feminist movement' by 192–180 votes, and its members decided, in November 1926, in spite of a vigorous speech by the future principal of Lady Margaret Hall, Miss Lucy Sutherland, that women's colleges should be levelled to the ground. Some unfortunate girls, emerging from a lecture in May 1923, found that their male colleagues had converted their bicycles into men's machines. In 1927 over 200 senior members successfully petitioned the Hebdomadal Council to impose a limitation on the number of women who were to be admitted to the university, a restriction not removed until 1956. The heads of the women's colleges still remained ineligible for the vice-chancellorship, and in other ways the university for some time continued to treat its female members as second-class citizens.

The war had seriously damaged the finances of the university. The colleges, though some of them enjoyed very substantial revenues, had been affected by the long continuance of the agricultural depression, leading to a fall in rentals. In any case their contribution to the expenses of the university remained small. The extension of the university's teaching facilities, more especially in science, had created a heavy burden on its resources which its current revenue was insufficient to bear. A decree was consequently passed on 6 June 1919, authorising the vice-chancellor to apply for a government grant, conditional on the university's readiness to co-operate with the government in an enquiry into its resources and the use made of them. Many were anxious at the loss of freedom which government assistance might entail. 'We do not want Oxford to voice the views of Whitehall as Berlin once did the views of Potsdam. Oxford stands for freedom; and if she is to fulfil her freedom as the inspirer, and guide of the higher national life and thought, she must be free to determine her own curriculum and her own life. . . . Are we to sacrifice our independence for the sake of saving ourselves the trouble of finding elsewhere the necessary funds for the equipment of our laboratories?' But the decree was carried, by 126 votes to 88, and 'so Oxford with the miners, has declared for nationalisation'; 'one might have hoped', a critic grimly noted, 'that in an ancient seat of learning there might have been found a mind and temper capable of looking beyond the advantage of the moment, but to the scientist, as to the miner, the vision of the State as a milch cow has proved too attractive.' The first grant was £30,000 and even in the 'thirties did not average as much as £100,000 a year.

Another indication of continuing concern with the efficiency and reputation of the older universities was reflected in the establishment of a royal commission, in part a sequel to the promised grant, under the chairmanship of Asquith, leading to the act of 1923. Its report was moderately conservative in character, and made few sensational charges, but it naturally raised the apprehensions of some at the possibility of further interference by the state. 'Reform a university', Lord Hugh Cecil, one of Oxford's burgesses, remarked with typical pungency, 'You may as well reform a cheese—there is a certain flavour about a university as there is about a cheese, springing from its antiquity, which may very easily be lost by mishandling.' Subsequently modifications were made in the composition and powers of Congregation. College contributions to university funds were regularised according to their wealth; though the assessment remained relatively low. The commissioners also defined the duties of professors, reorganised the faculties and required that entry to the university should always be by examination, either Responsions or its equivalent. Hitherto colleges had admitted candidates after taking their own examination, submitting their entrants to be admitted or matriculated by the vice-chancellor. Some saw in this new measure an erosion of the rights of the colleges. When the statute was at first introduced it was negatived by 75 votes to 16, but senior members realised that if the university did not itself take action, the statutory commission would, and the recommendation was eventually accepted in December 1924. Finally the commission made it possible for dons to retire with a pension, though some, appointed under the old statutes, continued to hold their fellowships until death.

In the period between the wars Oxford, like Cambridge, received very substantial sums from private benefactors, some of which helped appreciably to improve buildings and laboratories. Sir Basil Zarahoff endowed a chair of French, Arthur Serena, one of Italian; Mr Whitley gave £10,000 towards a chair of Biochemistry. The Sir William Dunn School of Pathology, built through the generosity of Dunn's trustees, was opened in 1927. The Rockefeller foundation gave generously for the development of the department of Biochemistry and towards the erection of the New Bodleian Library at the corner of Broad Street, designed, not wholly satisfactorily, by Sir Giles Gilbert Scott. The biggest single giver was an Oxford man, William Morris, later Lord Nuffield. A shy, fundamentally humble-minded man, he distrusted intellectuals; in making an early donation of £10,000 towards the foundation of a chair of Spanish, he had remarked that university education was comparatively useless for the would-be aspirant in commerce and industry. He expected results to follow close on the heels of decision, being less interested in long-term research than in its immediate benefits. His major benefactions were therefore to be to medicine; the establishment of the Nuffield Institute of Medical Research in 1935, the scheme for Dominion demonstratorships and clinical assistantships in 1936, the Nuffield Fund for Research in Opthalmology in 1941; the Nuffield chair of Anaesthetics.

But he proved also to be a generous benefactor to St Peter's College, opened as a hostel in 1928 and next year accepted by a vote of Congregation (by 260 to 60) as a permanent private hall. There was criticism at the establishment of what seemed to some to be a denominational foundation: 'If', as Reginald Lennard of Wadham put it in 1929, 'the idea is to get together a body of sincere Evangelical Christians, whether they are Churchmen or Nonconformists, the road is at once open to inquisitorial scrutiny of the precise shade and temper of the undergraduate's convictions.' But Nuffield, who was not a deeply religious man, obviously did not feel this to be a real danger and contributed handsomely to the new hall.

He was himself keen to found a new college which would be of a practical character. He was, however, dissuaded from establishing what would have been a college of accountancy and technology by the purposeful but austere master of Balliol, A. D. Lindsay, then vice-chancellor, founding in its stead a society to be mainly concerned with research and study in the social sciences. This was not fundamentally an object with which Nuffield himself very much sympathised, the less so as the college appeared to attract economists and politicians of radical views. Yet he gradually became reconciled to his 'Kremlin', having at least got his own way over its architecture which, like his cars, was workmanlike rather than distinguished, and on his death he made the college his residuary legatee. The outbreak of war had delayed its building which was not started until 1949.

The flavour of Oxford between the wars is not very easy to catch. Although no longer dominated by clericalism, it was still in many respects a conservative society, suspicious, sometimes with good reason, of precipitate change. One of the last bastions of the clerical order had been the examination in compulsory Greek. Immediately after the ending of the First World War a further effort was made to bring this requirement to an end. 'No doubt', the classical don, E. C. Marchant exclaimed, 'a few will lose the chance of learning Greek in their schooldays; but think of the thousands who will escape from a dismal and futile drudgery. Why should thousands be sacrificed to produce a Greek scholar here and there?' The preamble easily passed Congregation, by 123 votes to 63, in March 1919; but the temperature was rising, especially among the non-residents, at a threat which some construed to be directed at Oxford's position 'as the fountain-head of the intellectual life of the nation.' There were others who saw in the frontal attack on Greek an implied challenge to Christianity itself. The motion was referred to Convocation which rejected the proposed statute by 312 votes to 306. The narrow majority—and the realisation that the statute was supported by the resident dons—induced its protagonists to bring it forward again, this time with success, in March 1920.[1]

Twelve years later strong feeling was again aroused by a degree proposing the abolition of the compulsory examination in Holy Scripture known as 'Divvers'. An attempt was made to frustrate this move by making Scripture an additional and compulsory subject in Responsions, but the proposal put forward by N. P. Williams, the Lady Margaret professor of divinity, was vigorously opposed by the philosopher, Gilbert Ryle, and was lost by 19 (108–127). The temperamental conservatism of the Oxford don was shown in other ways. The socialist G. D. H. Cole's appointment as reader in economics in 1925 was much criticised, by,

---

[1] A rough analysis showed that of those who voted in favour of the statute 85 per cent were laity and 15 per cent clergy; of those against it, 46 per cent clergy and 54 per cent laity.

among others, the vice-chancellor, Joseph Wells of Wadham, who commented, though in Latin, that the appointment brought little credit on the university. Roger Fry, an eminently suitable candidate for the Slade professorship of Fine Art, was rejected in favour of a much inferior candidate because of the indiscretions of his private life. On Curzon's death in 1925 the university first elected Lord Milner as his successor and, then after his sudden death, preferred the mediocre Tory Lord Cave to the Liberal Asquith, a devoted son of Oxford.

The undergraduate population, like the seniors, seemed firmly placed in the age of normalcy. 'On the one hand', Osbert Lancaster writes of Oxford in the late 'twenties, 'were the hearties, grey-flannel trousered or elaborately plus-foured,[1] draped in extravagantly long striped scarves indicative of athletic prowess; on the other the aesthetes, in high-necked pullovers or shantung ties in pastel shades. . . . Apart and consciously aloof were the Bullingdon and their hangers-on, always in well-cut tweeds and old Etonian ties, or jodpurs, yellow polo-sweaters and hacking jackets.' But the majority of undergraduates knew neither the choice society of the Bullingdon Club nor that of Garsington Manor where, until her removal to London, Lady Ottoline Morrell presided over a mingled society of artistic and able undergraduates and members of the Bloomsbury coterie. Their horizons were bound by lectures and tutorials, by the river and the games-field. The undergraduate, normally a product of a public school, in his tweed sports-jacket, his grey flannel-trousers (which had soon replaced the seemingly daring vogue of Oxford 'bags'), brogue shoes and short hair was fundamentally a conformist (as he still is, if to a somewhat different set of values and to changed sartorial and tonsorial fashions), suspicious even of the wearing of suede or 'co-respondent' shoes, flamboyant ties or shirts.

There were, however, some indications that Oxford was becoming more politically conscious, and more critical than it had been of the traditional values. Economic depression at home and rising international tension abroad were beginning to pierce undergraduate complacency. To assist the unemployed, undergraduates for some years helped to run camps at Eynsham (for south Wales) and at Duncombe Park, Helmsby (for Durham and Yorkshire); but many thought such efforts mere palliatives and looked

---

[1] A correspondent, writing on 4 December 1930 deplored the presence in Convocation of two senior members 'attired in golfing knickerbocker suits, which, I understand, are vulgarly known as "plus-fours". We have grown accustomed to the scandalous vagaries of costume adopted by undergraduates—I lately met a junior member of the University clad in a commoner's gown, a cloth cap, plus-fours and an umbrella—but surely we might be spared similar revolting sartorial exhibitions in the University legislature.'

towards a period of genuine socialist government. In November 1932, the Union was persuaded by George Lansbury by 316 votes to 247 that socialism was the only solution to the problems facing Britain. In February 1933, it attracted the attention of the national press by passing a motion, by 275 votes to 153, that its members would 'in no circumstances fight for its king and country'; Quintin Hogg was the principal opponent, C. E. M. Joad, the proposer. There was an immediate furore and talk of a communist plot, a charge which it would have been difficult to sustain as at the time of the debate the few Communists at Oxford were attending another meeting addressed by the leader of the unemployed marchers. Nonetheless the motion represented the contemporary pacifism and liberalism of an increasing number of undergraduates. They much resented the attempt made by Lord Stanley of Alderley and Randolph Churchill to get the motion expunged, and turned their proposal down by 612 votes (138 to 750). In subsequent months the Union declared that it had no use for conventional morality (though typically the next year it was to deplore the decline of the family as an institution), voted for the abolition of capital punishment, and agreed that British rule operated to the detriment of native races.

The Union was, and is, no very good index to undergraduate opinion; but the temper of Oxford in the early 1930s was noticeably more radical than it had been, and brought some junior members into collision with the proctors. The proctors had banned a meeting of the Anti-War group, in part because it was likely to condemn the Oxford O.T.C., and when, in spite of the ban, the meeting was held at Ruskin College[1] those who were apprehended by the proctors were gated both for the rest of the term, and for the whole of the ensuing term, while the left-wing October Club, which had been largely responsible for arranging the meeting, was banned. Many criticised the harshness of the action taken by the proctors. The university Liberal Club at once passed a resolution protesting against the 'principle laid down by the university authorities disallowing public criticism of university institutions.'

For the moment domestic discontents took precedence of the darkening international scene. The university Labour Club published a manifesto, incorporating a number of radical demands: that undergraduates should be entitled to lead the life of the ordinary citizen in all non-academic activities:

---

[1] Ruskin College had been set up in 1899, through the generosity of Mr and Mrs Vrooman, to provide educational opportunities for working men. In 1913, though not a part of the university, it was approved by the university as a society for higher studies.

complete freedom of expression in all religious matters: equal status for men and women in the universities: the formation of clubs without proctorial permission: complete freedom of undergraduate publications: abolition of the limitations on the number of women in the university: the ending of existing restrictions on the undergraduate use of bars, hotels and restaurants. It further demanded the formation and recognition of an undergraduate representative council which the proctors should consult in doubtful cases affecting administration and through which undergraduates should be entitled to express their own wishes with regard to their own welfare. It was to take over 30 years for the majority of these demands to be implemented.[1]

More undergraduates were stirred by international politics than by domestic issues. A Union motion in 1935 to the effect that the proctorial system was an anomaly in a modern university and should be replaced by some measure of self-government was defeated by 14 votes (151–165). But the menace of Nazism, the aggressive tactics of Mussolini, and the outbreak of the Spanish Civil War attracted more attention, turned the politically conscious from university affairs (as the Hungarian crisis of 1956 was temporarily to do) and eroded the basic pacifism of the early 1930s. In Oxford fascist meetings led to violent clashes. The presence of German refugee scholars was a pertinent reminder to senior members of the menace of the intolerant régime in Germany.

When war broke out in 1939, the university was as deeply involved in the struggle against Nazism as it had been a quarter of a century earlier against the Kaiser. Yet there was none of the innocent enthusiasm which had emptied the colleges in 1914 nor was the university quite so void of undergraduates as it had been between 1914 and 1918. Some of the colleges and university buildings were requisitioned for war purposes; and a skeleton staff kept the traditions as well as the teaching of the university in being. Demobilisation in 1945 brought a flood of men to the university, many eager and enthusiastic to help the creation of the new world which it was hoped, as naively in 1945 as in 1919, that the ending of the war would initiate.

Post-war Oxford

If the Second World War was outwardly less of a watershed in Oxford's

---

[1] As early as 1893 Hilaire Belloc had proposed a motion at the Union that undergraduates should have some share in university government. He was opposed by F. E. Smith, and the motion was lost by 56 votes (114–70).

history than the First, it did represent a distinct break with the past, and this became more pronounced as the first flush of enthusiasm faded and a new generation of undergraduates, not old enough to remember the 'thirties and 'forties, came into residence. Although the colleges were *prima facie* financially independent (though indirectly subsidised by fees and the stipends paid to fellows as university lecturers), the very large annual grant made under the aegis of the University Grants Committee, likely to amount in 1976–7 to £12,278 million, made it no longer possible to argue that Oxford was not, financially at least, answerable to the nation. Besides, the pattern of entry to the university was itself slowly changing, if less radically than some thought to be desirable. The system of state grants, the extension of the school leaving age, and the increase in the number of boys and girls taking their advanced levels widened the potential field of entry. Finally the tremendous increase in scientific and technological studies raised the question as to how satisfactorily Oxford was coping with this particular problem.

A mood of introspection seized the university in the 'fifties and 'sixties. Some reforms of a piecemeal character had been introduced before the university decided to anticipate the possible setting up of another royal commission by appointing one of its own under the chairmanship of one of the most distinguished of its graduates, Lord Franks, formerly ambassador to Washington, and, from 1961, provost of Worcester.

In a judicious assessment of Oxford's short-comings and needs the Franks Commission made important recommendations. It suggested a significant modification of the university's administrative machinery. The choice of vice-chancellor was no longer to depend on a system of rotation among the heads of the colleges but was to be open, at least in theory, to any member of congregation; so far the nominating committee has shown little desire to select a vice-chancellor who is not the head of a college. The commission also recommended the strengthening of the powers of the university's elected cabinet, the Hebdomadal Council, a policy-making as well as the principal executive body, possibly to the detriment of the semi-democratic body of residents, Congregation. It also suggested the reconstruction of the General Board of the Faculties and the setting-up of a new institution, a Conference of Colleges, wider in its character than the already existing Senior Tutors' Committee, to try to regulate and harmonise College attitudes and policies, often so diverse.

The majority of the Franks proposals were accepted by Congregation, and evidently helped to promote the efficiency of the university and to bring its studies into line with the needs of the contemporary world. In one respect, however, the Franks report offered a challenge to Oxford's long established values, in that it exalted the university at the cost of the colleges by promoting the powers of faculty boards, and of the General Board of the Faculties in particular.

Another aspect of post-war Oxford fostered a similar development. As a result of the vast expansion of the teaching facilities of the university, more especially of appointments in the science faculties, many lecturers found that they had no college connections, forming a group of what was somewhat curiously called 'non-dons'. Without an interest in the colleges, and sometimes coming from non-collegiate universities, the non-dons clearly represented a challenge to the college system which could only be met by their assimilation within it. This was more easily said than done. In an effort to combat this problem new graduate societies were formed: Linacre, a continuation at graduate level of the former non-collegiate institution, St Catherine's Society (which had, in 1963, become a full undergraduate college, with impressive if stark buildings and equipment designed by the Danish architect, Arne Jacobsen), St Cross and Wolfson, the latter, originating as Iffley College, having had the good fortune to find a princely benefactor in Isaac Wolfson whose name it now perpetuates.[1] In 1962 the Harrison committee advised that it was undesirable in a collegiate university for so many senior posts to be extra-collegiate. Subsequently provision was made, in spite of severe criticism, for the non-dons to be distributed somehow or other among the existing colleges. This scheme, more especially where by reason of so-called 'entitlement' there seemed a possibility of coercion, raised considerable ill-feeling, for many dons felt, possibly with justification, that the intrusion of men who had few tutorial duties and no college interests would weaken the ethos of college life and so make a college, even more than it was already, little more than a luncheon and dining club. In practice the majority of the non-dons were assimilated without real difficulty into collegiate societies, but a residual problem remained.

There was one other change, coming into prominence in the 'seventies, which was bound to affect the character of the colleges and their life. This was the scheme for co-residence which would permit the hitherto male colleges to admit women as fellows and undergraduates. As early as 1964

[1] There was another graduate college, St Antony's, set up in 1948 through the benefaction of the Frenchman, Antonin Besse, of Aden, which catered mainly for students of modern history. Nuffield, also a graduate society, specialised in politics, economics, sociology and modern history.

New College had taken steps to change its statutes to admit women, but, as a result of representation by the women's colleges, it had decided to shelve the proposals for the time being. Since that date the tide of opinion, fostered by undergraduates and the younger dons, began to flow strongly in favour of co-residence. The movement was rooted in that fusion of emotional idealism and academic logic, so beloved of Oxford senior common rooms. It was argued pertinently enough that the ratio of women to men in the university was far too low, and that women ought not to be debarred, if they were intellectually qualified, from enjoying the benefits of an Oxford education because of the comparatively small number of places available to them. It was stressed that as more and more entrants to the university came from co-educational schools that a co-residential society would be more likely to be a more natural, better-balanced and healthier community than a single-sex one. What Evelyn Waugh once described as the 'hard bachelordom of English adolescence' was an increasingly rare phenomenon in England of the 'seventies. Contrariwise the critics of co-residence proffered the Burkian injunction that it was unreasonable, as well as unwise, to change radically the character of an institution, good in itself and rooted in centuries of tradition, simply to suit the fashionable radicalism of the moment. If there was a real demand for more opportunities for female education in Oxford, co-residence was manifestly not the answer since it sacrificed the interests of male candidates to Oxford and was likely, by 'creaming off' the better women to the male colleges, to be detrimental to the women's colleges. There were others, dons and undergraduates, who felt strongly, though they were sometimes unready to express such views publicly, that wholly male societies were pleasanter communities than co-residential ones.

In 1972 five men's colleges, Brasenose, Hertford, Jesus, St Catherine's and Wadham, changed their statutes to permit the admission of women as graduates and undergraduates in 1974. Two other colleges, Balliol and New College, amended their statutes to make this possible, announcing, however, they had no immediate plans for putting them into effect. Corpus changed its statutes to enable it to accept women as fellows and graduate students but not as undergraduates. The women's colleges, only so recently admitted to equal status with the men's colleges after so many hard battles, were naturally perturbed at a change which might easily reduce them again to second-class societies, their intake of undergraduates and fellows harmed by competition from the powerful male colleges. To safeguard their interests the university agreed that no other colleges should take any action to admit women until the experiment had been submitted to a scrutiny which the Hebdomadal Council agreed to initiate in 1977. It seems very likely that the review will be favourable and some other colleges will wish to change their statutes to become co-residential, with effect from 1979; in general, there is little reason to doubt that while a few colleges will remain single-sex societies, the number of colleges permitting co-residence will steadily increase.

The majority of undergraduates, unlike their predecessors half a century earlier, favoured this change, many arguing that colleges had been far too dilatory in taking positive action to make it possible. It was a development which accorded well with the more radical and liberal tone of under-graduate opinion of the 'sixties and 'seventies. The immediate post-war generation, in many ways unusually mature, had adapted itself with ease to university life, pertinacious of study, conservative by impulse, so much so that some forms of activity, as for instance attendance at college chapels, burgeoned in the late 'forties and 'fifties as they had never done in pre-war Oxford. But the ending of national service and the arrival of new genera-tions, for whom the conflict of 1939–45 was a mere historical episode, betokened a change of attitude.

Furthermore undergraduate society was experiencing a slow but steady social metamorphosis as public schoolmen ceased to be a preponderant influence in college life. Some colleges, notably Christ Church which still took 70 per cent of its entrants in 1960 from independent schools and Trinity which took 80 per cent, remained for some time bulwarks of public school entry; but elsewhere, the social range had become wider, with some consequential social tensions. Yet it would be misleading to stress the social divisions of modern Oxford, which are probably more perceptible to older senior members than to undergraduates, for though social cliques continued to exist, colleges formed homogeneous and socially fused societies nor were radicals drawn from any one type of school. The authentic uniform of the 1970s, the casual trousers, shirts and sweaters, the near shoulder-length hair, were less the prerogative of a social class than the mark of a generation which was more conscious of its identity than its predecessors.

Far more than in the past, influenced by the student movement in the wider world, many undergraduates were critical of the government and discipline of the university. Following the suppression by the proctors of critical reviews of university lecturers in the university magazine, *Isis*, an unofficial Student Representative Council was formed in 1961. Although on occasions its members displayed the doctrinaire arrogance, inseparable from the youthful revolutionary, its leaders in general showed a sense of responsibility; its committees circulated valuable reports on lodgings and mental health. As a result of the report of the Hart committee, the Student Representative Council, insecurely founded as it appeared to be, was eventually accorded official recognition. At the same time most faculties set up liaison committees with the junior members to discuss matters relating to the syllabus.

Naturally discipline was the principle target of undergraduate criticism, for the modern undergraduate claims a degree of independence of authority which his predecessors never envisaged. To many the proctorial system, often incorrectly identified simply with the disciplinary procedure of the university, void of any genuine court of further appeal, working in secrecy, and with power concentrated in the hands of two men, seemed a tyrannical and outworn relic of the past. In practice proctorial discipline was exercised wisely and sparingly. The number of those brought before the proctors was absurdly small, and, with very few exceptions, the penalties exacted were almost disturbingly light. Between 1 January 1965 and 19 February 1968, when the average number of students in the university was more than 10,000, some 386 undergraduates appeared before the proctors on various charges (omitting breach of motor regulations); of these 73 were dismissed, 132 admonished and eleven fined £10 or more. No undergraduate was actually sent down; though eight were rusticated, all but two for offences involving drugs. In the same period 64 junior members of the university were prosecuted by the city police, including 33 for obstructing a passage way by picketing, seven for theft, four for drugs, and one for intent to murder. Even so, since suspicions of the system were abundant, it was clearly desirable that any system of discipline involving junior members of the university should appear to them to be just and reasonable.

A university committee, set up following an incident in which several junior members organised a public demonstration against apartheid on the occasion of the visit of the South African ambassador, had already made recommendations modifying proctorial powers and had suggested the institution of an appeals tribunal. It was, however, decided in May 1968, after a year in which student protests and demands by students for participation in university government were a world-wide phenomenon, to appoint another committee under the chairmanship of Professor H. L. A. Hart, later principal of Brasenose, to consider the university's relations with its junior members. This committee recommended the annual revision of the university's disciplinary rules by a body composed of senior and junior members, thus giving the junior members some share in the making of them; it also sought to provide for regular channels of communication with faculties and faculty boards. These proposals, acceptable to the majority of the university, displeased the more conservative dons and the more radical undergraduates; but they went some way to meet the complaints of the middle-of-the-road undergraduates who formed the greater part of the university's population.

Although the walls of the colleges were occasionally daubed by graffiti, some witty, some obscene, all aesthetically deplorable, the university escaped more bitter manifestations of student trouble. The extreme wing of student radicalism, the O.R.S.S. (Oxford Revolutionary Socialist Students), affiliated to the national R.S.S.F. (Revolutionary Socialist Students Federation), though loud in its complaints, had a very small genuine following. Its aim was to disrupt and to destroy the university, its declarations characteristically naive and its testimony so full of radical jargon as to be unintelligible and sometimes illiterate. To the majority of undergraduates, liberal in their sympathies and far more socially concerned than their predecessors, its policy was for the most part distasteful. Ready as they were to criticise the university, what they wanted was a more meaningful and worthwhile relationship with its senior members. There were occasional sit-ins, but the atmosphere remained calm, in all probability because a collegiate society has at least the merit of sustaining some degree of dialogue between its junior and senior members.

What of the future? Since the ending of the Second World War, Oxford has experienced many major changes, the widening of its social composition, the fading impact of religion on its life, the expansion of its syllabuses, the foundation of some new societies, Linacre, St Cross, Wolfson, an increase in the number of its fellows, some, if limited, recognition of student representation, the admission of women to some of the men's colleges, increased dependence through the University Grants Committee on grants from the Treasury. It has been lightly singed, but not seriously burned, by the radical student movement of the sixties. In the seventies it is still experiencing something of a metamorphosis. But the historian possesses no crystal ball into which he can gaze into the future.

He can, however, with some confidence, suppose that there will be no relaxation in the rate of change. In 1920 Oxford and Cambridge were pre-eminent; the other universities were in many ways impoverished and inferior reproductions of their two richer cousins. In 1973 Oxford is only one among nearly 50 similar institutions, many of them with outstanding teachers and splendid amenities. There appears no fundamental reason why Oxford could not be reduced to a comparatively minor and provincial institution, starved of its funds (and so of some of the amenities which it is able to offer) by the ruthless confiscation of its endowments by the acquisitiveness of some radical régime, and so sink to the status of a second-rate comprehensive university.

It is, fortunately, more likely that some of the trends which we have observed in past decades will be carried further: the democratisation of Oxford's governing structure, the expansion of co-residence, a more centrifugal system of instruction, a further reduction in the autonomy of the colleges, possibly the conversion of the university into a purely graduate society. Unpleasing as some of these features may appear to those of a conservative temperament, they will not change the core of the place. 'Only in a dying state', the senior proctor, the historian E. L. Woodward, shrewdly observed on 21 March 1928, 'does each generation follow exactly the path laid down for it.' What is important is that the university should never lose sight of its basic *raison d'être*. 'All this elaborate provision for higher study and research', A. D. Lindsay reminded his hearers at the end of his vice-chancellorship, 'rests ultimately on a spiritual foundation, the conviction that in the minds of researchers, of teachers and of students knowledge has its own standards of integrity.' It is enough that, short of a nuclear holocaust, the spires and towers of Oxford may long continue to look down on a constant procession of men and women seeking the truths upon which the good of society must be founded.

Select Bibliography

GENERAL

There is a very comprehensive guide in *A Bibliography of Printed Works relating to the University of Oxford*, ed. E. H. Cordeaux and D. H. Merry, 3 vols., Oxford, 1968. The best history of the university is still Sir Charles Mallet, *A History of the University of Oxford*, 3 vols., Methuen, 1924-7. *The History and Antiquities of the University of Oxford* by Anthony Wood, ed. J. Gutch, 3 vols., 1792-6 is fundamental. *The Victoria County History of Oxford*, Oxford, 1954, incorporates accounts of all the colleges. Felix Markham, *Oxford*, Weidenfeld and Nicholson, 1967 is handsomely illustrated. W. A. Pantin's, *Oxford Life in Oxford Archives*, Oxford, 1972, is an attractive series of essays on different aspects of the university's history.

College histories of varying value were printed in the early years of this century; but more recent studies include: A. H. Smith, *New College*, Oxford, 1952; R. H. Hodgkin, *The Queen's College*, Oxford, 1949; W. C. Costin, *St John's College, 1598-1860*, Oxf. hist. soc., 1958; H. W. C. Davis, *Balliol College*, ed. R. H. C. Davis and R. Hunt, 1963; J. N. L. Baker, *Jesus College*, Oxford, 1971. There is useful material in W. G. Hiscock, *A Christ Church Miscellany*, Oxford, 1946.

On libraries: B. H. Streeter, *The Chained Library*, London, 1931; F. M. Powicke, *The Medieval Books of Merton College*, Oxford, 1931; Sir E. Craster, *History of the Bodleian Library, 1845-1945*, Oxford, 1952; Sir E. Craster, *History of All Souls College Library*, ed. E. F. Jacob, London, 1971.

W. Gaunt, *Oxford*, Batsford, 1965, is concerned with Oxford architecture; on this W. J. Arkell, *Oxford Stone*, London, 1947, throws some light.

Other books bearing on some aspects of Oxford life include: *Reminiscences of Oxford, 1559-1850*, ed. Lilian M. Quiller-Couch, Oxf. hist. soc., 1892; W. N. Hargreaves-Mawdsley, *A History of Academical Dress*, Oxford, 1963, pp. 60-106; G. D. Squibb, *Founder's Kin: Privilege and Pedigree*, Oxford, 1973.

MEDIEVAL OXFORD

The most authoritative work remains Hastings Rashdall, *The Universities of Europe in the Middle Ages*, ed. F. M. Powicke and A. B. Emden, Vol. III, Oxford, 1936. There is useful material in G. Leff, *Paris and Oxford Universities in the Thirteenth and*

Fourteenth Centuries, Wiley, 1968, and in H. C. Maxwell-Lyte, *A History of the University* (*to 1530*), London, 1886. A. B. Emden's *Biographical Register of Oxford* (*to 1500*), 3 vols., Oxford, 1957–9, provides a rich and fascinating quarry. For the medieval city, H. E. Salter, *Medieval Oxford*, Oxf. hist. soc., 1936.

On the halls: H. E. Salter, 'An Oxford Hall in 1424' in *Essays in History presented to R. L. Poole*, ed. H. W. C. Davis, London, 1927; A. B. Emden, *An Oxford Hall in Medieval Times*, Oxford, repr. 1968; W. A. Pantin, 'The halls and schools of medieval Oxford,' in *Oxford Studies presented to D. Callus*, Oxford hist. soc., 1964, pp. 31–100.

W. A. Pantin, *Canterbury College*, 3 vols., Oxford hist. soc. 1941–4, provides basic material for the study of a monastic college.

On the friars at Oxford: A. G. Little, *The Grey Friars at Oxford*, Oxf. hist. soc., 1892; W. A. Hinnebusch, *History of the Order of Preachers*, New York, 1966.

On teaching and scholarship: D. Callus, 'The Introduction of Aristotelian Learning in Oxford' in *Proceedings of the British Academy*, Vol. XXIX, 1944; *Robert Grosseteste*, ed. D. A. Callus, Oxford, 1955; A. G. Little and F. Pelster, *Oxford Theology and Theologians*, Oxf. hist. soc., 1934; D. E. Sharp, *Franciscan Philosophy at Oxford in the Thirteenth Century*, Oxf. hist. soc., 1930; B. Smalley, 'Robert Bacon and the early Dominican School at Oxford' in *Trans. Roy. Hist. Soc.* 1948; J. M. Fletcher, 'The Arts Teaching at Oxford, 1400–1520' in *Paedagogia Historia*, VII (2), Ghent, 1967.

John Wyclif's connection with Oxford is examined by J. A. Robson in *Wyclif and the Oxford School*, Cambridge, 1961.

On organisation: P. Kibre, *Scholarly Privileges in the Middle Ages*, Medieval Academy of America, 1961, pp. 268–330; *The Nations in the Medieval Universities*, Medieval Academy of America, 1948, pp. 160–166; A. B. Emden, 'Northerners and Southerners in the organisation of the university to 1509' in *Oxford Studies presented to D. Callus*, Oxf. hist. soc., 1964, pp. 1–13.

On the beginnings of humanism: R. Weiss, *Humanism in England during the fifteenth century*, 2nd edn., Blackwell, Oxford, 1957; R. J. Mitchell, *John Free*, London, 1955, ch. 2; F. Madan, 'The daily ledger of John Dorne, 1520', ed. C. R. L. Fletcher, *Collectanea*, 1st ser., Oxf. hist. soc., 1885.

Two scholarly essays by E. F. Jacob require mention: 'The building of All Souls College, 1438–1443' in *Historical Essays in Honour of James Tait*, ed. J. G. Edwards, V. H. Galbraith and E. F. Jacob, 1933, pp. 121–135; 'English University Clerks in the later Middle Ages' in *Essays in the Conciliar Epoch*, Manchester, 3rd edn., 1962, pp. 207–239.

Source material of value is to be found in the following publications of the Oxford Historical Society: H. E. Salter, *Medieval Archives of the University of Oxford*, 2 vols., 1917–19; *Epistolae Academicae Oxon.* ed. H. Anstey, 2 vols., 1898; *Registrum Cancellarii Oxon.*, ed. H. E. Salter, 2 vols., 1932; *Formularies which bear on the History of Oxford, c.* 1204–1420, ed. H. E. Salter, W. A. Pantin and H. G. Richardson, Oxf. hist. soc., 2 vols., 1942; *The Early Rolls of Merton College*, ed. J. R. L. Highfield, Oxf. hist. soc., 1964.

TUDOR AND STUART OXFORD

M. H. Curtis, *Oxford and Cambridge in Transition, 1558–1642*, Oxford, 1959, is a valuable study. There is useful material on early sixteenth-century Oxford in *The Letter Book of Robert Joseph, monk-scholar of Evesham and Gloucester College, 1530–32*, ed. H. Aveling and W. A. Pantin, Oxf. hist. soc., 1967. For the background, J. Simon, *Education and Society in Tudor England*, Cambridge, 1966. D. M. Loades, *Oxford Martyrs*, Batsford, 1970 recounts the trial of Cranmer and his associates. C. Plummer, *Elizabethan Oxford*, Oxf. hist. soc., 1886, prints excerpts from Tudor tracts on Oxford. I. G. Philip deals with 'Queen Mary's benefactions to the university' in *Bodleian Library Record*, 1954.

Hugh Kearney, *Scholars and Gentlemen, Universities and Society in Pre-Industrial Britain, 1500–1700*, Faber, 1970, is an important study. C. Hill, *The Intellectual Origins of the English Revolution*, Oxford, 1965, finds London, and Gresham College in particular, a more fruitful source than Oxford. I. Thomas discusses 'Medieval aftermath: Oxford logic and logicians of the 17th century' in *Oxford Studies presented to D. Callus*, pp. 297–311.

M. B. Rex, *University Representation, 1604–1690*, Allen and Unwin, 1964, traces the history of Oxford's burgesses. Laud's connection with Oxford is dealt with by H. R. Trevor-Roper, in *Archbishop Laud*, 2nd edn, Macmillan, 1962. *The Laudian Statutes* have been edited by J. Griffiths, Oxford, 1888.

The Diary of Thomas Crosfield, ed. F. S. Boas, Oxford, 1935, contains interesting material. F. S. Boas has also written *University Drama in the Tudor Age*, Oxford, 1914.

For the last half of the seventeenth century Anthony Wood, *Life and Times*, ed. A. Clark, 5 vols. Oxf. hist. soc., 1891–1910, is of fundamental importance. Other contemporary material includes J. R. Magrath, *The Flemings in Oxford*, 3 vols, Oxf. hist. soc., 1903–23; *Diary and Letter-Book of Thomas Brockbank*, ed. R. Trappes-Lomax, Chetham Soc., 1930. J. R. Bloxam prints relevant documents in *Magdalen College and James II, 1686–89*, Oxf. hist. soc., 1886.

D. C. Douglas, *English Scholars*, 2nd rev. edn., London, 1951, discusses the genesis of Anglo-Saxon studies at Oxford; W. G. Hiscock the work of *Henry Aldrich*, Oxford, 1960.

OXFORD IN THE EIGHTEENTH CENTURY

For the first three decades the *Remarks and Collections of Thomas Hearne*, ed. H. E. Salter and others, 10 vols., Oxf. hist. soc. 1885–1913, is of fundamental importance. W. R. Ward, *Georgian Oxford*, Oxford, 1958, is a scholarly consideration, mainly of Oxford's political history. Other books which throw light on Oxford in this period include: C. Wordsworth, *Social life at the English Universities in the Eighteenth Century*, Cambridge, 1874; C. Wordsworth, *Scholae academicae; some account of the studies at the English Universities in the Eighteenth Century*, Cambridge, 1877; *Studies in Oxford History*, J. R. Green and G. Roberton, ed. G. L. Stainer, Oxf. hist. soc., 1901; *Oxford during the Eighteenth Century*, ed. Mrs J. R. Green and K. Norgate, Macmillan, 1908; A. D. Godley, *Oxford in the Eighteenth Century*, Methuen, 1908. A suggestive essay is Lucy Sutherland, *Oxford in the Eighteenth Century*, Oxford, 1973. Contemporary works of use include: Z. C. von Uffenbach, *Oxford in 1710*, ed and tr. W. H. and W. J. C. Quarrell, Oxford, 1928; N. Amhurst, *Terrae-Filius*, 3rd edn., 1754; R. Newton, *University Education*, 1726; T. Salmon, *The Present State of the Universities*, London, 1744, pp. 25–460; J. Napleton, *Considerations on the public exercises*, Oxford, 1773; V. Knox, *Essays Moral and Literary*, 1782, and *Liberal Education*, 2 vols, 1788; *Letters of Richard Radcliffe and John James, 1755–83*, ed. Margaret Evans, Oxf. hist. soc., 1887; K. P. Moritz, *Travels*, London 1795, pp. 165–18.

On John Wesley: the material used came partly from the as yet unpublished Oxford diaries of Wesley (5 vols—in the course of being edited by R. Heitzenrater of Duke University, U.S.A.), utilised in V. H. H. Green, *The Young Mr Wesley*, Arnold, 1961. See also J. Wesley, *Journal*, Vol. I., ed. N. Curnock, London, 1909; and *Letters*, Vol. I., ed. J. Telford, London, 1931; L. Tyerman, *The Oxford Methodists*, Hodder and Stoughton, 1873. The expulsion of the Methodists from St Edmund Hall is recounted in S. L. Ollard, *The Six Students of St Edmund Hall*, 1911. On the Evangelical movement: J. S. Reynolds, *The Evangelicals at Oxford, 1735–1871*. Blackwell, Oxford, 1953.

For Woodforde: *Woodforde at Oxford, 1759–1776*, ed. W. N. Hargreaves-Mawdsley, Oxf. hist. soc., 1969.

NINETEENTH-CENTURY OXFORD

Contemporary, but not wholly reliable memoirs, include: G. V. Cox, *Recollections of Oxford*, 1870; W. Tuckwell, *Reminiscences*, 1901; T. Mozley, *Reminiscences*, 2 vols., 1912. Two novels which illuminate undergraduate life in unreformed Oxford: C. M. Westmacott, *The English Spy*, by Bernard Blackmantle, 2 vols., edn., 1907; Cuthbert Bede (Edward Bradley), *The Adventures of Verdant Green*.

The most recent, scholarly study of nineteenth-century Oxford is W. R. Ward, *Victorian Oxford*, Frank Cass, 1965.

The best study of the Oxford Movement remains R. W. Church, *The Oxford Movement*, Macmillan, 1891. There is ample biographical material: G. Faber, *The Oxford Apostles*, Faber, 1936; W. Liddon and J. O. Johnston, *E. B. Pusey*, 4 vols., 1893–97; R. D. Middleton, *Newman at Oxford*, London, 1950; G. Battiscombe, *John Keble*, Constable, 1963.

On university reform: *Oxford University Commission, Report of Her Majesty's Commissioners*, London, 1852; *Report of a Committee of the Hebdomadal Board and evidence upon the recommendations*, Oxford, 1853; M. Pattison, *Suggestions on Academical Organization*, 1868; *Universities Commission. Report of the Commissioners appointed to enquire into the property and income of the Universities of Oxford and Cambridge*, 3 vols., London, 1874. Two important recent studies are E. G. W. Bill and J. F. A. Mason, *Christ Church and Reform, 1850–1867*, Oxford, 1970, and E. G. W. Bill, *University Reform in Nineteenth-Century Oxford, A study of Henry Halford Vaughan*, Oxford, 1973.

There is biographical material in R. D. Middleton, *Dr Routh*, Oxford, 1938; N. Wymer, *Thomas Arnold*, London, 1953; T. W. Bamford, *Thomas Arnold*, London, 1953; G. Faber, *B. Jowett*, Faber, 1957; M. D. Jeune, *Pages from the diary of an Oxford lady, 1843–1862*, ed. M. J. Gifford, Oxford, 1932; Sir C. Oman, *Memoirs of Victorian Oxford*, London, 1941.

Two institutions established in the nineteenth century: C. Hollis, *The Oxford Union*, London, 1965; R. D. Burnell, *The Oxford & Cambridge Boat Race, 1829–1953*, London, 1954.

On studies: C. H. Firth, *Modern Languages at Oxford, 1724–1929*, London, 1929; *Modern History at Oxford, 1724–1841* in the *English Historical Review*, 1917; *Modern History at Oxford, 1841–1919* in *English Historical Review*, 1920; H. G. Hanbury, *The Vinerian Chair and Legal Education*, Oxford, 1958; F. H. Lawson, *The Oxford Law School, 1850–1965*, Oxford, 1967.

For Gladstone at Oxford: *Gladstone's Diary*, Vol. I., ed. M. D. Foot, Oxford, 1968; S. G. Checkland, *The Gladstones, a family biography, 1764–1851*, Cambridge, 1971.

For Pattison: much of the illustrative material has been taken from the mainly unpublished letters from Pattison to his sister, Eleanor, given to Lincoln College by Eleanor's daughter, Lady de Sausmarez, subsequently mislaid and only rediscovered in 1972 (they formed the basis of an article by F. C. Montague, 'Some Early Letters of Mark Pattison' in the *Bulletin of the John Ryland Library*, 1934). For other information see M. Pattison, *Memoirs*, 1885, ed. J. Sparrow, 1973; V. H. H. Green, *Oxford Common Room*, Arnold, 1957; J. Sparrow, *Mark Pattison and the Idea of a University* Cambridge, 1967.

TWENTIETH-CENTURY OXFORD

The material is diverse. Biographical material is contained in L. R. Farnell, *An Oxonian Looks Back*, London, 1934; H. A. L. Fisher, *An unfinished autobiography*, London, 1940; E. L. Woodward, *Short Journey*, 1942; G. B. Grundy, *Fifty-five years at Oxford*, London, 1945; R. F. Harrod, *The Prof.*, *a personal memoir of Lord Cherwell*, London, 1959; A. L. Rowse, *A Cornishman at Oxford*, Cape, 1965; C. M. Bowra, *Memoirs*, Weidenfeld and Nicolson, 1966; T. F. Higham, *Dr*

Blackiston recalled, Blackwells, Oxford, 1967; Drusilla Scott, *A. D. Lindsay*, Blackwells, Oxford, 1971.

On the admission of women: Annie Rogers, *Degrees by degrees*, Oxford, 1938; Vera Brittain, *The Women at Oxford*, London, 1960.

On university reform: G. N. Curzon, *Principles and methods of university reform*, Oxford, 1909; *Royal Commissions on Oxford and Cambridge Universities Report* (CMD 1588), London, 1922; *Franks Report on Oxford University*, 2 vols., Oxford, 1966.

W. Elmhirst, *A Freshman's Diary* 1911–12, Blackwells, Oxford, 1969 is an invaluable account of undergraduate life.

More recent studies of Oxford include: T. Greenidge, *Degenerate Oxford*, London, 1930; K. Briant, *Oxford Limited*, London, 1937; J. Betjeman, *An Oxford University Chest*, London, 1938; N. Longmate, *Oxford Triumphant*, London, 1954; J. C. Masterman, *To Teach the Senators Wisdom*, London, 1952; Dacre Balsdon, *Oxford Life*, Eyre and Spottiswoode, 1957; D. Potter, *The glittering coffin*, London, 1960; M. Beadle, *These ruins are inhabited*, New York, 1961; Dacre Balsdon, *Oxford Now and Then*, Duckworth, 1970.

Appendix: Undergraduate entries at Lincoln College, 1680–1920

	Admissions	G-Commoners	Servitors		Admissions
1680–89	130	8	29	1800–09	46
1690–99	102	5	31	1810–19	75
1700–09	104	6	33	1820–29	125
1710–19	100	12	34	1830–39	130
1720–29	91	6	21	1840–49	150
1730–39	87	7	20	1850–59	125
1740–49	71	10	18	1860–69	180
1750–59	65	2	7	1870–79	177
1760–69	60	4	5	1880–89	198
1770–79	54	1	—	1890–99	214
1780–89	60	—	—	1900–09	280
1790–99	52	—	—	1910–19	261

The figures illustrate the steep decline in the university entry, affecting more particularly the children of the aristocracy and gentry, and poorer commoners, which occurred in the eighteenth century. No gentlemen-commoners were admitted after 1777 nor servitors nominated after 1763 (bible-clerks, included in the numbers of servitors, continued to be appointed irregularly). The drop in entries for 1850–59 reflects the aftermath to the scandalous rectorial election of 1851. The final figure demonstrates the effect of the Great War on the undergraduate entry (1915, 6, 1916, 2, 1917, 2, 1918, 4, followed by a very large intake in 1919, 98).

Index